"These distinguished authors have provided an excellent guide for any teacher (Jewish or non-Jewish) to encourage student engagement with the immense variety of engaging Jewish literature. Thanks to this important work, Jewish children's books will finally be discovered by a non-Jewish audience who will be delighted to have these top educators help open up a new literary world for their students."
 —**Lisa Silverman, retired director, Sperber Jewish Community Library; curator, Jewish Journal Streaming Guide**

"Because bigotry, antisemitism, and racism continue to find their way into our schools and society, the need for authentic representation and respect for children's identities and communities is greater than ever before. Beautifully written and creatively organized, *Enduring Questions* includes cultural insights, suggested literature, and curricular resources to enrich the understanding of the Jewish experience for students and teachers of all backgrounds. This book will be cherished by educators and families who work towards a future that is inclusive and multicultural."
 —**Sonia Nieto, professor emerita in language, literacy, and culture at the College of Education, University of Massachusetts, Amherst**

"This compelling and thorough book shares the range of Jewish children's literature: stories of love, stories of memory, stories that evoke laughter and tears. But what remains with readers most is that which sets out to reason why Jewish children's literature matters for *all* children, how the identities of Jewish people have been broadened, and what places these books have in the wider context of what we read together. The practical curricular connections are supported with honest insights from teachers who share their experiences. From establishing the current state of the field to offering resources to study further, this book will guide readers who know the topic well as well as those who need introduction. For all, this book affirms and inspires as it establishes the necessary place of Jewish children's literature for all readers."
 —**Junko Yokota, director, Center for Teaching through Children's Books; professor emerita, National Louis University**

"Carefully structured and engagingly written, *Enduring Questions* helps to make the particulars of Jewish difference legible on the American cultural landscape. This is a practical guide for incorporating Jewish literature at all stages of the curriculum from preschool through elementary school, regardless of the level of teachers' and students' familiarity with Jewish history and practice. Deftly harnessing the energy of the stories themselves, the authors lead readers on a journey far beyond the Holocaust narratives that dominate the limited Jewish content in most mainstream educational settings. Of particular value are the sidebars in teachers' own words describing how they deployed a given text in the classroom and how students in a variety of settings received and spoke back to the stories."

—Miriam Udel, associate professor of Yiddish language, literature, and culture; Department of German Studies and Director of Tam Institute of Jewish Studies, Emory University

"*Enduring Questions* expands awareness of Jewish books for children beyond the typical focus on the Holocaust or Hanukah. The authors provide cogent reasons for using Jewish books as an integral part of multicultural literature with children. The authors weave in Jewish learning that will support teachers with choosing and using Jewish books with their students. In each chapter, the authors provide teacher testimonies of using specific titles with their students. In addition, the authors provide excellent examples of enduring questions for each book they present. Finally, the appendices are valuable resources for all educators."

—Ted Kesler, associate professor, elementary and early childhood education, Queens College, City University of New York

Enduring Questions

Using Jewish Children's Literature in Classrooms

David Bloome, Evelyn B. Freeman,
Rosemary Horowitz, and Laurie Katz

ROWMAN & LITTLEFIELD
Lanham • Boulder • New York • London

Published by Rowman & Littlefield
An imprint of The Rowman & Littlefield Publishing Group, Inc.
4501 Forbes Boulevard, Suite 200, Lanham, Maryland 20706
www.rowman.com

86-90 Paul Street, London EC2A 4NE, United Kingdom

Copyright © 2023 by David Bloome, Evelyn B. Freeman, Rosemary Horowitz, and Laurie Katz

All rights reserved. No part of this book may be reproduced in any form or by any electronic or mechanical means, including information storage and retrieval systems, without written permission from the publisher, except by a reviewer who may quote passages in a review.

British Library Cataloguing in Publication Information Available

Library of Congress Cataloging-in-Publication Data

Names: Bloome, David, author. | Freeman, Evelyn B. (Evelyn Blossom), 1948– author. | Horowitz, Rosemary, author. | Katz, Laurie, author.
Title: Enduring questions : using Jewish children's literature in classrooms / David Bloome, Evelyn Freeman, Rosemary Horowitz, and Laurie Katz.
Description: Lanham : Rowman & Littlefield, [2023] | Includes bibliographical references and index. | Summary: "This book introduces preschool and elementary teachers to a broad range of high-quality children's literature books and stories and provides them with background information so that they can use Jewish children's literature thoughtfully with their students"—Provided by publisher.
Identifiers: LCCN 2022027724 (print) | LCCN 2022027725 (ebook) | ISBN 9781475865356 (cloth) | ISBN 9781475865363 (paperback) | ISBN 9781475865370 (epub)
Subjects: LCSH: Children's literature—Study and teaching (Preschool) | Children's literature—Study and teaching (Elementary) | Judaism—Study and teaching (Preschool) | Judaism—Study and teaching (Elementary) | Jewish children—Books and reading. | Jewish literature.
Classification: LCC LB1527 .B58 2023 (print) | LCC LB1527 (ebook) | DDC 372.64/044—dc23/eng/20220824
LC record available at https://lccn.loc.gov/2022027724
LC ebook record available at https://lccn.loc.gov/2022027725

Dedication

On August 7, 2021, our friend, colleague, and coauthor Rosemary Horowitz died from cancer. Rosemary was a professor of English at Appalachian State University in Boone, North Carolina. She was the author of several books including the edited collection *Elie Wiesel and the Art of Storytelling* (McFarland Press, 2006), *Memorial Books of Eastern European Jewry: Essays on the History and Meanings of Yizker Volumes* (McFarland Press, 2011), and *Women Writers of Yiddish Literature* (McFarland Press, 2015). She was an outstanding teacher; codirector of the Appalachian State University Center for Judaic, Holocaust, and Peace Studies; and she worked with the U.S. Holocaust Memorial Museum, among many other accomplishments.

Rosemary Horowitz

David and Laurie had known Rosemary since she was a doctoral student in the early 1990s; Evie got to know her when we were all involved with the National Council of Teachers of English Jewish Caucus. We were all concerned about the lack of Jewish children's literature in P–12 classrooms, and we were concerned about misinformation and inappropriate pedagogies for teaching Holocaust literature. This was one of the areas in which Rosemary had great expertise. We decided to organize a few panels on the topic of Jewish children's literature for P–12 classrooms, and it was those panels that led to this book.

Despite the seriousness of the topic, talking together about Jewish children's literature was joyful and full of learning. Even against a background of so much horror and hate—too much of which continues in one form or another, against too many people, Jewish and other—our conversations about Jewish children's literature focused on beauty, family, wonder, *tikkun olam* (repairing the world), community, friendship, and what we have come to call enduring questions.

We miss her.

We have dedicated this book to her and hope it is worthy of her memory.

Contents

Acknowledgments		ix
Permissions		xi
Introduction: Why and How to Use Jewish Children's Literature in the Preschool and Elementary School Classroom		1
1	What Makes Jewish Children's Literature Jewish?	11
2	What Is Our Story? What Is Our History? A History of Jewish Children's Literature	25
3	What Is Love? Stories of Family, Friendship, Animals, and Nature	41
4	What Is Time? Jewish Rites and Holidays through Jewish Children's Literature	57
5	What Is Wisdom and What Is Foolishness? Humor in Jewish Children's Literature	79
6	What Is Evil? How Might We Respond to Evil? Jewish Children's Literature, Anti-Semitism, and the Holocaust	103
7	What Is Justice? What Is a Righteous Person to Do? Jewish Children's Literature and the Pursuit of Tikkun Olam	131
8	How Might We Imagine Life for Ourselves Together in the World? Using Jewish Children's Literature in Multicultural Education	151

Glossary	167
Appendixes	
Appendix A: Select List of Jewish Children's Literature Organized by Topics/Themes	173
Appendix B: Select Resources for Using Jewish Children's Literature in the Preschool through Elementary Classroom	189
Appendix C: Select List of Professional and Scholarly Books and Articles on Jewish Children's Literature	193
Index	195
About the Authors	203

Acknowledgments

In 2002, the Jewish Caucus of the National Council of Teachers of English (NCTE) was established. The four of us who have written this book were among its first members and officers. One of the first issues that the NCTE Jewish Caucus tackled was the need to make classroom teachers across the United States and elsewhere, preschool through high school, aware of the broad range of Jewish children's and young adult literature available and how that literature might enhance the depth of their teaching and their students' learning. Numerous conversations throughout those years have helped form the conceptualization of this book.

We are grateful to the members of the NCTE Jewish Caucus for all of the conversations about Jewish children's literature and how it might be used in classrooms. We are also grateful to NCTE more generally for valuing discussions of Jewish children's literature and for providing space for such discussions.

We want to acknowledge conversations early in the genesis of this book with Roxanne Henkin, Debi Goodman, and Yetta Goodman. More recently, we have benefited from the advice and comments of Paula Ressler, Becca Chase, Ruth Lowery, Lisa Silverman, and Ari Bloomekatz on an early draft of this book. They shared their wisdom and experience with us and helped us sharpen our vision and language. We also want to acknowledge the assistance of Alice Levine, who helped us identify Jewish children's literature in which Jews of color were included in more than a trivial manner. Whatever flaws remain are solely our responsibility.

We have greatly benefited from eighteen outstanding educators across the United States who volunteered to work with us: Annelyn Baron, Emily Bauman, Lily Blackburn, Marie Boozer, JoAnne Boulware, Tammy

Dalling, Renée Gilpin, Julie Johnson, Renee Klein, Katie Konrad, Maggie McCormick, Katy McKenney, Liz Paige, Susan Polos, Betsy Shuler, Audrey Stafford, Allison Volz, and Stephanie Whitfield. Each used one of the books we have discussed with their students and reported back to us on how they used the book and how their students responded. They have shared their insights and their instructional acumen and creativity. We are honored to have their efforts represented in the book.

In addition to these teachers' valuable input, we were fortunate to have the input of children who talked to us about many of the books. They shared their love of reading and how the books inspired their imaginations. We thank them for the special times they spent with us.

The artwork on the cover was created by Jerome "Jerry" Harste. Jerry brings to his artwork a sensitivity to and appreciation of children engaged in reading. Jerry is known as a literacy scholar as well as an artist. Over his thirty years at Indiana University, Jerry received many awards and distinctions for his expertise in the teaching and learning of reading and writing. He takes children seriously, and it shows in both his artwork and publications as a scholar. We are extremely fortunate and grateful to have his artwork and insight on the cover.

We appreciate the guidance and assistance of our editor, Carlie Wall, who has been supportive of this book from the beginning.

Permissions

We thank the Center for Judaic, Holocaust, and Peace Studies at Appalachian State University for permission to reprint the photograph of Rosemary Horowitz. The photograph was taken by Dr. Thomas Pegelow Kaplan. We thank the Association of Jewish Libraries for permission to reprint the document "Excellence in Jewish Children's Literature." The document © 2021 is reprinted by permission of the Association of Jewish Libraries, http://jewishlibraries.org/.

Permissions for Text

From *Day of Delight* by Maxine Rose Schur. © 1994 by Maxine Rose Schur. Reprinted by permission of the author.

From *New Year at the Pier* by April Halprin Wayland. © 2009 by April Halprin Wayland. Used by permission of the author, who controls all rights.

From *Rifka Takes a Bow* by Betty Rosenberg Perlov. © 2013 by Betty Rosenberg Perlov. Reprinted with permission of Kar-Ben Books, a division of Lerner Publishing Group, Inc. All rights reserved. No part of this text excerpt may be used or reproduced in any manner whatsoever without the prior written permission of Lerner Publishing Group, Inc.

From *Golemito* by Ilan Stavans. © 2013 by Ilan Stavans. Reprinted by permission of the publisher, NewSouth Books.

From *My Grandfather's Coat* by Jim Aylesworth. © 2014 by Jim Aylesworth. Reprinted by permission of the publisher, Scholastic Press.

From *Onions and Garlic* by Eric A. Kimmel. © 1996 by Eric A. Kimmel. Reprinted by permission of the author.

From *Dear Mr. Dickens* by Nancy Churnin. © 2021 by Nancy Churnin. Reprinted by permission of the publisher, Albert Whitman & Company.

From *Gittel's Journey* story by Lesléa Newman, pictures by Amy June Bates. Text © 2019 by Lesléa Newman. Illustrations © 2019 by Amy June Bates. Used by permission of Abrams Books for Young Readers, an imprint of Abrams, New York. All rights reserved.

Permissions for Book Covers

Cover illustration from *Always an Olivia: A Remarkable Family History* by Carolivia Herron. Illustrated by Jeremy Tugeau. © 2007 by Carolivia Herron. Art © 2007 by Lerner Publishing Group, Inc. Reprinted by permission of Kar-Ben Publishing, a division of Lerner Publishing Group, Inc. All rights reserved. No part of this image may be used or reproduced in any manner whatsoever without the prior written permission of Lerner Publishing Group, Inc.

Cover illustration from *Berchick*, written by Esther Silverstein Blanc, illustrated by Tennessee Dixon. © 1989 by Tennessee Dixon. Reprinted by permission.

Cover illustration from *Between Parents* by Hersh Dovid Nomberg. Cover illustration by Issachar Ber Ryback. © 2021 by Farlag Press. Reprinted by courtesy of Farlag Press.

Cover illustration from *Hannah's Way* by Linda Glaser. Illustrated by Adam Gustavson. Text © 2012 by Linda Glaser. Illustrations © 2012 by Adam Gustavson. Reprinted by permission of Kar-Ben Publishing, a division of Lerner Publishing Group, Inc. All rights reserved. No part of this image may be used or reproduced in any manner whatsoever without the prior written permission of Lerner Publishing Group, Inc.

Cover illustration from *Janusz Korczak's Children* by Gloria Spielman. Illustrated by Matthew Archambault. Text © 2007 by Gloria Spielman. Reprinted by permission of Kar-Ben Publishing, a division of Lerner Publishing Group, Inc. All rights reserved. No part of this image may be used or reproduced in any manner whatsoever without the prior written permission of Lerner Publishing Group, Inc.

Cover illustration from *One City, Two Brothers*, illustrated by Aurélia Fronty. © 2007 by Aurélia Fronty. Reprinted by permission of the publisher, Barefoot Books.

Cover illustration from *Too Far from Home* by Naomi Shmuel. Illustrated by Avi Katz. Text © 2000 by Naomi Shmuel. Illustrations © 2000 by Avi Katz. First published as *Rainbow Child* in 2000 by Hakibbutz Hameyuchad/Sifriyat Poalim Publishing. Reprinted by permission of Kar-Ben Publishing, a division of Lerner Publishing Group, Inc. All rights reserved. No part of this image may be used or reproduced in any manner whatsoever without the prior written permission of Lerner Publishing Group, Inc.

Cover illustration from *When Jessie Came Across the Sea.* Text © 1997 by Amy Hest. Illustrations © 1997 by P. J. Lynch. Reproduced by permission of the publisher, Candlewick Press, Somerville, MA.

Introduction

Why and How to Use Jewish Children's Literature in the Preschool and Elementary School Classroom

When Ezra was young, his father used to read to him Isaac Bashevis Singer's story *Naftali the Storyteller and His Horse, Sus*. Set many years ago in Eastern Europe at a time when peddlers traveled from town to town and village to village selling wares, Naftali peddled books; but mostly he told stories. His horse, Sus, would pull their wagon into a town or village where they would be greeted by children eager for a story. And Naftali would oblige and share a story he had just heard in a previous town or that he had read in one of his books. The children's eyes would grow large and their imaginations fly.

Year after year Naftali and Sus would travel across the land, telling stories and selling books until they grew too old to endure the weariness of a book peddler's life. They settled on the estate of a wealthy man who loved stories. There, Naftali told stories, and Sus would graze. Eventually Sus died. When Naftali buried Sus, he placed a hickory stick on the grave.

Although peddlers often used a hickory stick to whip their horses, Naftali had never done so. The stick had no use. That is, until Naftali used it to mark Sus's grave. The stick grew into a tree, and Naftali would sit under the tree reading and thinking. Eventually, Naftali died and was buried next to Sus.

Naftali the Storyteller and His Horse, Sus resonates with many Jews and others, both adults and children. Although the story does explicitly include Jewish customs (Naftali and Sus did not travel on Shabbat), it is more so the Jewish values of a life spent with books, stories, community, family, and love that invite people to hear and read the story as much with their heart as with their mind. Ezra would ask for the story to be read to him over and over, and each time, just as it would get to the part where Naftali and Sus retired to the estate, he would begin to cry quietly and not stop until well after the reading had been completed. And then he would ask for the story to be read again.

When Ezra's sister, Sharon, was a young girl, one of her favorite stories was *Berchick* by Esther Silverstein Blanc. Berchick is a colt that was raised by a Jewish family homesteading in Wyoming. Hard times hit the family, and they had to sell their farm and all their horses, including Berchick. But Berchick escaped his new owners and returned to his family. However, he could not stay with them as the family needed to move into town. So, they told Berchick to run away and be free. He does.

Then, sometime later, after they have moved to town, a friend tells the family he saw Berchick running with a herd of wild horses, healthy and free. "That is what is most important," the mother says, speaking for all of them.

Berchick is a favorite story because it includes many of the elements that appeal to children everywhere: loving families, children like themselves involved in adventures, and a special animal who is more a member of the family than a pet. *Berchick* also has elements that resonate especially with many Jews. It recognizes that the Jewish experience in America is broad and diverse. Not many people realize that Jewish families were also homesteaders in the West.

It also acknowledged the desire to be accepted as part of the community, as neighbors and friends, without needing to hide being Jewish. It contains perseverance through hard times, through strong family ties and sacrifice. It involves the bittersweet experience that too many Jewish families have experienced, if not in one generation, then in another. In order to be free and safe and to make a life for oneself and one's family, sometimes family members and friends need to part ways. Sharon liked to read *Berchick* silently by herself. Perhaps she imagined herself there in Wyoming with Berchick.

Sharon and Ezra's younger brother, Bernie, loved *The Carp in the Bathtub* by Barbara Cohen. Set in a small apartment in New York City in the early twentieth century, a family with two small children prepares for Pesach (also called Passover). The mother buys a large carp and puts it in the bathtub until she is ready to kill it and turn it into gefilte fish (a dish often eaten at Pesach). But while the mother is out shopping, the children—who have become very fond of the carp and want to save it from being ground up into gefilte fish—take it out of the bathtub, carry it to a neighbor's apartment, and hide it in the bathtub there.

When their father comes home, the children tell him about the carp, hoping to enlist his aid. But he tells them that the carp cost a lot of money, and they will need to use the carp to make gefilte fish for Pesach. They cannot afford to let the carp go, and they cannot keep it in their neighbor's bathtub (as she will eventually need to take a bath). The children return the carp to their apartment and while they are at school, their mother makes gefilte fish.

The appeal of the book is obvious: children who get into a bit of mischief but are essentially good and a loving family celebrating Jewish life. For many Jews in the United States, their American history begins in New York where they, their parents, grandparents, or great-grandparents arrived at Ellis Island, having crossed the Atlantic escaping the pogroms, anti-Semitism, and violence in Europe. The largest Jewish immigration occurred from the 1880s through the 1920s.

The Carp in the Bathtub tells a piece of that history with humor and joy, a bit of unpleasant reality (the fish is killed, turned into gefilte fish, and eaten), and a good deal of nostalgia. The story invokes the Jewish holiday of Pesach that is itself a story, the story of the exodus of Jews from Egypt, a story of freedom. Humor, joy, a loving family, a bit of mischief, suspense, some unpleasant realities, and a wonderful holiday—what is there not to like?

Ezra, Sharon, and Bernie did not find the stories described above at school. The only Jewish children's literature at school was Holocaust literature: Jane Yolen's *The Devil's Arithmetic*, *Anne Frank: The Diary of a Young Girl*, and Elie Wiesel's *Night*, among others. These are important books for all children to read. As we explain in chapter 6, Holocaust children's literature is an important part of Jewish children's literature. Neither Jewish nor non-Jewish children should be shielded from the horror, the fear, the hatred, the death, and the evil of the Holocaust alongside the courage of Jews and some Christians; but the Holocaust is only a part of the Jewish experience. It is rare to find in schools, in children's literature courses in teacher education programs, or professional organizations, Jewish children's literature beyond Holocaust children's literature.

Ezra, Sharon, and Bernie, among other Jewish children, are being denied a literary heritage because of the absence of Jewish children's literature in their school. Deny a people their literature, and you deny them their humanity; present their literature as a single dimension (e.g., as just Holocaust literature), and you turn them into a caricature and a stereotype. The loss of a literary heritage here is not just a loss for Jewish children. Fail to share a people's literature with others, and you fail to connect each people's humanity with that of others, diminishing the whole human community. Ezra, Sharon, and Bernie should not have to wonder why their literature and humanity are absent in the classroom (nor should any child have to so wonder), and they should not be denied the right to share it with others.

This book is about the use of Jewish children's literature in preschool through grade 6 classrooms. It is for all teachers regardless of whether any of their students are Jewish. Using Jewish children's literature can expose students to stories that will provoke their imaginations, deepen their aesthetic and emotional experiences with children's literature, and engage them in philosophical inquiries about the nature of being human, the nature of good and evil, and open up discussion about how to imagine a life among others in the world.

At the end of his collection of *Stories for Children*, Isaac Bashevis Singer, a winner of the Nobel Prize for Literature, writes:

> No matter how young they are, children are deeply concerned with the so-called eternal questions: Who created the world? Who made the earth, the sky, people, animals? . . . Children think about and ponder such matters as justice, the purpose of life, the why of suffering. They often find it difficult to make peace with the idea that animals are slaughtered so that man can eat them. They are bewildered and frightened by death. They cannot accept the fact that the strong should rule the weak. . . . If I had my way, I would publish a history of philosophy for children, where I would convey the basic ideas of all philosophers in simple language. Children, who are highly serious people, would read this book with great interest. In our time, when the literature for adults is deteriorating, good books for children are the only hope, the only refuge. Many adults read and enjoy children's books. We write not only for children but for their parents. They, too, are serious children. (337–38)

Using Jewish children's literature as part of a broad-based, diverse program of children's literature expands students' appreciation of the human condition, deepens their awareness of history, helps them counter stereotypes and forms of hatred that include but go beyond anti-Semitism, and helps them obtain a broader conception of the Jewish experience beyond being victims of the Holocaust. Perhaps most important, Jewish children's literature can engage children in what Singer called "eternal" questions.

Although eternal questions can never be fully or finally answered, asking eternal questions and struggling with them yields insights into ourselves, others, and the human condition and its diversity. Because eternal questions endure from generation to generation and are the kinds of questions that are important to embrace whether we are children or adults, we call them enduring questions. Asking enduring questions—struggling with them either by yourself or with others—not only brings us closer to wisdom, it also makes us more sensitive to others and invites us to what Jews call *tikkun olam* ("repair the world").

ABOUT THIS BOOK

This book discusses the use of Jewish children's literature in the preschool through grade 6 classroom. It provides information and recommendations about children's books that teachers might share with their students and keep in their classroom libraries. But perhaps most important, it provides a framework about the use of Jewish children's literature as an opportunity for all children, both Jewish and non-Jewish, to be philosophers and engage in dialogue and debate about enduring questions. To be clear: every classroom should have a broad range of children's literature that exposes children to a wide range of cultures, histories, geographies, families, languages, sexual orientations, and people with diverse talents and strengths (including people with different abilities). Jewish children's literature should be part of the multicultural literature collection in every classroom.

It is not enough for teachers just to expose children to multicultural literature. They need to guide children in how reading multicultural literature can inform them; open their minds to diverse ways of thinking, living, caring, and loving; and engage them in exploring enduring questions. As educators and lovers of children's literature, the literature we read and the discussions we have with children about enduring questions give all of us much to think about, more insightful understandings of others and of the world, humility, and perhaps even some guidance for our own lives.

This book focuses on Jewish children's literature originally written in English or translated into English. Jewish children's literature has been written in many languages including English, Hebrew, Yiddish, Spanish, Ladino, Russian, Polish, and others. Some Jewish children's stories were not so much translated as "retold" in English. (Appendix A contains a select list of bilingual Jewish children's literature: English/Yiddish, English/Hebrew, English/Ladino, English/Arabic.)

Chapter 2 briefly describes a history of Jewish children's literature in the United States. Opinions are diverse about some of the Jewish children's literature discussed in this book. For example, some Jews may object because, in their opinion, Jewish children should only be exposed to stories from the Torah (the Hebrew name for the first five books of the Hebrew Bible known in English as the Old Testament) and other Jewish religious texts. Some Jews may object to a particular children's book because their experience with Jewish life differs from what is represented. This book takes an expansive view of Jewish children's literature, valuing the range of Jewish experiences in America (and around the world) and valuing the diversity of imagination shared in Jewish children's literature.

The book begins, in chapter 1, with a discussion of what makes Jewish children's literature Jewish. Chapter 2 provides a history of Jewish children's literature. These are topics that teachers need to explore (and not only about Jewish children's literature but about children's literature in general). These two chapters provide a background so that teachers are better able to help students ask enduring questions: Who are we? What is our story? What is our history? What is our purpose?

Chapter 3 asks, "What is love?" In Jewish children's literature, this question is explored in many contexts: family, friendship, love for animals and nature, community, and more. But across all these contexts, love—in the Jewish context—is not so much a feeling as a set of acts toward the other. For example, one Jewish story—*Two Brothers*, retold by Chris Smith—is of two grown brothers who each worked the fields that they had inherited from their father. One brother had a family, and the other brother lived by himself. Each brother was worried about the other. The brother without a family thought that because his brother had a family that his needs were greater. Thus, rather than split the crop equally, his brother should receive more. So, one night he started taking some of the crop and carried it to his brother's house so his brother would have more. The brother with the family was worried about his brother who had no family to take care of him when he became old. Thus, his brother's needs were more than his own. So, that very same night he decided to bring some of the crop to his brother's house. Only after daybreak did the brothers see each other; they immediately understood that each was giving the other extra crop, and they embraced.

Most certainly the brothers had feelings for each other, but the love was in their acts toward each

ONE CITY, TWO BROTHERS: A STORY FROM JERUSALEM

[A folktale, with both Jewish and Arabic roots, tells the story of two brothers who show how much they care for each other by sacrificing for each other.]

I read this book to my class of first graders. They were very moved by the two brothers behaving so generously toward each other. I asked them, "What is most hard for you to share?" We drew pictures and wrote about what or who is most hard to share. Carl said, "I like to be first in line ALWAYS." Shani replied, "I don't like to share clothes with my sister." From Janell, "It is hard for me to share friends." Sean replied, "My books." Valerie said, "I don't like sharing my mom and dad with my sister."

We followed up in our class circle. I asked them, "So, you expressed that _____ was really hard to share. Have you noticed that sharing is clearly SO hard for children, and even some adults?" After we discussed this question, I asked, "So what does it take then, do you think, to share this item or these special people you care so much about, even though it is really hard?" Frank replied, "Take a breath and wait five seconds." Shani said, "I can't share my clothes, I'll run out." Janell asked, "Can I play, too?" Sean replied, "When I am on Book 2, I could let my brother read Book 1 of *Alien Next Door*." Through our discussion of the book, we explored our experiences with sharing what is most important to us and how we get to have choices in the way we respond. We wrestled with how difficult the struggle is when it comes to sharing what is most important.

Emily Bauman, first grade teacher, private independent school, Utah other. This story has many versions. One, adapted by Fawzia Gilani-Williams and titled *Yaffa and Fatima: Shalom, Salaam*, is about two women farmers, one Jewish and one Muslim. They act out their love for each other by secretly giving each other dates they had picked from their date trees, only to realize the other had done the same.

Chapter 4 asks, "What is time?" Jews mark the passing through the year with holidays creating a yearly cycle of affirmation of community, a relationship with nature, a commitment to justice and freedom, and engagement with memory and history. Rites mark the passing of time weekly, monthly, yearly, and across the life cycle. These rites connect the individual to the community and to those who have come before and who will live after us.

Chapter 5 begins with the question, "What is wisdom and what is foolishness?" Jewish humor undermines the privilege of the powerful and wealthy, allows us to look at our foibles and shortcomings, and makes accessible complex philosophical issues. Jewish humor is serious reading.

Chapter 6 asks, "What is evil and how might we respond to evil?" This chapter discusses the use of Jewish children's literature to address evil, anti-Semitism, and the Holocaust. Too often children's literature has appropriated the Holocaust inaccurately and has occasionally trivialized the Holocaust. In some cases, children's literature has appropriated the Holocaust for universalist themes, almost overlooking that it happened to Jews and was part of a long, evil history of anti-Semitism. Jewish life has a long tradition in bearing witness to evil and injustice. This is one driving force behind Jewish children's literature about the Holocaust and anti-Semitism. Bearing witness is not easy, and Jewish children's literature about the Holocaust, anti-Semitism, injustice, and hate is often painful and uncomfortable.

Chapter 7 asks a series of related questions: "What is justice? What is a righteous person to do?" The concept of tikkun olam is part of the core values of Jewish life and culture. It may be roughly translated as "repair the world," but many Jews use tikkun olam to mean "pursuit of social justice." Within the concept of tikkun olam is an important subtlety, the obligation to be involved in repairing the world and pursuing social justice. But what does that obligation mean? This is an important enduring question.

Chapter 8 asks, "How might we imagine life for ourselves together in the world?" This is the heart of classroom education, to help young children imagine and craft lives for themselves both now and in their future. The chapter focuses on designing curriculum and instruction that uses Jewish children's literature as part of a broadly diverse collection of children's literature for engaging children as serious philosophers and as people who act on the worlds in which they live. The chapter is written so that it applies to teachers who have many, few, or no Jewish children in their classrooms.

It discusses how Jewish children's literature might be integrated with other diverse children's literature and with learning experiences that go beyond the reading of literature.

Throughout the book are brief inserts from teachers on how they used a particular book in their classrooms. These personal reflections provide ideas about how Jewish children's literature might be used in educational settings.

At the back of the book are three appendixes that may be useful. They are:

- A list of select Jewish children's literature organized around traditional elementary school educational themes, with the appropriate grade level indicated.
- A select list of resources that will be helpful in using Jewish children's literature.
- A select list of scholarly books and articles about Jewish children's literature that provide insightful literary analyses and historical information.

We also want to share with you some stylistic choices we have made. The first concerns how the name of God is represented. In Judaism there are many ways to represent the name of God. This topic provokes some debate and a great variation in what Jews do in representing the name of God. In this book, we have decided to represent the name of God as "God." We have further decided not to use pronouns. It is not just that many pronouns are gendered, but also that pronouns suggest that God is like a person; or if the pronoun "It" were used, like an object. Jews define God in many ways. Many Jews, both currently and historically, do not have a belief in God or view such a belief as central or necessary to a vibrant Jewish community and culture. How to represent the name of God can, itself, be viewed as an enduring question.

Another stylistic choice concerns how to designate authorship. Many Jewish stories are retold stories. Sometimes the retelling is a near match to the original; but sometimes the retelling varies in substantive ways, so much so that one could say it is a different story. Some might even argue that retelling a story is a very creative act, tantamount to authoring itself. We believe that it is important that authors acknowledge their sources, and we are pleased that almost always the authors do so. They may acknowledge their sources in an introduction or in notes to the reader at the end. Should people who are retelling a story be called authors or retellers? We have chosen to call them authors but indicate that their authorship is a retelling.

It is our view that Jewish children's literature is currently experiencing a boom. Many new Jewish children's books are being published, and many Jewish children's stories are being translated from Yiddish, Hebrew, Ladino, Spanish, and other languages into English. Much of the artwork in Jewish children's picture books is exciting, engaging, and worthy of display in the finest art museums. (If you would like to see a sample of that artwork, look at *Monsters and Miracles: A Journey through Jewish Picture Books.*)

Although we are enthusiastic about Jewish children's literature and its use in classrooms, we have concerns that need to be noted. Too few books show the racial diversity of Jews and Jewish families in the United States. Jews of color constitute 12–15 percent of all Jews in the United States, and approximately 20 percent of all Jewish households in the United States have at least one member who is a person of color (Kelman, Tapper, Fonseca, & Saperstein, 2019). Jewish children of color need to see themselves in the books they find in their classrooms. In addition, too few books show Jews and members of Jewish families who identify as lesbian, gay, bisexual, transgender, queer, and/or nonbinary. Too few books show Jewish children and Jewish adults with differing abilities. It is our hope that in the coming decade, these gaps will be addressed with high-quality, authentic Jewish children's literature.

The books we have selected to discuss in the chapters are of high quality, authentic, and appropriate for use by teachers in a preschool through elementary educational setting. We focus on books and stories that teachers and librarians could read aloud during sharing time and that could engage educators and students in serious conversations. We have also included books that could be used with a classroom reading group and books that would be useful to have in a classroom or school library. Some books of Jewish children's literature are more appropriate for home libraries than for use by educators. We have also selected books that teachers and librarians can easily find and purchase. Many wonderful Jewish children's literature books are, unfortunately, out of print (although many are still easy to obtain). If you have a favorite Jewish children's literature book and do not find it discussed in the chapters or listed in any of the appendixes, please know that it is also probably one of our favorites. Wonderful Jewish children's literature books are so plentiful that we could not discuss them all.

FINAL INTRODUCTION COMMENTS

Ezra, Sharon, and Bernie are now grown adults with their own families and children. They are sharing with their children the books they loved when they were children. Every year brings new books, new Jewish children's literature, and it is hard to say who is enjoying reading them more—the children, their parents, or their grandparents. After all, we never grow too old, and we are never too young to pursue enduring questions. It matters little that we have no answers. It is in the asking, the seeking, and in the dialogue that we find ourselves and each other and the pursuit of tikkun olam.

Perhaps, in the not-too-distant future, the books that give Ezra, Sharon, Bernie, and their children such joy and that engage them in enduring questions will be found in preschool and elementary educational settings across the nation. Such books, used in combination with other multicultural children's literature, engage all children—Jewish and non-Jewish—in exploring enduring questions and in providing everyone with more diverse and complex representations of Jewish people and their lives. It is our hope that when they go to school, Jewish children will not wonder whether they have to leave being Jewish at home.

WORKS CITED

Children's Literature

Blanc, Esther Silverstein. *Berchick*. Illustrated by Tennessee Dixon. Volcano, CA: Volcano Press, 1989.

Cohen, Barbara. *The Carp in the Bathtub*. Illustrated by Joan Halpern. New York: Lothrop Lee & Shepard, 1972.

Frank, Anne. *The Diary of a Young Girl*. Translated by Barbara Mooyaart-Doubleday. New York: Modern Library, 1952.

Gilani-Williams, Fawzia. *Yaffa and Fatima: Shalom, Salaam*. Illustrated by Chiara Fedele. Minneapolis: Kar-Ben, 2017.

Singer, Isaac Bashevis. *Naftali the Storyteller and His Horse, Sus; and Other Stories*. Illustrated by Margot Zemach. New York: Farrar, Straus & Giroux, 1976.

Smith, Chris. *One City, Two Brothers*. Illustrated by Aurélia Fronty. Concord, MA: Barefoot Books, 2007.

Wiesel, Elie. *Night*. Translated by Stella Rodway. London: MacGibbon & Kee, 1960.

Yolen, Jane. *The Devil's Arithmetic*. New York: Viking Kestrel, 1987.

References

Kelman, A. Y., A. H. Tapper, I. Fonseca, and A. Saperstein. *Counting Inconsistencies: An Analysis of American Jewish Population Studies, with a Focus on Jews of Color*, 2019. Retrieved April 4, 2022, from https://www.jewishdatabank.org/content/upload/bjdb/2019_Counting_Inconsistencies_Methodological_Appendix_Focus_on_Jews_of_Color.pdf.

Singer, I. B. "Are Children the Ultimate Literary Critics?" In I. B. Singer, *Stories for Children*, 332–38. New York: Farrar, Straus & Giroux, 1984.

Stavans, I., N. Sokol, and T. Gozani. *Monsters and Miracles: A Journey through Jewish Picture Books*. Eric Carle Museum, Amherst, MA, and Skirball Cultural Center, Los Angeles, 2010.

Chapter 1

What Makes Jewish Children's Literature Jewish?

"Gittel," Mama put her hands on Gittel's shoulders and looked her in the eye. "Home is not safe for us. You are going to America to have a better life."

"By myself?" Gittel's voice came out in a squeak. She was only nine years old. How could she go to America without Mama?

This passage is from the award-winning *Gittel's Journey: An Ellis Island Story* by Lesléa Newman. When Gittel's mother is denied passage on the boat to America due to an eye infection, nine-year-old Gittel must travel alone from Eastern Europe to meet her relatives in New York.

A lengthy author's note explains that the book is based on the true story of two individuals, the author's grandmother and a close family friend. Although the time period is the early 1900s, Gittel's story resonates not only with Jewish children, many of whose families immigrated to the United States in the late nineteenth and early twentieth centuries, but also with children who are recent immigrants to the United States, the current situation of migrant children at the U.S. borders, and displaced children around the world.

The book prompts many enduring questions: Why do people leave home? How does it feel to be a stranger in a new land? How can a child show kindness to a peer new to this country who doesn't know English?

This chapter discusses this question: "What makes Jewish children's literature Jewish?" A response to this question is complex, requiring an understanding of the historical, social, cultural, political, ethnic, linguistic, and religious contexts of Jewish lives. Too often, Jews are simply defined as belonging to a different religion or celebrating different holidays. Such a simple definition of Jews has problems. Hundreds of books discuss the questions "What is a Jew?" and "Who is a Jew?," which have been vigorously debated for centuries. Although variations exist, Jews share a culture, a history, a sense of belonging, and an ethnicity. The words available in English for defining what is a Jew and what is Jewish are inadequate. Many Jews are frustrated by government forms, such as the U.S. Census, which require them to check "Jewish" as religion, rather than ethnicity or culture. Some Jews define being Jewish as a nationality. It is perhaps easier to think of Jews as a "people" who are diverse racially, ethnically, culturally, linguistically, and religiously; who share a broad history that is worldwide; and who recognize each other as belonging despite differences. Racial diversity is also apparent among Jews worldwide and in the United States.

Diversity is also reflected in various ways that Jews identify and practice Judaism. Within Judaism are several denominations, which differ based on their interpretation of Jewish law and their approach to tradition and rituals. The major denominations in the United States are Orthodox, Conservative, and Reform. Other Jews in the United States affiliate with smaller denominations such as Reconstructionist, Jewish Renewal, Humanistic Judaism, and Bundist. Many Jews in the United States do not affiliate with any denomination. They may not know their heritage

GITTEL'S JOURNEY

[Gittel and her mother plan to immigrate to America together, but when her mother is stopped by a health inspector, Gittel must make the journey alone.]

I introduced *Gittel's Journey* to my first graders by having them stand up and pretend they were going on a long journey. Then I told them to put their chairs directly in front of them to block them and act as an obstacle. I proceeded to ask them to take a few steps forward. They were stuck! I told them to try again. Clearly, they couldn't move; some laughed at the attempt to do so. I told them we still had to go on our journey and needed to problem solve how to do this. Students talked about going around the chair, climbing over it, moving the chair, and one small six-year-old even demonstrated how to go under the chair.

Then, we moved to the carpet and read our story about a young girl who also faced obstacles along her way. As Gittel faced each new obstacle, we stopped and drew a picture and wrote a word to represent it. After the story, we discussed how Gittel persevered and overcame each obstacle during her journey.

My students were enthralled with the imagery of candles and candlesticks and how they were joined together when mother and daughter were as well. Connections were made to our newest English learners who have recently moved to Montana from Mexico and Honduras and who speak Spanish, languages—Hebrew, Yiddish, and Ladino—or the rich literature written in these languages, including children's literature.

Many non-Jews in the United States have little or no experience with Jewish people or Jewish communities. They may live in regions of the United States where few Jewish people live and may not have the opportunity to interact with Jews. Their knowledge about Judaism may be nonexistent. For other non-Jews, their knowledge may be limited to the musical *Fiddler on the Roof*, reading a book on the Holocaust, or from stereotypes on popular media such as television.

but many speak little English like Gittel, who comes to America speaking only Yiddish. One student referenced God and how happy God is when we overcome hard things and find happiness, like Gittel finally being together with her mother again. We discussed Gittel's attributes (e.g., courage and persistence, and what helped overcome her obstacles). At the end of the book, my students were blown away that this was, in fact, a true story. The influence of one girl's courage in the face of obstacles then made an even greater impact.

Renée Gilpin, first-grade teacher, public school, Montana

With the wide range of books that constitute Jewish children's literature for children ages three through twelve and the diversity within Judaism, how do educators know if a book provides an authentic representation of the Jewish experience? This question does not have an easy answer. Unfortunately, not one source, website, or book provides a simple way for separating authentic from non-authentic Jewish experience. Reading what different people have to say about the Jewish experience and its representation in Jewish children's literature provides information, perspective, and understanding. Children—including Jewish children—are not in the position to know whether a story provides an authentic account of Jewish life; this responsibility rests with educators and librarians. In the next section, some suggestions are shared to guide you in selecting Jewish children's books in the classroom.

A book such as *Gittel's Journey* is an excellent touchstone for what makes a story or book high-quality Jewish children's literature. So, too, are the other books and stories described throughout this book and in the list of Jewish children's literature organized by themes/topics in appendix A. This chapter provides a beginning for teachers to think about the question and feel more confident in making judgments about which books to share with children (and which books to avoid). After defining Jewish children's literature, criteria are suggested to use in evaluating quality Jewish children's books.

WHAT IS JEWISH CHILDREN'S LITERATURE?

We agree with Silver (2008), who defines an authentic Jewish children's literature book as one "characterized by its specifically Jewish dimensions, namely Jewish time, place, characters, and themes" (1). More specifically, we define Jewish children's literature as

> any book for children that represents authentic Jewish experience including its culture, history, religion, languages, and the day-to-day life of Jewish people around the world through specific themes, characters, settings, plots, or content.

A Jewish children's book can be in any genre or format: realistic fiction, historical fiction, fantasy, picture book, folktale, poetry, informational book, biography, or graphic novel. Although the setting could be anywhere Jews have lived—and Jews have lived everywhere—what establishes the setting as Jewish is how it is framed historically. So, the setting could be New York City and the many different Jewish neighborhoods there, the result of the large immigration of Jews through Ellis Island in the 1870s through the 1920s. It could be a *shtetl* (small village) or *shtot* (city) in Eastern Europe, where many Ashkenazi Jews lived before the Holocaust in World War II. It could be a town in Spain, South America, or Turkey, where Sephardic Jews lived for centuries both before and after the Spanish Inquisition and other persecutions; North Africa or countries in the Middle East where Mizrahi Jews have lived; or in Israel and Palestine. It could be Wyoming—as in *Berchick*—with the few Jews who were homesteading there barely able to gather a *minyan* (ten Jewish adults needed for some religious rituals). In recent history, Jews have lived in large numbers in the United States, Israel, France, Canada, Mexico, South Africa, Australia, Argentina, Russia, and other areas of the world.

The time period may be contemporary or in the past. For example, *Letters from Rifka* by Karen Hesse is a historical novel based on the immigration experience of the author's great-aunt. This outstanding book, winner of both the National Jewish Book Award and the Sydney Taylor Award, provides readers insights into the immigration experience of the Jews in the early 1900s. Written in the format of letters from Rifka to her cousin Tovah, Rifka shares her thoughts and feelings as she leaves Russia in 1919 to arrive eventually at Ellis Island in 1920.

An example of a contemporary story is the biography of beloved Supreme Court Justice Ruth Bader Ginsburg, who died in 2020. In *I Dissent: Ruth Bader Ginsburg Makes Her Mark* by Debbie Levy, readers immediately learn that Ginsburg is Jewish. Although it is now rare, at the time of her youth it was not unusual for signs in hotels and motels to state, "No Dogs or Jews Allowed." As a child, Ginsburg saw such a sign. As she became an adult, she did not forget how such a sign made her feel, and her experiences with anti-Semitism and prejudice more generally shaped her commitment to justice. First as a lawyer and then as a judge, she fought prejudice and unfairness through the law and through the courts.

Not all children's literature written by a Jewish author would necessarily be considered Jewish children's literature if the book does not include Jewish characters or Jewish content. For example, children's author William Steig, the son of Polish Jewish immigrants, wrote award-winning books for children and created the Shrek character, originally introduced in the book *Shrek!* and then popularized in film and a Broadway musical. But Steig's books do not focus on Jewish themes. The character Curious George and the books about him were written by Hans and Margret Rey. The Reys, German Jews living in France during World War II, escaped Paris on bicycles, bringing the manuscript about a mischievous monkey with them. Other award-winning children's authors are Jewish, notably Maurice Sendak and Ezra Jack Keats, but not all their books would be considered Jewish children's literature. For instance, Sendak's *Where the Wild Things Are* would not be considered Jewish children's literature, but his illustrations for *In Grandpa's House*, a book by Sendak's father, Philip Sendak, about his life and originally written in Yiddish, would.

Conversely, an author need not be Jewish to have penned an outstanding book for children with Jewish content. *Number the Stars* by Lois Lowry received the National Jewish Book Award, the Newbery Medal, and the Sydney Taylor Book Award. This historical novel about the friendship between ten-year-old Danish friends, one Jewish and one Christian, takes place during World War II and describes ways that the Danish resistance saved most of Denmark's Jews. The book is dedicated to Lowry's friend Annelise Platt, whose childhood experiences inspired the book. Another example is the book by award-winning historian Jerry Stanley, *Frontier Merchants: Lionel and Barron Jacobs and the Jewish Pioneers Who Settled the West*. This well-researched informational book describes how the Jacobs brothers began a general store in 1867 in Tucson and then established the first bank in Arizona.

Jewish children's literature includes books from many countries written in English as well as books written in other languages that have been translated into English. Swedish author Annika Thor has written award-winning historical novels such as *A Faraway Island* and its sequel, *The Lily Pond*, about two Jewish sisters who are sent from their Austrian home to a remote island in Sweden to ensure their safety during World War II. Israeli author Uri Orlev writes in Hebrew and has received the coveted Hans Christian Andersen Award. His books have been translated into English and received numerous awards, with such titles as *The Island on Bird Street* (also made into a feature film) and *Run, Boy, Run*. Stories written for children in Yiddish have been translated into English and adapted or retold for today's young people. For example, the story "Oyb Nisht Nokh Hekher" by the famous Yiddish author I. L. Peretz has been translated under the title *Even Higher* and has retellings for children by Barbara Cohen (1987), Eric Kimmel (2009), and Richard Ungar (2007). Ungar's book received the National Jewish Book Award.

WHY USE JEWISH CHILDREN'S LITERATURE? SELECTING AUTHENTIC, QUALITY JEWISH CHILDREN'S BOOKS

Teachers may question why, if no Jewish children are in their classroom or community, they should choose to include Jewish children's literature. The response to this question is the same as the answer to why we include any kind of diverse literature in the classroom. Rudine Sims Bishop (1994) has expressed it well:

> Literature educates not only the head, but the heart as well. It promotes empathy and invites readers to adopt new perspectives. It offers opportunities for children to learn to recognize our similarities, value our differences, and respect our common humanity. Children need literature that serves as a window onto lives and experiences different from their own, and literature that serves as a mirror reflecting themselves and their cultural values, attitudes and behaviors. (xiv)

The nonprofit organization We Need Diverse Books states, "We recognize all diverse experiences, including (but not limited to) LGBTQ+, Native, people of color, gender diversity, people with disabilities, and ethnic, cultural, and religious minorities" (https://diversebooks.org/about-wndb/). In brief, Jewish children are diverse. As a religious, cultural, and ethnic minority in the United States, Jewish children need that mirror to see themselves and their experiences in books (including the diversity among Jewish children), whereas non-Jewish children need that window to look into and view the history, culture, customs, languages, diversity, and religion of Jewish people. All children, regardless of religion, race, ethnicity, culture, sexuality, gender identity, and language(s), benefit from discussing enduring questions that diverse books explore.

The document that the Association of Jewish Libraries prepared, titled "Excellence in Jewish Children's Literature" (found at the end of this chapter), is an excellent guide to selecting authentic, quality Jewish children's literature. The Association of Jewish Libraries sponsors the Sydney Taylor Award for children's literature. This award honors Sydney Taylor, the author of the *All-of-a-Kind Family* series, a breakthrough in Jewish children's literature and considered the first Jewish-themed children's book in the United States that crossed over into the mainstream. The first book in the five-book series, published in 1951, is still in print today, as are the other four. As you think about selecting Jewish children's books to share with children, you might consider several criteria. These include books that engage children in your class, support the curriculum, reflect literary merit, include the diversity of Jewish children and families, and authentically represent Jewish content.

Books that engage children in your class are ones that encourage children to think about enduring questions and to pose their own questions. They are books that spark the children's imagination, prompt thoughtful discussion, and foster reader response in a variety of ways—through art, drama, writing, music, and other creative outlets. Teachers also want to select books that are age-appropriate for their classroom. As a teacher, you know the children you teach and what books would best support their cognitive, language, and social-emotional development. You also are sensitive to the range of individual differences among children. The interests of children in your class may vary—the topics that excite them, or the kinds of books they prefer. So, in selecting books for your classroom library, to read aloud, to share as part of your curriculum, or to recommend to a specific student, you will be guided by your children, both as individuals and as a classroom community.

Your school district's curriculum and the content you are expected to teach will also influence the books you select. Jewish children's books can be shared across subject areas to be integrated into your existing curriculum. For example, if you are studying biographies, you can include books about famous Jewish Americans such as the doctor who discovered the polio vaccine; his story is told in *The Polio Pioneer: Dr. Jonas Salk and the Polio Vaccine* by Linda Elovitz Marshall.

Children may not be aware that the actor who played *Star Trek*'s Spock was Jewish, born to immigrant parents from Ukraine. They can learn more about him in *Fascinating: The Life of Leonard Nimoy* by Richard Michelson. When you study Thanksgiving, you might consider sharing *Molly's Pilgrim* by Barbara Cohen, about a Russian-Jewish immigrant child who struggles to find acceptance in school. Her classmates learn that the Pilgrims based Thanksgiving on the Jewish holiday of Sukkot, the Feast of the Tabernacles. The movie version of the book received an Oscar for Best Short Film. If you are doing a theme study on immigration, you could read aloud the beautiful picture book *When Jessie Came Across the Sea* by Amy Hest. Thirteen-year-old Jessie, who lived with her grandmother, travels alone across the Atlantic to America and a new life. The historically authentic illustrations by P. J. Lynch garnered him the Kate Greenaway Medal, the United Kingdom's equivalent of the Caldecott. As you celebrate Black History Month, your students may be surprised to learn about organizations of Black Jews and of the active role that Jews have played in the civil rights movement. You might share *Always an Olivia: A Remarkable Family History* by Carolivia Herron who recounts, in a fictionalized picture book, her African American and Jewish heritage. Or you might read aloud *As Good as Anybody: Martin Luther King, Jr., and Abraham Joshua Heschel's Amazing March toward Freedom* by Richard Michelson, which describes the friendship between Martin Luther King Jr. and Rabbi Heschel, and their shared commitment to justice.

We always want to share books of high literary quality with children in our classroom. These books reflect the beauty of language, strong themes, engaging plots, and identifiable characters. They raise deep questions without right or wrong answers for children to think about and discuss with their peers. Quality books also serve as mentor texts for children's own writing and can be of any genre—picture books, novels, biography, informational books, graphic novels, and poetry.

Professional sources provide criteria and guidelines to assess the literary quality of a children's book (see *Charlotte Huck's Children's Literature: A Brief Guide* by Barbara Kiefer, Cynthia Tyson, Bettie Parsons Barger, Lisa Patrick, and Erin Reilly-Sanders; *Literature and the Child* by Lee Galda, Lauren Liang, and Bea Cullinan; and *Children's Books in Children's Hands* by Charles Temple, Miriam Martinez, and Junko Yokota). There are also book awards and lists of outstanding books that are indicated as high quality. Many professional organizations also provide yearly lists of outstanding books as well as individual book awards. Commercial outlets such as the *New York Times* publish lists of outstanding children's books. If a book has received some kind of recognition, you can usually feel confident about its literary merit.

EVALUATING JEWISH CONTENT

The Association of Jewish Libraries Guide, "Excellence in Jewish Children's Literature," provides helpful criteria for judging Jewish content. First, whether a book is fiction or nonfiction, "accuracy is essential" in representing Jewish content. People, places, dates, holidays, customs, and other Jewish elements need to be based on factual information. If the book is a picture book, the illustrations also need to portray Jewish content accurately.

A second criterion on the AJL Guide is "authenticity," which means that "Jewish beliefs, characters, settings, and experiences should be portrayed without sentimentality, distortion or stereotyping, in words or illustrations." An example of a book meeting this criterion is the award-winning *The Inquisitor's Tale* by Adam Gidwitz, the fast-paced adventure fantasy about three children on a quest to save the Jewish Talmud. An extensive author's note provides information about Judaism in the Middle Ages in Europe. An example of a book that does not meet this criterion is *Shmelf the Hanukkah Elf.* The book describes Shmelf, one of Santa's new elves, who cares for Jewish children and travels on a Jewish reindeer to bring presents to Jewish children. The book has been criticized for equating Hanukkah with Christmas and misrepresenting the meaning and significance of Hanukkah (Connor, 2016; Silverman, 2016).

Accuracy and authenticity are often challenging to determine. Many critics ask if the author is an insider (a Jewish person) or an outsider (someone who is not Jewish). Being an insider provides the author more credibility for understanding cultural subtleties, not just surface-level features. As noted earlier in this chapter, an outsider can write an outstanding Jewish children's book, and some of these authors have received Jewish book awards. Recently, Jonathan Auxier received the Sydney Taylor Award and other recognitions for *Sweep: The Story of a Girl and Her Monster*, the story of the chimney sweep, Nan, and her golem. Set in late-nineteenth-century London, the story was inspired by the Jewish legend of the Golem of Prague, the clay giant who protected the Jews in 1580. As Lehman (2005) points out, "authors who write outside their own religion have a special obligation not only to verify the accuracy of facts . . . but also to create authentically the more subtle nuances or impressions of the religion being depicted" (12).

Here are several approaches to consider in assessing accuracy and authenticity. First, check the credentials of the author, usually found on the book's dust jacket. Does the author have the appropriate background or experience to have written a book about Jewish people? Often the book may include acknowledgments or recognition of an expert who has reviewed the book for accuracy. In her acknowledgments for *Hammerin' Hank Greenberg: Baseball Pioneer*, Shelley Sommer recognizes Stephen Greenberg, Hank Greenberg's son, for reviewing the manuscript. Or there may be an author's note with further explanations or a list of resources that the author consulted in writing the book.

You can also read reviews of the book that have appeared in professional journals. These reviews are written by people who have knowledge and expertise on the content of the book as well as its literary merit. Some resources specifically review Jewish children's books, such as *Tablet* magazine, the *Association of Jewish Libraries Review*, and the Jewish Book Council. It is easy to obtain information online about a book's author and to access reviews of the book.

In addition to accuracy and authenticity, consider additional criteria in judging Jewish content. The Association of Jewish Libraries lists criteria for "depth of Jewish content," the extent to which the book includes content that is specifically Jewish. The AJL Guide notes, "Contemporary Judaism is pluralistic and this is reflected in children's books. The content may range from fully observant to marginally Jewish." One book's main character may be Jewish but otherwise doesn't include many references to Jewish culture and history, whereas another book's central plot, theme, or setting is Judaism.

For example, compare how Jewish content is represented in two picture books, both considered fine examples of Jewish children's literature. In *Rabbi Benjamin's Buttons* by Alice B. McGinty, a congregation presents its beloved rabbi with a special holiday vest. Members of the congregation also cook so much food for the rabbi on each Jewish holiday that the buttons start to pop off. A glossary of terms and recipes for Jewish holiday food is included. On the other hand, in *A Scarf for Keiko* by Ann Mapaspina, set in Los Angeles in 1942, a Jewish family and Japanese family are neighbors and friends. When the Japanese family is sent to an internment camp, the young Jewish boy, Sam, makes a special present for his friend Keiko. Although references to Jewish customs are limited to Shabbat observance, Jewish values such as lovingkindness and justice and righteousness are emphasized. Both of these books were named Sydney Taylor Book Award Notable Books, but their depth of Jewish content differs.

The criterion "positive focus and values" in the AJL Guide emphasizes a perspective that is rooted in Jewish values "that have special emphasis in the Jewish tradition and are often tied to Jewish texts" such as the Hebrew Bible or Talmud. In *The Jewish Values Finder: A Guide to Values in Jewish Children's Literature* (Silver, 2008), annotations of Jewish children's books are organized by important Jewish values such as "justice and righteousness," "lovingkindness," "remembrance," and "repairing the world."

The AJL Guide notes, "Whether serious or lighthearted, Jewish children's literature should have something Jewish to say to readers." For example, the Yiddish folksong "I Had a Little Overcoat" is the basis for two award-winning children's books. In the Caldecott Medal book *Joseph Had a Little Overcoat*, author/illustrator Simms Taback includes the words and music to the song. The story reflects widely repeated Jewish wisdom that we always have a way to create something out of nothing (see also "Shlomo the Tailor" by Rabbi Stacy Schlein in *Three Times Chai* by Laney Katz Becker, 2007). Jim Aylesworth retells this folk song in the Sydney Taylor Book Award recipient *My Grandfather's Coat*. In this retelling, the conclusion, "nothing left at all, nothing that is, except for this story," reflects the Jewish value of the importance of story in Jewish history and culture.

The Jewish content of "sensitivity" focuses on the awareness that diversity exists in Judaism. Not all Jews are of Eastern European descent, not all Jews live in urban areas, not all Jews are white, and not all Jews are observant.

It is important for a book to dispel stereotypes that people may have about Jews and Judaism. It is also critical that the book doesn't generalize in such a way that children will believe that all Jews think, feel, and behave in the same way.

A classic example is the award-winning novel, *The Return* by Sonia Levitin, the story of Desta, her brother, and sister who live in a small, isolated community of Ethiopian Jews and who make the long, dangerous journey to the Sudan, where they are airlifted to Israel. The book is based on the actual Operation Moses, the airlift of hundreds of Ethiopian Jews into Israel in the 1980s. Jewish diversity exists in the United States as portrayed in the award-winning *Lucky Broken Girl* by Ruth Behar. In this novel, inspired by the author's life, Ruthie Mizrahi is a Jewish Cuban immigrant in New York in the 1960s. Her injuries in a car accident require that she spends one year in a full-body cast.

It should be noted that a book may not meet all these criteria perfectly, but the criteria provide some guiding principles when reviewing books to share with children in the classroom. In the following chapters, books are described that we consider quality Jewish children's literature based on the criteria that have been discussed.

Memory is an important concept in Jewish culture and life. *Zachor*, the Hebrew word for remember, appears nearly two hundred times in the Hebrew Bible (https://www.myjewishlearning.com/article/zachor-why-jewish-memory-matters/). The importance of collective memory in the Jewish religion is reflected in rituals, holiday observances, religious texts, memorial books (in Yiddish called *Yizker Bikher*), and story. Jewish children's literature is one way to remember not only historical events, but also to remember holidays, customs, life-cycle events, ethics, and values. Within the context of memory and history, Jewish children's literature provides a way to ask and discuss enduring questions. Educators play a critical role in their students' lives. We invite you to share a Jewish children's book with your students—their responses may surprise you as you discuss enduring questions together.

WORKS CITED

Children's Literature

Auxier, Jonathan. *Sweep: The Story of a Girl and Her Monster.* New York: Abrams, 2018.

Aylesworth, Jim. *My Grandfather's Coat.* Illustrated by Barbara McClintock. New York: Scholastic, 2014.

Becker, Laney Katz. *Three Times Chai: 54 Rabbis Tell Their Favorite Stories.* Millburn, NJ: Behrman House, 2007.

Behar, Ruth. *Lucky Broken Girl.* New York: Nancy Paulsen Books, 2017.

Cohen, Barbara. *Even Higher.* Illustrated by Anatoly Ivanov. New York: Lothrop, Lee & Shepard, 1987.

———. *Molly's Pilgrim.* Illustrated by Michael J. Deraney. New York: Lothrop, Lee & Shepard, 1983.

Gidwitz, Adam. *The Inquisitor's Tale: Or, The Three Holy Children and Their Magical Dog.* New York: Dutton, 2016.

Herron, Carolivia. *Always an Olivia: A Remarkable Family History.* Illustrated by Jeremy Tugeau. Minneapolis: Kar-Ben, 2012.

Hesse, Karen. *Letters from Rifka.* New York: Henry Holt, 1992.

Hest, Amy. *When Jessie Came Across the Sea.* Illustrated by P. J. Lynch. Cambridge, MA: Candlewick, 1997.

Kimmel, Eric A. *Even Higher.* Illustrated by Jill Weber. New York: Holiday House, 2009.

Levitin, Sonia. *The Return.* New York: Atheneum, 1987.

Levy, Debbie. *I Dissent: Ruth Bader Ginsburg Makes Her Mark.* Illustrated by Elizabeth Baddeley. New York: Simon & Schuster, 2016.

Lowry, Lois. *Number the Stars.* Boston: Houghton Mifflin, 1989.

Malaspina, Ann. *A Scarf for Keiko.* Illustrated by Merrilee Liddiard. Minneapolis: Kar-Ben, 2019.

Marshall, Linda Elovitz. *The Polio Pioneer: Dr. Jonas Salk and the Polio Vaccine.* Illustrated by Lisa Anchin. New York: Knopf Books for Young Readers, 2020.

McGinty, Alice B. *Rabbi Benjamin's Buttons.* Illustrated by Jennifer Black Reinhardt. Watertown, MA: Charlesbridge, 2014.

Michelson, Richard. *As Good as Anybody: Martin Luther King, Jr., and Abraham Joshua Heschel's Amazing March toward Freedom.* Illustrated by Raul Colón. New York: Knopf, 2008.

———. *Fascinating: The Life of Leonard Nimoy.* Illustrated by Edel Rodriguez. New York: Knopf, 2016.

Newman, Lesléa. *Gittel's Journey: An Ellis Island Story.* Illustrated by Amy June Bates. New York: Abrams, 2019.

Orlev, Uri. *The Island on Bird Street.* Translated by Hillel Halkin. Boston: Houghton Mifflin, 1983.

———. *Run, Boy, Run.* Translated by Hillel Halkin. Boston: Houghton Mifflin, 2003.

Sendak, Maurice. *Where the Wild Things Are.* New York: Harper & Row, 1963.

Sendak, Philip. *In Grandpa's House.* Illustrated by Maurice Sendak. New York: Harper & Row, 1985.

Sommer, Shelley. *Hammerin' Hank Greenberg: Baseball Pioneer.* Honesdale, PA: Calkins Creek, 2011.

Stanley, Jerry. *Frontier Merchants: Lionel and Barron Jacobs and the Jewish Pioneers Who Settled the West.* New York: Knopf Books for Young Readers, 1998.

Steig, William. *Shrek!* New York: Farrar, Straus & Giroux, 1990.

Taback, Simms. *Joseph Had a Little Overcoat.* New York: Viking, 1999.

Taylor, Sydney. *All-of-a-Kind Family*. Illustrated by Helen John. Westchester, IL: Follett, 1951.

Thor, Annika. *A Faraway Island*. Translated by Linda Schenck. New York: Delacorte Books for Young Readers, 2009.

———. *The Lily Pond*. Translated by Linda Schenck. New York: Delacorte Books for Young Readers, 2011.

Ungar, Richard. *Even Higher.* Toronto: Tundra Books, 2007.

References

Association of Jewish Libraries. "Excellence in Jewish Children's Literature," https://jewishlibraries.org/excellence-in-jewish-childrens-lit/

Bishop, R. S., ed. *Kaleidoscope: A Multicultural Booklist for Grades K–8.* Urbana, IL: National Council of Teachers of English, 1994.

Connor, A. Review of Shmelf the Hanukkah Elf. *School Library Journal*, 2016. Retrieved April 26, 2002, from https://www.slj.com/review/shmelf-the-hanukkah-elf.

Galda, L., L. A. Liang, and B. E. Cullinan. *Literature and the Child*. Boston: Cengage Learning, 2017.

Kiefer, B., C. Tyson, B. P. Barger, L. Patrick, and E. Reilly-Sanders. *Charlotte Huck's Children's Literature: A Brief Guide*. New York: McGraw-Hill, 2022.

Lehman, B. A. "Religious Representation in Children's Literature." In D. L. Henderson and J. P. May, eds., *Exploring Culturally Diverse Literature for Children and Adolescents*, 11–21. Boston: Allyn and Bacon, 2005.

Patt, A. "Zachor: Why Memory Matters." *My Jewish Learning*. Retrieved April 26, 2022, from https://www.myjewishlearning.com/article/zachor-why-jewish-memory-matters/.

Silver, L. R. *The Jewish Values Finder: A Guide to Values in Jewish Children's Literature.* Chicago: Neal-Schuman Publishers, 2008.

Silverman, L. "Story of 'Shmelf' Not Welcome on Every Jewish Library Shelf." *Jewish Journal*, 2016. Retrieved April 26, 2022, from https://jewishjournal.com/culture/arts/books/213173/

Temple, C., M. Martinez, and J. Yokota. *Children's Books in Children's Hands: A Brief Introduction to Their Literature*. New York: Pearson, 2018.

We Need Diverse Books. Our definition of diversity. Retrieved April 26, 2022, from https://diversebooks.org/about-wndb/

EXCELLENCE IN JEWISH CHILDREN'S LITERATURE

A Guide for Book Selectors, Reviewers, and Award Judges

INTRODUCTION When evaluating children's books of Jewish content, book selectors, reviewers and book award judges always look for outstanding literary and artistic quality. Equally important is the merit of the book's Jewish content. Few books will meet all of the criteria for excellence identified in this guide but the books of Jewish content that librarians select, reviewers praise and judges award should approach the highest standards in both general literary criteria and those applied to Jewish children's literature.

JUDGING JEWISH CONTENT

ACCURACY

Accuracy is essential in dates, spelling, identification of objects, and empirically verifiable facts. Interpretations are based on reputable scholarship. Conflicting points of view are balanced. The author's point of view, if partisan, is clearly stated. The depiction of historical periods, events or processes is not distorted or over-simplified. Careful research and editing are evident.

AGE-APPROPRIATENESS

A distinction must be made between "picture books", i.e., those aimed at younger readers, and "illustrated books," which are for older readers. Picture books are usually characterized by short sentences, playful language, and concepts complemented by clear, concrete illustrations. In illustrated books, the subject matter is more serious or abstract, the theme and language more sophisticated, and the illustrations may be somber or dark.

AUTHENTICITY

Jewish beliefs, characters, settings, and experiences should be portrayed without sentimentality, distortion or stereotyping, in words or illustrations. Authenticity is achieved when individuals are shown interacting with Jewish belief, tradition, history, and practice in a manner that is both truthful and respectful, although the perspective may be satirical or critical. Sometimes, there will be no explicit Jewish content, as in stories by the Hasidic masters that imply or assume a Jewish setting, characters, theme or audience.

Prepared by an AJL Task Force comprised of Linda R. Silver, Cheryl Banks, Ellen Cole, and Lisa Silverman in 2003. Reformatted in 2021.

DEPTH OF JEWISH CONTENT

Contemporary Judaism is pluralistic and this is reflected in children's books. The content may range from fully observant to marginally Jewish. In the former, Torah values are central and virtually all aspects of life are portrayed from a Jewish perspective. In more mainstream books, Jewish individuals are found in secular stories. Setting, theme, plot development, climax and denouement do not depend on the character as a Jew but on a person who happens to be Jewish.

POSITIVE FOCUS AND VALUES

Jewish values are those that have special emphasis in the Jewish tradition and are often tied to Jewish texts. However universal they may be, there is a particularly Jewish way of looking at them and they are a vital, living force in Jews' lives. Whether serious or lighthearted, Jewish children's literature should have something Jewish to say to readers. While positive content is desirable but not always possible, a positive Jewish focus will tell the reader "L'chaim, choose life."

SENSITIVITY

Literature of Jewish content should promote respect for and understanding of Judaism. The use of Christological terms like "A.D." and "Old Testament" should be avoided, along with Christian interpretations of the Bible and proselytizing. It should also be recognized that not all Jews are Caucasian or Ashkenazic in origin. Sensitivity to this issue includes an awareness of cultural and racial differences among Jews, as well as differing levels and forms of Jewish observance.

Jewishlibraries.org

Figure 1.1. Excellence in Jewish Children's Literature

Chapter 2

What Is Our Story? What Is Our History?

A History of Jewish Children's Literature

> Once upon a time there lived a merchant who had three sons: Gedalyah, Hananyah, and Getzel. Getzel was the youngest. His father and brothers call him "Getzel-Nahr," which means "Getzel the Fool." Getzel wasn't stupid, but he was kindhearted and trusting—unfortunate qualities in a merchant. (Kimmel, 1996)

So begins this retelling of *Onions and Garlic: An Old Tale*, retold by Eric Kimmel with illustrations by Katya Arnold. In this tale, Getzel wants to prove himself to his father and begs to be sent on a trade mission. His father gives him onions to trade because they are not worth much. So, Getzel sets sail, but nowhere can he find buyers for the onions.

After being shipwrecked, Getzel arrives in a country that has never before seen or tasted onions. Getzel prepares a meal using his onions and is lauded for this delicacy by the king. In this land, diamonds are plentiful and not worth much, so the king trades diamonds for Getzel's onions. When Getzel returns home with the diamonds, his greedy brothers decide to take garlic to this country that had never seen onions, expecting a trade of riches similar to their brother's. The king does love the garlic and, in trying to think of a suitable item to trade, decides to give the brothers the country's most precious commodity—onions!

Children laugh at the ending and delight in this folktale that prompts many enduring questions: What is greed? What is humility? Why are different items considered valuable in different places? Getzel's father and brothers call him "the fool." Why do we describe others with hurtful names?

In addition to fostering discussion of enduring questions, *Onions and Garlic* also represents the way that Jewish children's literature has evolved.

In this chapter, some significant events and milestones in the history of Jewish children's literature are described, specifically oriented to the needs of preschool and elementary school teachers in the United States. Although this book focuses on Jewish children's literature in English, it is important to note that Jewish children's literature has been written in (and translated into) many languages—the Jewish languages of Hebrew, Yiddish, and Ladino, as well as other languages including German, Spanish, French, and Polish. Throughout this book, Jewish children's literature in languages other than English is noted because of the importance of recognizing the multilingual corpus of Jewish children's literature and that children in U.S. classrooms speak a broad range of languages. Learning about the evolution in Jewish children's literature provides context and background to understanding Jewish children's literature today.

EARLY SOURCES OF JEWISH CHILDREN'S LITERATURE

The history of *Onions and Garlic* dates back to the Aggadah, the collection of stories found in the Talmud, which was compiled in the fourth century. The Talmud is a sacred text in which rabbis discuss Jewish laws and their various interpretations. The Talmud consists of two parts: the Mishnah, a compilation of Jewish laws; and the Gemara, the commentaries on the Mishnah. Throughout these texts, the rabbis pose enduring questions, pondering over what these laws mean and presenting a diversity of opinions and perspectives on them.

The Talmud also includes the Aggadah, commentaries on biblical narratives and people. One of these commentaries in the Aggadah is the basis for the *Onions and Garlic* tale. The famous Hebrew poet Hayyim Nahman Bialik wrote a version of the tale, *Knight of Onions, Knight of Garlic*, that was translated into English in 1939. Most recently, PJ Library published a version of *Onions and Garlic* by Rebecca Sheir in 2019. Many contemporary Jewish children's books originate in historical texts and stories.

Throughout their history, Jews have relished in retelling their experiences and asking enduring questions through story. Jewish storyteller Peninnah Schram (1984) wrote, "Because it has remained an integral part of Jewish religion and society, storytelling in Jewish life continues to be an ongoing effective way of transmitting a cultural heritage and thereby of sharing the values of a people" (33). The story of Jewish literature for children travels back in time and across the globe.

The history of Jewish literature for children begins with stories from the Hebrew Bible that were shared with children. Stories based on commentaries from the Talmud were also written, and Judaism has a large body of folktales based on these stories. These folktales and stories from sacred texts were intended to instruct and enculturate children to Jewish values and *mitzvot* (commandments). Jewish folktales can be found around the world from Eastern Europe, Israel, northern Africa, and other locales where Jews have lived (and Jews have lived everywhere). Recently the Talmud has been featured in the multiple award-winning *The Inquisitor's Tale: Or, The Three Magical Children and Their Holy Dog* by Adam Gidwitz, a rollicking adventure set in the Middle Ages, about three youths on a quest to save the Talmud from being burned.

The evolution of modern Jewish children's literature reflects, in part, the evolution of children's literature in general. In addition to exciting the imagination and fostering values, children's literature has increasingly addressed the complex issues of modern and contemporary life. The conceptions of the child—and of the child as reader—have changed. Children are viewed as complex readers who often address difficult issues in their literature. High-quality children's literature encourages children to think deeply about human relationships and who they are in a world that offers many dichotomies: kindness and cruelty, joy and sorrow, loneliness and friendship, fear and hope. Topics in children's literature reflect contemporary society: courage, love, death, prejudice, war, violence, and others—topics that lend themselves to enduring questions.

Contemporary authors have taken historical Jewish books and reworked them into children's books. For example, award-winning author/illustrator Uri Shulevitz fictionalizes the original *Book of Travels* by Benjamin of Tudela, written in Hebrew in the 1100s, to create *The Travels of Benjamin of Tudela: Through Three Continents in the Twelfth Century.* Young readers today embark on a pictorial journey with Benjamin of Tudela, Spain, who traveled for fourteen years to Italy, Greece, Persia, and other countries. Children may ask and discuss why someone would want to wander away from home for so many years. Knowing that his travels would entail dangers and unknowns, did Benjamin make an appropriate decision in setting out on his journey? What did Benjamin learn on his travels? How did he benefit from them?

Although the Spain of Benjamin of Tudela's time had a thriving Jewish community, Jews were expelled from Spain in 1492 during the Spanish Inquisition (see the discussion of Gail Carson Levine's *A Ceiling Made of Eggshells* in chapter 6). Spanish Jews (Sephardim) migrated to Italy, Greece, Turkey, Northern Africa, and elsewhere. Persecution of the Jews continued for centuries in Europe through the Holocaust and World War II, and in some places continues. In Europe, stories appropriate for children were often being told in Yiddish, the language spoken by Jews in Eastern Europe. Rabbi Nachman of Breslov (1772–1811) was known for his teachings and stories, which were written down by his students. One of his famous stories, *The Rooster Prince of Breslov*, as retold by Ann Redisch Stampler, is discussed in chapter 5.

In the nineteenth century, well-known Yiddish authors for adults such as Sholom Aleichem (the pen name of Solomon Naumovich Rabinowitz) and I. L. Peretz wrote stories for children. Sholom Aleichem's story "Dos Meserel" (in English, "The Penknife"), originally published in 1887, is generally thought to be the first modern Yiddish story written for children (Bar-El, 2008). Some authors penned stories in languages other than Yiddish. For example, Jewish authors in Poland wrote in Polish for both Jewish and non-Jewish children. Janusz Korczak wrote the popular book *Król Macius Pierwsy* (King Matt the First) in 1923. The book was translated into English and published in 1986. A paperback version was released in 2015.

THE INFLUENCE OF IMMIGRATION TO THE AMERICAS

An influence on Jewish children's literature is the migration of Jews from Europe and elsewhere to North and South America. Jews have immigrated to North and South America since the sixteenth century. The first synagogue was established in Recife, Brazil, in 1636, and Touro Synagogue was established in Rhode Island in 1773 by Sephardic Jews of Spanish and Portuguese descent. A wave of Jews from Germany occurred between 1820 and 1880. From 1880 to 1920, a huge migration of Jews came from Eastern Europe to the Americas.

The experiences of Jews in the Americas have been told through Jewish children's literature. Some of these stories reflect personal experiences of authors and poets, and some resemble the stories that had been written in Europe. Other stories, however, focus on the Jewish immigrant experience. Similar to other immigrant groups, Jews have struggled with poverty, anti-immigrant sentiments, anti-Semitism, and the tension between becoming Americanized and modernized versus maintaining their culture and distinct ethnic and religious identity. The literature written for children shares these themes.

Poets and authors have immigrated to the United States, and many continued to write in Yiddish such as Sholom Aleichem, Mani Leib, Isaac Bashevis Singer, and Kadya Molodowsky. As Miriam Udel (2020) notes, "Yiddish children's literature, deeply preoccupied as it is with the themes of identity, narrow escapes, fortuitous twists of fate, and the exercise of power, seems more relevant now than ever" (14). Many works for children by these early Yiddish writers have been translated into English. For example, Mani-Leib's classic story poem, *Yingl Tsingl Khvat* (Young Tongue Scamp), first published in 1918, was translated by Jeffrey Shandler and published in 1986 in English. In 2020 a book of poems by Kadya Molodowsky, *Vu Di Velt Hot Nor an Ek* (Through an Endless Stretch of Land) was published in Yiddish by a Swedish publisher. It has been translated into English by Yairs Singer, who also illustrated the volume, which is now available in a bilingual version of English and Yiddish.

Another important development in Jewish children's literature occurred in 1888 when the Jewish Publication Society of America (today known as the Jewish Publication Society) was founded as a nonprofit publisher of Jewish texts in English. Although widely known for its translations of the Hebrew Bible, the company also produced books for children. Prior to World War I, the purpose of the early books was "didactic: to inculcate Jewish belief, knowledge, identity, and pride in young people as a way of ensuring that they would remain fully Jewish while becoming fully American" (Silver, 2008, 2).

MODERN JEWISH CHILDREN'S LITERATURE

Modern Jewish children's literature in the United States is viewed as originating with the publication in 1935 of *The Adventures of K'tonton* by Sadie Rose Weilerstein and illustrated by Jeannette Berkowitz (Silver, 2008). Written in English, K'tonton is considered the Jewish Tom Thumb, a tiny boy whose adventures occur in a Jewish home and community. In her preface, Weilerstein credits Nobel Prize–winning Hebrew author S. Y. Agnon with the inspiration for his character Gadiel, the little rabbi. *The Adventures of K'tonton* is composed of individual short stories, many of them about the Jewish holidays. This book is considered the first example of modern Jewish children's literature because "it delivered its theme or message more subtly, with playful, child-centered attitudes, fanciful plots, exuberant characters . . . and a goal of engaging readers' emotion" (Silver, 2008, 2).

During this time period, Jewish children's books in the United States were written in Yiddish as well as English. Madsen (2006) notes that "the first children's book about the Holocaust was written before the event" (38). In 1940 Yankev Glatshteyn wrote *Emil un Karl* in Yiddish for students who attended Yiddish-speaking schools in the United States. The story, set in Vienna in 1940, describes the friendship of two 9-year-old boys, one Jewish and one non-Jewish, who are both separated from their families and must survive the terrible events occurring around them. At the time it was written, the novel was considered realistic fiction because it reflected the current time period. In 2006 the book was translated into English by Jeffrey Shandler and published as *Emil and Karl*. The book received starred reviews in book review publications and was named a Sydney Taylor Book Award Notable Book.

After the Holocaust and World War II, one of the tasks that Jewish children's literature faced was helping Jewish and non-Jewish children learn about the Holocaust. Doing so requires a delicate balance between representing the horror of the Holocaust and not traumatizing children but giving them hope. Perhaps the most well-known book to bring the Holocaust to the attention of American children was *Anne Frank: The Diary of a Young Girl*. First published in Dutch in Holland in 1947, the diary was translated into English by Barbara Mooyaart-Doubleday and published in both the United States and Great Britain in 1952. In 1955, the diary was adapted for the stage in a play version, followed by the movie in 1959. Today, the diary has been translated into more than sixty languages. The secret annex where Anne Frank hid during the war and where she wrote her diary is now part of the Anne Frank House, a museum in Amsterdam. More than one million people from all over the world visit the museum each year. (Holocaust literature for children is discussed in chapter 6.)

When *All-of-a-Kind Family* by Sydney Taylor was published in 1951, as noted in chapter 1, it became the first modern Jewish children's book to cross over into the mainstream of children's literature publishing. The story of an immigrant family with five daughters living in New York at the beginning of the twentieth century appealed to Jewish and non-Jewish readers alike. The series includes five books. Heidi Estrin (2004) explains, "Taylor's books reach past those ethnic boundaries with a universal family story and characters everyone can care about. . . . For over fifty years, readers have loved the adventures and the closeness of the family in the stories" (5).

In honor of this groundbreaking book and in memory of its author, the Association of Jewish Libraries established the Sydney Taylor Book Award in 1968 to recognize outstanding Jewish children's books. The first recipient of the award in 1968 was *The Endless Steppe* by Esther Hautzig, the memoir of the author's life growing up in a Siberian labor camp during World War II. (Winners of the Sydney Taylor Book Award can be found at https://jewishlibraries.org/wp-content/uploads/2022/01/stbaallawardwinnersever.pdf.)

A more recent milestone for Jewish children's literature in the United States was the establishment of Kar-Ben Publishing in 1974. Two friends, Judyth Groner and Madeline Wikler, founded Kar-Ben in order to produce copies of *My Very Own Haggadah*, a children's Passover Haggadah that they had created. For the next twenty-seven years, Kar-Ben published more than 150 Jewish children's books, created by eighty authors and illustrators, and increased the titles of Jewish-themed books in the marketplace. The company provided the opportunity for Jewish authors and illustrators to create

Jewish-themed books for wide distribution. Since 2001, Kar-Ben Publishing has been a division of Lerner Publishing Group and publishes at least twenty-four new titles each year of both fiction and nonfiction for children. It is significant that a major children's book publisher has an imprint dedicated to Jewish-themed books.

CHILDREN'S BOOK AWARDS IN THE UNITED STATES

Since *All-of-a-Kind Family*, Jewish children's literature has continued to be published by mainstream children's book publishers. Jewish children's literature has received national attention and prominence as Jewish authors, illustrators, and books have received prestigious children's book awards in the United States such as the Newbery, Caldecott, and Mildred L. Batchelder Awards. This recognition has brought Jewish children's literature to the attention of a wide range of audiences. Nobel Prize recipient Isaac Bashevis Singer received a Newbery Honor for *Zlateh the Goat and Other Stories* in 1967; it was illustrated by Maurice Sendak, who received the Caldecott in 1964 for *Where the Wild Things Are*. Singer again received Newbery Honor recognition in 1969 for *When Shlemiel Went to Warsaw and Other Stories*, illustrated by Margot Zemach; she would receive a Caldecott in 1974 for *Duffy and the Devil*, written by Harve Zemach. In 1973 Johanna Reiss's *The Upstairs Room*, the fictionalized autobiography of the author's life concealed in Holland during World War II, was named a Newbery Honor Book. More recent Newbery titles with Jewish content are mentioned throughout this book.

At the same time, other Jewish illustrators were gaining prominence and receiving the Caldecott Award for books that didn't necessarily have Jewish content: Ezra Jack Keats for *The Snowy Day*, in 1963; Uri Shulevitz for *The Fool of the World and the Flying Ship*, written by Arthur Ransome in 1969; and William Steig for *Sylvester and the Magic Pebble* in 1970. In the 1970s, several Jewish children's books were named Caldecott Honor books: *The Golem: A Jewish Legend* by Beverly Brodsky McDermott and *It Could Always Be Worse* by Margot Zemach. Other Caldecott Honor books followed; and in 1997, *Golem* by David Wisniewski received the Caldecott Medal.

The inception of the Mildred L. Batchelder Award by the American Library Association in 1966 marked an important milestone for Jewish children's literature. This award, given to the publisher for the best book for children translated from another language into English, introduced children to many Jewish children's books written in other countries and in languages other than English. In 1972, *Friedrich* by German author Hans Peter Richter received the award. This book, set in Germany during World War II, is told from the perspective of a German boy whose Jewish friend Friedrich faces increasing persecution. Israeli author Uri Orlev has received the Batchelder Award four times for his historical novels, based on personal experiences during the Holocaust—most notably *The Island on Bird Street*, which has been made into a movie. In 1996, Orlev also received the prestigious Hans Christian Andersen Award, sponsored by the International Board on Books for Young People, considered by many the "Nobel Prize" for children's literature.

Swedish author Annika Thor's *A Faraway Island* was honored in 2010 and describes the experiences of two Austrian sisters who are sent to live with a Swedish family on a remote island during World War II. A story of the friendship between a Jewish boy and a Palestinian boy in an Israeli hospital, *Samir and Yonatan*, by Israeli author Danielle Carmi, received the Batchelder Award in 2001. These books, written by authors around the world, enable children in the United States to experience varied perspectives on Jewish history and culture.

ISRAELI AUTHORS PUBLISHED IN THE UNITED STATES

The story of Jewish children's literature travels to Israel, which has a thriving children's literature presence. These books are originally written in Hebrew and reflect the diversity of Jews living in Israel and within Israeli society as well as the issues of the day. For example, the critically acclaimed book *Too Far from Home* by Naomi Shmuel and illustrated by Avi Katz recounts the story of an Israeli girl, Meskereen, who has an Ethiopian Jewish mother and an American Jewish father. Meskereen faces racial prejudice when the family moves from a village where many of the inhabitants are Ethiopian Jews to a suburb of Tel Aviv. The book has been translated into English and resonates with any child from any background who has moved and needs to adapt to new circumstances.

In order to encourage translation of Hebrew books into other languages, the Institute for the Translation of Hebrew Literature has worked to promote and disseminate Hebrew children's literature in translation worldwide since 1962. Through its work, Hebrew books for children and adults have been translated into eighty-two languages. For example, *Samir and Yonatan* is one of its books. As noted in the discussion of the Batchelder Award, the works of Israeli children's authors have been translated into English and received critical acclaim in the United States.

Israeli children's literature, of course, has its own history, distinct from Jewish children's literature in the United States. Levin Kipnis, who died in 1990 at age ninety-six, is considered the father of Israeli children's literature, with eight hundred stories and six hundred poems. He received several prestigious awards including the Israel Prize in 1978 for "devoting his life to the development of children's literature in Hebrew" (*New York Times*, June 23, 1990). The Kipnis Center for Children's Literature at Levinsky Teachers College is named for him.

Israeli author Leah Goldberg's books are considered classic Hebrew language children's literature. Goldberg died in 1970. Written in 1959 and still popular today, *A Flat to Rent* has been translated into English under the title *Room for Rent* with illustrations by Shmuel Katz. This picture book focuses on a five-floor apartment inhabited by animals. When the fifth-floor resident, Mr. Mouse, mysteriously leaves, a new renter must be found. When all the prospective renters meet the neighbors, they believe something is wrong with the neighbors, until the dove arrives. Dove decides to rent the flat, and the neighbors live in harmony. The book's theme of tolerance and understanding is timeless and important today.

The works of many other Israeli children's authors are available in English. For example, Gila Almagor wrote *Under the Domim Tree* (1995), a fictionalized account of her experiences in an Israeli youth village in 1952, for children who survived the Holocaust. The book was the recipient of the National Jewish Book Award.

THE TWENTY-FIRST CENTURY

As Jewish children's literature in the United States entered the twenty-first century, it continued to include a broad range of genres from the Hebrew Bible and Talmud stories, retellings of folktales, realistic stories of everyday life, picture books, biography, memoir, fantasy, informational books, and graphic novels.

A milestone for Jewish children's literature occurred in 2005 when the Harold Grinspoon Foundation initiated the PJ Library, a Jewish engagement program that sends free books to Jewish children from six months to twelve years old. The program is now in the United States, Canada, United Kingdom, Australia, Brazil, Mexico, Russia, Ukraine, and Israel. Books in countries in which the primary language is not English are printed in the country's official language. PJ Library has created awareness of many Jewish children's books as well as encouraged authors to write new books that could be part of the program's collection.

The activities of Jewish organizations support and celebrate Jewish's children's literature. The Jewish Book Council sponsors the National Jewish Book Award, now in three categories: children's picture book, middle-grade literature, and young adult literature. The Association of Jewish Libraries'

Sydney Taylor Book Award is also now in three categories: younger readers, older readers, and teen readers—and includes a list of notable books in those categories.

Current trends in Jewish children's literature reflect those in general children's literature. The importance of diversity and inclusion of all kinds in children's books exists in Jewish children's literature. Interfaith families, settings in various regions of the United States, children with special needs, Jews living around the world, and Jews of color are all featured in current Jewish children's books.

For example, in *Hanukkah Moon* by Deborah da Costa, Isobel learns about Jewish Mexican holiday traditions from her Aunt Luisa, who recently arrived from Mexico. Set in 1947, *Stealing Home* by Ellen Schwartz recounts how nine-year-old Joey, an orphaned biracial boy, overcomes bullying to establish a relationship with his mother's Jewish family. In *Always an Olivia: A Remarkable Family History*, Carolivia Herron presents a fictionalized account of her family's Jewish and African American heritage in the Geechee Islands, Georgia. In *The Length of String* by Elissa Brent Weissman, Imani, an adopted Black Jewish girl, seeks her roots as she prepares for her bat mitzvah and finds a deep connection with her great-grandma, who was also adopted when she traveled alone to the United States to escape the Holocaust.

ALWAYS AN OLIVIA: A REMARKABLE FAMILY HISTORY

[An elderly Black grandmother passes on the story of the family's Jewish roots and their flight from the Spanish Inquisition to her young granddaughter, Carol Olivia. One daughter in each generation is given the name Olivia, from the Hebrew *Shulamit* (meaning peace) to honor the Jewish part of their ancestry.]

I used this book with my fifth-grade class as part of an English language arts unit on nonfiction reading based on the signposts that Kylene Beers and Robert Probst developed in their book *Reading Nonfiction*. My class is racially and ethnically diverse. I introduced the genre of nonfiction by explaining and giving an example from *The Life and Times of the Honeybee* by Charles Micucci to show students how to use this genre to surprise themselves and make the subject matter more meaningful. Then, I presented *Always an Olivia* in the following ways:

- "This book is in the genre of historical fiction, told like a fiction story but based on true events in the author's life. Carol Olivia (notice the author's name) is hearing a story about her family from her great-grandmother. (Does this happen in your family?) She knows her family is Jewish. (What does that mean?)"

- After reading the first page, we discuss the students' surprise that the characters are both Black and Jewish. We also compare two slavery events noted in the book.

The trend of picture-book biographies for all ages is also evident in books about Jews from all walks of life. These biographies are discussed throughout other chapters and a list can be found in appendix A. Another trend in children's publishing, graphic novels, is also evident in Jewish children's literature. Several of these books have been recognized by Sydney Taylor Book Awards. The Hereville series by Barry Deutsch, for middle-grade readers, features superhero Mirka, an Orthodox girl, and her adventures. The first book, *Hereville: How Mirka Got Her Sword*, was a Sydney Taylor Book Award winner. The second book, *Hereville: How Mirka Met a Meteorite*, was a Notable Book; and the third book, *Hereville; How Mirka Caught a Fish*, was an Honor Book. Another Sydney Taylor Award–winning graphic novel is *White Bird: A Wonder Story* by R. J. Palacio. This book focuses on Julian, a character from the best-selling book *Wonder*, who learns how his Jewish grandmother, Sara, was hidden by a family in a French village during the Nazi occupation of France (a list of graphic novels can be found in appendix A).

This brief history of Jewish children's literature has only touched on the highlights of this robust past. It is important also to pay attention to the artwork in Jewish children's literature—much of it is stunningly beautiful and engrossing. More information on art in Jewish children's books can be found in *Monsters and Miracles: A Journey through Jewish Picture Books* by Ilan Stavans, Neal Sokol, and Tal Gozani. The covers of a book invite readers to open the book's pages and enter worlds that have been created. The sampling of covers from Jewish children's books represents a diversity of language, illustrators, countries, and aesthetics in the books—revealing a wealth of storytelling.

The story of Jewish children's literature continues to evolve as new trends emerge in general children's literature and as new issues and concerns occur within the Jewish world. Jewish children's books, as the chapters in this book discuss, prompt deep thought and provide children the means to ponder enduring questions.

- "As I read this book to you, I'm going to stop and have you talk with people at your table about what surprises you. Write down your ideas. You may use words or quick sketches. Record what surprises you, and at end of the book, compare the surprises."
- "Discuss what you want to know more about." Following are a few of the comments from the students: "Why would people be killed just because they are Jewish?" "It surprised me that they kicked out the Jewish people." "Why are they white when the storyteller is Black?" "I didn't know Jews were hated before Hitler."

Marie Boozer, fifth grade, public school, Ohio

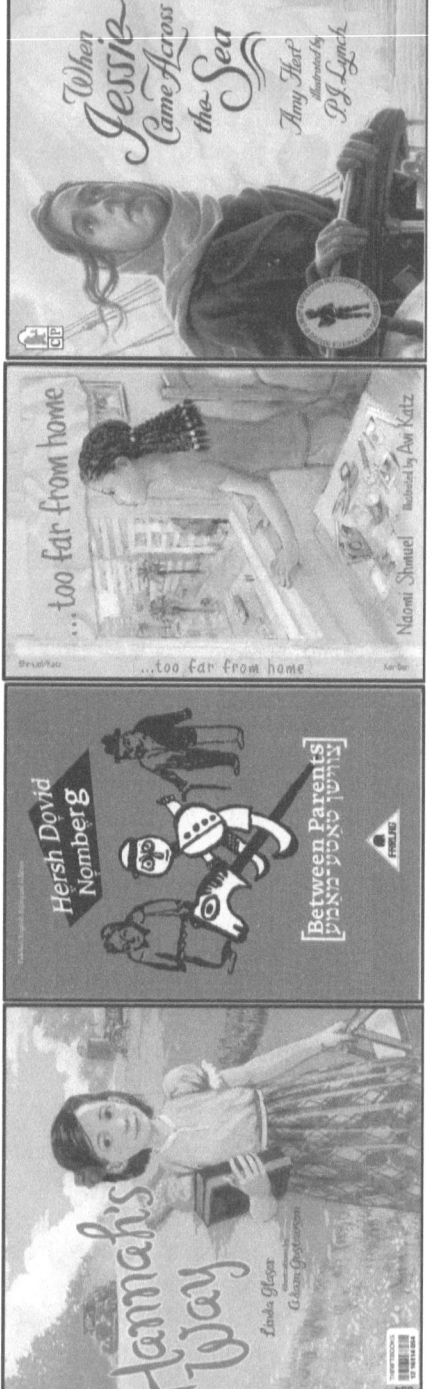

Figure 2.1. Book Covers
Permission for each cover is listed on the permissions page.

WORKS CITED

Children's Literature

Almagor, Gila. *Under the Domim Tree.* Translated by Hillel Schenker. New York: Simon & Schuster, 1995.

Bialik, Hayyim Nahman. *Knight of Onions and Knight of Garlic.* Illustrated by Emanuel Romano. Translated by Herbert Danby. New York: Hebrew Publishing Co., 1939.

Carmi, Daniella. *Samir and Yonatan.* Translated by Yal Lotan. New York: Scholastic, 2000.

da Costa, Deborah. *Hanukkah Moon.* Illustrated by Gosia Mosz. Minneapolis: Kar-Ben, 2007.

Deutsch, Barry. *Hereville: How Mirka Caught a Fish.* New York: Abrams, 2015.

———. *Hereville: How Mirka Got Her Sword.* New York: Abrams, 2010.

———. *Hereville: How Mirka Met a Meteorite.* New York: Abrams, 2012.

Frank, Anne. *Anne Frank: The Diary of a Young Girl.* Translated by Barbara Mooyaart-Doubleday. New York: Modern Library, 1952.

Gidwitz, Adam. *The Inquisitor's Tale: Or, The Three Holy Children and Their Magical Dog.* New York: Dutton, 2016.

Glatshteyn, Yankev. *Emil and Karl.* Translated by Jeffrey Shandler. New Milford, CT: Roaring Brook Press, 2006.

Goldberg, Leah. *Room for Rent.* Illustrated by Shmuel Katz. Translated by Jessica Sitbon. Jerusalem: Gefen, 2017.

Groner, Judyth, and Madeline Wikler. *My Very Own Haggadah.* Minneapolis: Kar-Ben, 1983.

Hautzig, Esther. *The Endless Steppe.* New York: Harper & Row, 1968.

Herron, Carolivia. *Always an Olivia: A Remarkable Family History.* Illustrated by Jeremy Tugeau. Minneapolis: Kar-Ben, 2012.

Keats, Ezra Jack. *The Snowy Day.* New York: Viking, 1962.

Kimmel, Eric A. *Onions and Garlic: An Old Tale.* Illustrated by Katya Arnold. New York: Holiday House, 1996.

Korczak, Janusz. *King Matt the First.* Translated by Richard Lourie. New York: Farrar, Straus & Giroux, 1986.

Leib, Mani. *Yingl Tsingl Khvat.* Illustrated by El (Lazar) Lissitzky. Translated by Jeffrey Shandler. Mt. Kisco, NY: Moyer Bell, 1986.

Levine, Gail Carson. *A Ceiling Made of Eggshells.* New York: HarperCollins, 2020.

McDermott, Beverly Brodsky. *The Golem: A Jewish Legend.* Philadelphia: Lippincott, 1976.

Molodowsky, Kadya. *Vu di velt hot nor an ek/Through an Endless Stretch of Land.* Translated by Yaira Singer. Sweden: Olniansky Tekst, 2020.

Orlev, Uri. *The Island on Bird Street.* Translated by Hillel Halkin. Boston: Houghton Mifflin, 1983.

Palacio, R. J. *White Bird: A Wonder Story.* New York: Knopf Books for Young Readers, 2019.

———. *Wonder*. New York: Knopf Books for Young Readers, 2012.
Ransome, Arthur. *The Fool of the World and the Flying Ship*. Illustrated by Uri Shulevitz. New York: Farrar, Straus & Giroux, 1968.
Reiss, Johanna. *The Upstairs Room*. New York: Crowell, 1972.
Richter, Hans Peter. *Friedrich*. Translated by Edite Kroll. New York: Holt, 1970.
Schwartz, Ellen. *Stealing Home*. Toronto: Tundra Books, 2006.
Sendak, Maurice. *Where the Wild Things Are*. New York: Harper & Row, 1963.
Sheir, Rebecca. *Onions & Garlic*. Illustrated by Sabina Hahn. Agawam, MA: PJ Library, 2019.
Shmuel, Naomi. *Too Far from Home*. Illustrated by Avi Katz. Minneapolis: Kar-Ben, 2000.
Shulevitz, Uri. *The Travels of Benjamin of Tudela: Through Three Continents in the Twelfth Century*. New York: Farrar, Straus & Giroux, 2005.
Singer, Isaac Bashevis. *When Shlemiel Went to Warsaw and Other Stories*. Illustrated by Margot Zemach. Translated by Elizabeth Shub. New York: Farrar, Straus & Giroux, 1969.
———. *Zlateh the Goat and Other Stories*. Illustrated by Maurice Sendak. Translated by Elizabeth Shub. New York: Harper & Row, 1966.
Stampler, Ann Redisch. *The Rooster Prince of Breslov*. Illustrated by Eugene Yelchin. Boston: Clarion, 2010.
Steig, William. *Sylvester and the Magic Pebble*. New York: Simon & Schuster, 1969.
Taylor, Sydney. *All-of-a-Kind Family*. Illustrated by Helen John. Westchester, IL: Follett, 1951.
Thor, Annika. *A Faraway Island*. Translated by Linda Schenck. New York: Delacorte Books for Young Readers, 2009.
Weilerstein, Sadie Rose. *The Adventures of K'Tonton*. Illustrated by Jeannette Berkowitz. New York: National Women's League of the United Synagogue, 1935.
Weissman, Elissa Brent. *The Length of a String*. New York: Penguin Random House, 2018.
Wisniewski, David, *Golem*. New York: Clarion, 1996.
Zemach, Harve. *Duffy and the Devil*. Illustrated by Margot Zemach. New York: Farrar, Straus & Giroux, 1973.
Zemach, Margot. *It Could Always Be Worse*. New York: Farrar, Straus & Giroux, 1976.

References

Bar-El, A. "Children's Literature: Yiddish Literature." In D. H. Gershon, ed., *YIVO Encyclopedia of Jews in Eastern Europe*, 322–26. New Haven, CT: Yale University Press, 2008.
Estrin, H. "Why Is *All-of-a-Kind Family* an Important Book?" in *The All-of-a-Kind Family Companion*. New York: Association of Jewish Libraries, 2004.
Madsen, C. "Ending on a Question Mark: Yankey Glatshteyn's Novel for Children." *Pakn Treger* 51 (2006): 38–40.

New York Times. Levin Kipnis, author, 96, obituary, 2020. Retrieved April 29, 2022, from https://www.nytimes.com/1990/06/23/obituaries/levin-kipnis-author-96.html.

Schram, P. "One Generation Tells Another: The Transmission of Jewish Values through Storytelling." *Literature in Performance* 4, no. 2 (1984): 33–45.

Silver, L. R. *The Jewish Values Finder: A Guide to Values in Jewish Children's Literature.* Chicago: Neal-Schuman, 2008.

Stavans, I., N. Sokol, and T. Gozani. *Monsters and Miracles: A Journey through Jewish Picture Books.* Eric Carle Museum, Amherst, MA, and Skirball Cultural Center, Los Angeles, 2010.

Udel, M. *Honey on the Page.* New York: New York University Press, 2020.

Chapter 3

What Is Love?

Stories of Family, Friendship, Animals, and Nature

In Sydney Taylor's *All-of-a-Kind Family*, a Jewish family in early 1900s New York sits down to Shabbat dinner. The family is strictly observant of Jewish traditions and Jewish commandments. After washing his hands in the ritual fashion, the father starts the evening's observance with the special weekly blessing for his wife. Then, he blesses the wine and the ceremonial bread, the *challah*, and following that, the family eats a typical Friday night meal.

After supper is finished and the cleaning done, the family engages in quiet activities in accordance with the Shabbat tradition, which provides a respite from the routine of daily grind. It is tradition not to work on the Sabbath, and highly observant Jews follow that commandment strictly. Resting and not working on Shabbat reminds Jews that they are human and not beasts of burden. Strictly observant Jews do not work on Shabbat. As lighting candles is considered work, the family lit the candles before sundown and read as long as possible by candlelight before going to sleep. The picture Sydney Taylor paints of the family is one of serenity, respect, and love.

The concept of love as expressed in Jewish children's literature is the focus of this chapter. Besides looking at stories about families, books about friends, animals, and nature are discussed. Each story discussed lends itself to engagement in what can be called enduring questions. As explained in the introduction, enduring questions ask us to think deeply about what it means to be human and what it means to be in this world with others. Enduring questions can never be fully or finally answered, nor is there just one correct answer. It is in the discussion of and struggling with enduring questions that insights are generated into ourselves, others, and the human condition and its diversity. As noted in the introduction, asking enduring questions—struggling with them either by yourself or with others—not only brings us closer to wisdom, but it also makes us more empathetic with others.

WHAT IS LOVE? PEACE IN THE HOME

Sacred Jewish books such as the Torah and the Talmud, among other books of Jewish philosophy and life, note the importance of *shalom bayit*. Shalom bayit, which translates literally as peace in the home, is better understood as the creation of a loving family that is respectful of all its members. Respect is foundational, because all people should be treated with dignity and respect. The family in Sydney Taylor's *All-of-a-Kind Family* provides one example of shalom bayit. The family lives in a stable household in a Lower East Side neighborhood of New York City in the early twentieth century.

Although Taylor wrote four other *All-of-a-Kind* books, the first in the series has been the most successful. The story centers on a family of five girls and their parents. The adventures of the girls are told as a series of vignettes. The descriptions of Jewish observances and holidays offer a glimpse into the religious beliefs of the family. Glimpses into their domestic, social, and economic life are also given. Insights into the family's values are presented as the conclusion of the tale. Although outdated in many ways, with family life overly romanticized, children still enjoy reading the *All-of-a-Kind Family* books. In one chapter, after the mother has given birth to five daughters, she finally has a long-awaited son. The mother wonders whether her daughters will be upset by the new baby boy. The mother tells the girls that the birth of their brother will not disrupt the happiness of the family. She frames the change in the life of the family by noting that closeness, love, kindness, and loyalty are its real foundation.

When seven-year-old Hannah read *All-of-a-Kind Family*, she enjoyed the book immensely even though she recognized the difference between that family and real families with all of their diverse configurations. What was it about *All-of-a-Kind Family* that so engaged Hannah? Maybe it was the expression of *shalom bayit*, peace, love, and respect among the family members even as Hannah recognizes and rejects the gender stereotypes. One of the enduring questions to discuss after reading *All-of-a-Kind Family* is what makes a family a family? Who gets to decide? Does a family have to be happy to be a family? What might it take for a real family—one that has to address all the complexities, difficulties, and hard times of daily life—to be a place of shalom bayit? Can there be love in a family without respect and loyalty? What do respect and loyalty within a family look like?

The love between children and parents is central to another Jewish children's book, *Rifka Takes a Bow*, written by Betty Rosenberg Perlov and illustrated by Cosei Kawa. In the story, Rifka's mother and father are actors in the Yiddish theater. Historically, Yiddish theater was vibrant in New York City during the early years of the twentieth century. In the story, Rifka accompanies her parents to work from time to time and watches them prepare their makeup and costumes, as well as watches them act, sing, and dance.

When her father takes her under the stage to see the props, she is scared because of the dark. He calms her fears in a loving way, telling her, "Piff-Paff! Not to worry!" At the end of the story, Rifka inadvertently walks on the stage during a performance. Her parents and the audience are stunned by her appearance, but she repeats the words that her father said to her under the stage: "Piff-Paff! Not to worry!" The audience claps and cheers at Rifka's courage and poise, both of which she has learned from her family. She decides right then and there to go into the theater herself, thereby following the life of her parents.

At one level, *Rifka Takes a Bow* is a simple story about a young girl hanging out with her parents at their jobs in the theater and making a mistake by walking out on stage during a performance. We can all admire how well she handled her mistake and wish we had parents who would be so understanding. But at another level, it offers serious, enduring questions to ponder. A theater is all about pretending. The props and the sets are all fake. What's real and what's not real? Was Rifka's bow real? Was the poise and courage she displayed real or just a show? Does it matter whether it was real or pretend?

When Rifka went below the stage to where the props were stored, her fear was real. But there really wasn't anything to fear from the props, so what was Rivka afraid of? Was she afraid of what she imagined was there, and what was actually there? Does our imagination sometimes make us afraid of what is not real? Many of us, including young children, feel pressure to put on an act, to act as if we are happy and as if everything is just fine—when maybe it is not. Why and where does it happen? Families are often thought of as places of comfort, love, and respect, and where everyone can relax and be who they are. But are families always that way?

Adopting Ahava by Jennifer Byrne tells the story of Jonathan on his eighth birthday. His two moms take him to the animal shelter to adopt a dog—Jonathan's big birthday present. While he considers which dog to adopt, readers learn that Jonathan was himself adopted. A flashback in the story shows where Jonathan lived in foster and group homes, being passed up for adoption because he was not a baby. Finally, he is adopted by Mama Rachel and Mama Jessica, and he begins to learn Hebrew and read from the Torah. When they go to adopt a dog, instead of choosing a puppy, Jonathan chooses a three-year-old dog that everyone is passing by. He names the dog Ahava (which means "love" in Hebrew). The four of them—Jonathan, his two moms, and Ahava—celebrate both the birthday and the adoption.

When the story was read to five-year-old Diane, she was riveted by the issue of adoption. She commented that Jonathan feels better because Ahava is also adopted, so he is not alone. When asked why Jonathan named the dog Ahava, Diane said it was because they loved each other. She was then asked, "Who loves each other?" "They all love each other, silly" ("silly" being Diane's way of saying someone is asking a question with an obvious answer).

For older children and adults, *Adopting Ahava* is a simple story of a happy, loving family. But for five-year-old Diane, and perhaps for other preschoolers and kindergarteners, the issue of adoption may tap into a deep-seated fear—being without a family. The question for Diane and other preschoolers prompted by the story is not so much what is a family but rather how can it be that some children are without a family? Without people who love them?

Aware that family life is not always easy, some authors write about the ways in which family members experience hardship and behave toward each other in times of poverty, separation, or war. An example is *Sparks Fly Upward* by Carol Matas, a story inspired by the members of her family who moved from Odessa to Saskatchewan, Canada, in the early 1900s to live in a farming community funded by Baron Hirsch. Hirsch, a philanthropist, donated money to Jewish resettlement colonies in Argentina, Canada, and Palestine. In the novel, set in Winnipeg in 1910, a Jewish Russian family loses their farm as a result of a fire and is forced to move to the city.

Twelve-year-old Rebecca recounts how her family members—twenty-one people including her grandmother and grandfather, her mother and father, her siblings, aunts, uncles, and cousins—struggle to adjust to their new life. At one point in the story, Rebecca's parents are so poor that they decide to place their three children in foster care. Rebecca, the oldest, is placed with a Ukrainian family in Canada, the Kostaniuks. As her parents leave the Kostaniuk house, they part from their daughter in a heartbreaking fashion. Rebecca's mother asks Rebecca to forgive her. By asking Rebecca for forgiveness, Mama seems aware that her actions are undermining the primacy of the family and shalom bayit. Although separated, the family hopes to be together again in the future, perhaps by the Jewish New Year (Rosh Hashanah).

For Jews, family separation has often been a necessity of survival. In Rebecca's case, economic survival necessitated separation. Pogroms (systematic violence and murder of Jews) and attempted genocide (such as occurred in the Holocaust) have often required Jewish parents to separate from their children in order to secure their children's survival. Can a family still be a family if they are forced to separate? If the children are sent away to be raised by others? If so, what makes a family a family? What gets lost when children are necessarily separated from their parents and their siblings and from other members of their family? Can what is lost ever be fully recovered?

Immigration also separates families, bringing anxiety and a longing for reunion. *Feivel's Flying Horses* by Heidi Smith Hyde and illustrated by

Johanna van der Sterre is a case in point. This story is based on the lives of Jewish woodcarvers from Eastern Europe who originally carved religious items such the holy arks for Torahs but who in America carved secular items such as carousel horses in amusement parks. The father in the story, Feivel, is working in the Brooklyn-based amusement park Coney Island to earn enough money to bring his wife and four children to America. As he finishes each horse, he carves the name of a family member in a concealed spot on the horse as a tribute to that person. After three years of work, the job is complete. When Mr. Nathanson, the owner of the carousel, turns it on for the first time, he asks Feivel to get on for a ride. Feivel declines. He prefers to wait until his wife and four children immigrate to the United States and can join him. When they finally do arrive, they all ride the carousel together.

As they ride the horses named for them, Feivel feels that his sacrifice of working and waiting has made everything right. But has it? What was lost during all those years when Feivel was separated from his family? Serious, enduring questions need to be asked about family separation that poverty and violence necessitate. What does such separation do to a family? To shalom bayit? What does it do immediately, and what does it do over the long term? What responsibilities do the rest of us have regarding such family separations? Immigration policies in the United States and elsewhere have often made family separation worse, allowing one member of a family to immigrate but not the rest of the family. Is this ethical? Is this moral? What obligations do the rest of us have to help families stay together? To helping them create shalom bayit?

Hersh Dovid Nomberg's novel *Between Parents* tells the story of eleven-year-old Yitskhok whose parents have divorced. His mother is getting remarried and sends Yitskhok by train to his father, who lives in another town. The morning after he arrives at his father's house, his father sends Yitskhok back by train. Arriving back at his mother's home, he hugs his mother, and they both sob. The man who married his mother paces back and forth, seemingly upset that Yitskhok had come back.

Between Parents is a brief bilingual novel, about thirty pages written in both English and Yiddish. There is no romanticization of family life or sentimentality. No shalom bayit. It is a harsh story but a story that too many children live. The sparse text makes it easy to see the world through Yitskhok's eyes. Why doesn't anyone want Yitskhok? He dreams about finding money, enough money to bring his mother and father back together and for all of them to live happily. It is not a dream that has any chance of coming true. What obligations do parents have to their children? What are the material obligations? What are the emotional obligations? What if parents are not able to meet those obligations? Can shalom bayit really be commanded? What obligations do other family members, teachers, and friends have to children like Yitskhok when their parents cannot meet (or do not want to meet) their obligations for shalom bayit in the family?

WHAT IS LOVE? FROM GENERATION TO GENERATION

Another Jewish principle guiding family life is the special qualities of intergenerational love, in Hebrew called *l'dor vador*. L'dor vador can be translated as from generation to generation. But it means more. Each generation has an obligation to share and pass down Jewish heritage and values to the next and future generations. Doing so is not only a matter of education, but also of caring and of love. In some families, intergenerational love is shared through activism, some by passing on stories to their children. Some choose another way.

With its focus on a grandfather and his granddaughter, *Gathering Sparks*, winner of the Sydney Taylor Book Award in 2011, written by Howard Schwartz and illustrated by Kristina Swarner, is an example of a book on intergenerational love. The narrator explains that one night when the grandfather and granddaughter were outside together, the child starts asking questions about the stars. The grandfather tells her a folktale attributed to the fourteenth-century Rabbi Luria about how the stars were the result of ships carrying a cargo of light. When the ships broke up, the light they carried scattered into the sky as stars and landed elsewhere. We are required to gather the sparks of light and restore the order of the world. Our good works, kindness, compassion, and other loving behavior help restore the original order. The grandfather tells his granddaughter that whenever she does a good deed, a spark in the sky is set free and can be seen, for example, in the eyes of her baby sister or elsewhere in the world.

The love between this grandfather and his granddaughter is perhaps best seen by contrasting the grandfather's story with what children are typically told about why they should do the right thing. Ask children, and they are likely to tell you that they will be punished if they do not do the right thing, or that their parents forced them to do the right thing. Or they may say that they treat people nicely because they want people to treat them nicely.

But this is not what the grandfather does. He and his granddaughter are outside, looking up at the night sky. The stars are beautiful, but they are more than that. They are the potential and the resource for the beauty of kindness and doing good in the world—at least that's what the story about them suggests.

So where does doing good lie? Does it lie in our fear of punishment from parents, teachers, others, the police, or God? Does it lie in ourselves, within each person? Does it lie in the universe just waiting to be gathered? Does it lie in the stories that we tell? Does it make a difference where doing good lies? Does it matter that the story comes from the grandfather and not from someone else, such as the girl's parents? What is the love that the grandfather is showing his granddaughter by telling her that story?

Bagels from Benny by Aubrey Davis with illustrations by Dušan Petričić, winner of the 2003 Sydney Taylor Book Award, is another grandfather–grandchild story. Benny's grandfather owns a bakery, where Benny works before school. One day, a customer thanks the grandfather for his bagels. When the grandfather deflects the customer's appreciation and Benny questions that response, the grandfather said that God should be thanked, not him. That thought stays in Benny's mind all day. He decides to show his gratitude by taking the bagels to the place where people speak to God, the synagogue. Week after week on Friday, Benny takes the bagels to the synagogue and places them in the ark. Each time, the bagels disappear. Benny believes that God ate the bagels. What Benny does not know is that a poor man with a hungry family found the bagels

BAGELS FROM BENNY

[Benny loves helping at his grandpa's bakery. Benny decides to give bagels to God and leaves them for God at the synagogue. A person in need finds the bagels and believes that God has provided them for him and his family.]

After reading *Bagels from Benny*, I posed various questions about the content and writing of the text including, "How do you think Benny feels about placing the bagels in the ark?" Some of the students' responses included, "God hears Benny." "Benny was afraid he would get into trouble." "Benny was scared that synagogue workers were the only people around." "Benny was walking quietly." I asked, "What thoughts do you have after the man in a tattered coat said that he would not need bagels from the ark?" They responded, "Benny thought about crying because God does not eat bagels. People do." "Benny was sad because he wanted to give more." "Benny was happy because he was helping others in need." "Benny wanted to still take bagels for the man."

I asked, "What words can you tell me about this story?" They responded, "Benny loved to ask questions and wonder." "Benny and his grandpa helped those in need." "Benny and God made the bagels from the wheat that was created on Yom Shlishi."

We paired *Bagels from Benny* with the book *Strega Nona Harvest* by Tomie dePaola and *In God's Hands* by Lawrence Kushner and Gary Schmidt. *Bagels from Benny* there in the ark. He believes that God is providing the bagels. He takes the bagels for his family.

One day, Benny's grandfather becomes curious about his grandson's actions and follows him to the synagogue. Benny's grandfather sees the poor man entering the sanctuary and taking the bagels from the ark. As he does so, the poor man says aloud that he has found work and will not need the food from heaven anymore. He also promises to help others as he has been helped.

will help us to experience the value of acting compassionately.

We followed up our discussions of the books by making a Venn diagram comparing the books. Also, the kindergartners created a flier for their family to help them discuss how they can earn *tzedakah* to buy bagels. The kindergartners and I plan to walk to our city's food pantry and deliver bagels.

Annelyn Baron, kindergarten,
private Jewish school, Ohio

At first, Benny is upset that the hungry man was the actual recipient of the bagels and not God. The grandfather tells Benny it is not so simple. By his actions, Benny unintentionally benefits a person in need. Does it matter that Benny did not realize that what he was doing was feeding a hungry person and his family? Where does the good in this good deed lie? Does it lie in Benny's actions? Does it lie in the coincidence that the poor man just happened to visit the synagogue and the ark at the right time? Was it a coincidence? Do such coincidences happen a lot? Are they rare? What does it say about our world whether they happen a lot or rarely? At first, Benny is upset that the bagels he left for God have been taken by someone. Then, Benny's grandfather talks with him. Benny seems to change—but just what is it in Benny that changes?

Another book about intergenerational ties is *When Zaydeh Danced on Eldridge Street*, written by Elsa Rael with illustrations by Marjorie Priceman. The story takes place during the early twentieth century on Eldridge Street, a block in the Lower East Side neighborhood of New York City. For many Jewish immigrant families of the period, the Lower East Side was their first home in America. As the story opens, the reader learns that the main character, Zessie, is afraid of her stern grandfather (the Yiddish word for grandfather is *zaydeh*). Visiting with her grandparents on the day of her brother's birth, Zessie feels that her grandfather is testing her as usual with his questions. Zessie's grandfather tells Zessie that the day is the Jewish holiday of Simchas Torah, and that he is going to a holiday party at his synagogue in the evening. He invites her to accompany him, and she accepts.

When the two enter the synagogue, Zessie is very surprised at the festivities. One particular surprise concerns the grandfather himself. He is smiling and dancing with the congregants. During the ceremony, Zessie asks him about the Torah and what it means to Jews. Zessie's grandfather is moved by her question and later that night tells her father that he should be proud of a child who is so curious and who wants to learn.

Zessie was afraid of her grandfather until she accompanied him to the synagogue; why did Zessie's fear change? Was she wrong to have been afraid of her grandfather before? Zessie's grandfather always tests her with questions; is that an expression of love? When Zessie goes to the synagogue with her grandfather, she asks the questions—just the opposite of what usually happens, which is that the grandfather asks her the questions. Does this make a difference? Is there something different between the grandfather asking questions of Zessie and Zessie asking questions of her grandfather? Are Zessie's questions an expression of love for her grandfather? Has Zessie changed? If so, how?

The story *Zayde Comes to Live* by Sheri Cooper Sinykin and illustrated by Kristina Swarner is told from the perspective of a granddaughter. The story examines the Jewish concept of death. The story opens with a grandfather who, near the end of his life, moves in with his family. Rachel, the granddaughter, is aware that her grandfather is too weak to play with her or to read to her because he is dying. Wondering what will happen to him, she asks her friends about death. The answers given by her Christian and Muslim friends do not comfort her because she is Jewish. She then asks the rabbi. He says that at death her grandfather will join his ancestors in an afterlife.

Although Judaism does not have a clear dogma about the afterlife, the rabbi's explanation provides Rachel with a measure of comfort. Finally, she talks with her grandfather directly. He mentions the circle of life and says that his body will return to the earth. He says his spirit will live on because his love will stay with her and so, too, her memories of him. Rachel realizes that the conversation she is having with her grandfather, their hugs, and his smell of peppermint and lime are also memories that she will have. After he dies, Rachel realizes that all the members of her family will remember the time spent with her grandfather during his life. They will tell stories about him and share their memories. She realizes that even in dying, he is creating a memory for her.

Stones for Grandpa by Renee Londner with illustrations by Martha Avilés is similar to *Zayde Comes to Live*. *Stones for Grandpa* begins one year after a young boy's grandfather has died. The young boy and his family are unveiling the headstone, and they lay stones on top of it. Leaving stones is a Jewish custom. This custom has different explanations. Leaving a stone is a permanent way of noting that people who cared about the deceased person were present as a sign of respect, memory, and love. (In general, Jews do not leave flowers at a grave site, nor are they appropriate at a funeral. Flowers eventually die, but stones remain forever.) The young boy has many memories of his grandfather but worries that over time he will forget those memories. His mother assures him that he will not forget them and the illustration shows them together looking at a photo album. The books prompt enduring questions: Why are the memories we have of grandparents so important? What do these memories give us? What's the connection between memories and love?

WHAT IS LOVE? BEYOND THE FAMILY

Beautiful Yetta: The Yiddish Chicken by Daniel Pinkwater and illustrated by Jill Pinkwater concerns a chicken in Brooklyn who, on the way to the butcher, breaks out of her crate and runs down the street. By escaping, Yetta saves herself from the soup pot as well as from the roasting pan. Although free, she is lost and lonely in the city until she rescues a parrot from a cat. At that point, a flock of parrots befriends her. Despite the fact that Yetta speaks Yiddish and the birds speak Spanish, Yetta becomes their protector. They become her community.

Obviously, this book is not about chickens or parrots. At times either individuals or a group of people find themselves in difficult, even dangerous situations from which they must escape. A child might be escaping from an abusive family; or immigrants might be fleeing from violence and genocide, such as the immigration of Jews from Russia to escape the pogroms and genocide. When they do escape—if they escape—they find themselves lost.

In the case of individuals, who will take them in? Who will be their friend? Who will be their family? In the case of a group, the people in that group are asking similar questions: Who will take them in? How will others act

> **BEAUTIFUL YETTA: THE YIDDISH CHICKEN**
>
> [A clever chicken escapes becoming chicken soup but now is lost in Brooklyn, New York.]
>
> I read *Beautiful Yetta* to my multiage third- and fourth-grade classroom. The students learned from home, and I met with them on Zoom.
>
> I introduced the book by explaining that it contained three languages, Yiddish, Spanish, and English. Yiddish was a new language to most of my students. The story is told in English, but Yetta's dialogue is written in Yiddish, and the parrots speak Spanish. The speech bubbles show the English translation and the Hebrew characters. Many of my students speak more than one language, and learning about new languages is especially interesting to them.
>
> After reading the story, we talked about four big questions:

toward them? Friendly, indifferent, or hostile? Will they be able to stay together as a family? As a community? Will they be able to maintain their culture and language?

For both individuals and for groups, the situation is made more difficult if they do not speak the language or know the culture of the place to which they have escaped. Yetta and the parrots become a community, a family. But this only happens after Yetta saves them. Is this what is necessary to be accepted? Do those escaping from terrible situations need to prove their worth by performing a heroic act? What obligations, if any, do we have to people who are escaping from frightening situations? Jewish culture, like many cultures, commands Jews to be kind and generous to strangers and to those in need.

Jews are reminded again and again in a broad range of Jewish books and customs that they have often been strangers in a strange land. Indeed, in Jewish literature and in Jewish folklore, the prophet Elijah is said to disguise himself as a beggar and a stranger to test how well Jews treat the least well-off. For example, in I. L. Peretz's story "The Magician" (retold by Uri Shulevitz in a picture book also titled *The Magician* and retold by Susan Kusel with the title *The Passover Guest*), a stranger shows up in town near the holiday of Pesach (also called Passover). The stranger performs many magic tricks, and no one can figure out how he does those tricks.

1. In this story, why do you think some of the animals were unkind to Yetta?
2. Why do you think it's important to treat people and animals with respect and kindness?
3. All animals and people are created differently. What makes you curious when you meet someone who is different?
4. What are the big ideas the author wants you to understand in this book?

Their responses showed connections to Yetta and the importance of being open to ideas and people that are new to them. Our final project was to pretend that Yetta had come to our community and create a house for her that would make her feel welcome. The students could use any materials they had at home or create on their iPads.

While they were sharing their creations, I was struck by how thoughtful they were in considering what would make Yetta feel welcome. They included essentials such as food bowls, a coop for sleeping, and a place for the parrots to live alongside her. They also added a welcome sign and a confetti cannon to make her feel special. We will return to this book.

Julie Johnson, third/fourth grade, public school, Ohio

On the first night of Pesach, when everyone should be having a seder (a wonderful meal during which the story of the Jews' exodus from slavery in Egypt is told), a poor couple find themselves without money or other resources to make a seder. They had found a silver spoon that they could sell to get money to have a plentiful seder. Instead, they gave the money from selling the spoon to the town charity to help the poor.

As evening comes (the time when Jewish holidays begin), they hear a knock on the door, and it is the magician. The poor couple invite him into their house but tell him that although they do not have money for a seder, they will share what they have. The magician tells them not to worry, and he magically provides all they need for a wonderful seder meal. The poor couple do not know what to make of this magic, so they hurry to the rabbi to ask what they should do. The rabbi tells them that if they can actually feel the food, then it is real and not a trick. If it is real, they can eat the food. They go home, the food is still there, but the magician is gone. They feel the food. It is real, so they sit down to a wonderful Pesach meal. All of the different versions of this story are similar.

At a surface level, this is a story about goodness being rewarded. The couple gave money to the town charity when they needed it themselves for their seder meal, and they never became bitter over being poor, so they were rewarded. But beyond the surface level, enduring questions are present to ponder. What if the couple were not rewarded for their charity and continued joy in their life despite their poverty and not having enough for a seder meal? What if being generous is not rewarded? Indeed, is it correct to label an act—such as giving to a charity—generous if you are expecting a reward? What if good acts are never rewarded; does that make the people who do good acts fools? The famous Rabbi Hillel said, "If I am not for myself who will be; if I am only for myself, what am I?" How does one strike the right balance between meeting one's own needs and meeting the needs of others? When the magician knocked on their door, the couple had very little to share, but offered to share what little they had. In Judaism, it is a *mitzvah* to be generous and kind to strangers. But what does it mean to be kind and generous to strangers? How far should one go?

The short story "Zlateh the Goat," written by Isaac Bashevis Singer (who won the 1978 Nobel Prize for Literature), tells the story of a family that must sell their goat, named Zlateh, because they are poor and do not have enough money to provide for the family. The story can be found in the Newbery Honor Book, *Zlateh the Goat and Other Stories* by Isaac Bashevis Singer and illustrated by Maurice Sendak. This book was also named a Best Illustrated Children's Book by the *New York Times*.

The members of the family are devastated by the decision, but they have to accept it. The oldest boy, Aaron, is given the task of taking the animal to the butcher. As the boy and goat set out, the goat appears confused because the road is unfamiliar, yet she remains trusting. The goat trusts Aaron because she has never experienced any harm from him or anyone else. As the two proceed to town, a major snowstorm develops. Aaron finds shelter in a haystack for himself and the goat. For the next three days, the goat keeps Aaron warm with her body, gives him her milk, comforts him with her presence, and provides companionship. During the time in the haystack, Aaron vows never to give up Zlateh. When the storm passes, the two emerge from the haystack and walk home. After Aaron tells his family about Zlateh's kindness, the family members change their mind about selling her. As it happens, their financial situation is not so desperate as the father's business begins to improve.

The story of "Zlateh the Goat" could be about the relationship between animals and humans. What should the relationship be between people and animals? It is not at all unusual for people to love their pets (and reciprocally; it certainly seems as if their pets love them back). We would all find it hard to butcher and eat a pet. But most people do not find it difficult to eat a hamburger or chicken leg. Is there a contradiction here? What are our obligations to animals? Not just to our pets, but to all animals? Not only did Aaron have love for the goat, but the goat had love for him. If animals can love people, what does that mean about the natural world? If animals can have emotions such as love, does that mean that the natural world—or at least parts of it—has a spiritual dimension?

Of course, the story "Zlateh the Goat" can be read as not about animals, per se, but about people and their relationships to the natural world more broadly. Even in harsh climates, the world takes care of us. It feeds us and protects us from harsh weather. When we look at a sunrise or a starry night, the world can comfort us. Yes, we do have to till the earth and build shelter, but plants grow, and nature provides materials for us to build houses and other kinds of shelter; never mind providing medicinal plants and ingredients that can make us healthy when we are ill. What is our relationship to the natural world? What are our obligations to it?

Jews have an injunction against needless destruction; it is called *bal tash'chit* (do not destroy). In the Torah, Jews are instructed to preserve fruit trees because those kinds of trees provide food. Understood narrowly, this commandment refers simply to specific fruit-bearing trees. However, more recently, people who are concerned with preserving nature have understood the passage more broadly. They have expanded the commandment. They hold that the need to recycle, reuse, and reduce is especially pressing. Some Jews use the principle of bal tash'chit as the basis for an obligation to safeguard the world at large. The injunction to preserve fruit trees because they provide food—and similarly to preserve the natural world because it provides what is needed to preserve life—would seem to be a utilitarian value. But is our relationship just utilitarian, or is there (or should there be) an ethical aspect to our relationship with the natural world? If there is an ethical obligation, what is it, and what does it demand of us?

FINAL THOUGHTS ON WHAT IS LOVE? AND ENDURING QUESTIONS

In *A Basket Full of Figs*, a Jewish folktale, based on a Talmudic story, retold by Ori Elon and illustrated by Menahem Halberstadt, an old man digs a hole to plant a fig tree. The emperor who is passing by laughs at the old man. The emperor tells the old man that he will not live long enough to see the fig trees grow and yield fruit. The old man shrugs off the emperor's criticism and derisive laughter and tells him that even if the old man does not live long enough, his children and grandchildren will enjoy the trees and their fruit. It turns out that the old man does live long enough to see the trees bear fruit, but that does not seem to be what's important.

In the last picture of the book, the old man is lying on the ground looking up at the sun through all of the trees he has planted. What he sees, however, are not figs but the faces of his children and grandchildren. Would we—should we—call that love? Can a person have love for people the person has not yet met? Who do not yet exist? What kind of love is it? Can it be a reciprocal and mutual kind of love? Can the person feel love back? Or is it all in the person's mind? Simply in their imagination? Do our answers to these questions change if we view the old man not as an individual but rather as a symbol? What if the old man were a symbol of a whole generation? What would it mean if a whole generation of people planted trees or did other things not for their own benefit but for the benefit of future generations? Would that be love? If so, how should the receiving generation return the love?

There are, of course, no final answers to the question "What is love?" Using Jewish children's literature and other children's literature to explore the question "what is love?" asks each of us to reflect on how we act with others. This includes how we act and interact with family, friends, animals, strangers, and even future and past generations.

WORKS CITED

Children's Literature

Byrne, Jennifer. *Adopting Ahava*. Illustrated by Oana Vaida. Sicklerville, NJ: My Family! Product/Dodi Press, 2013.

Davis, Aubrey. *Bagels from Benny*. Illustrated by Dušan Petričić. Toronto, ON: Kids Can Press, 2003.

Elon, Ori. *A Basket Full of Figs*. Illustrated by Menahem Halberstadt. Translated by Gilah Kahn-Hoffmann. Barnsley, England: Green Bean Books, 2017.

Hyde, Heidi Smit. *Feivel's Flying Horses*. Illustrated by Johanna van der Sterre. Minneapolis: Kar-Ben, 2010.

Kusel, Susan. *The Passover Guest*. Illustrated by Sean Rubin. New York: Holiday House, 2021.

Londner, Renee. *Stones for Grandpa*. Illustrated by Martha Avilés. Minneapolis: Kar-Ben, 2013.

Matas, Carol. *Sparks Fly Upward*. New York: Clarion, 2002.

Nomberg, Hersh Dovid. *Between Parents*. Translated by Ollie Orkus and David Kennedy. Farlag Press, 2021.

Peretz, I. L. "The Magician." In Esther Hautzig (translator), *The Seven Good Years and other Stories of I. L. Peretz*, 37–46. Illustrated by Deborah Kogan Ray. Philadelphia: Jewish Publication Society, 1984.

Perlov, Betty Rosenberg. *Rifka Takes a Bow*. Illustrated by Cosei Kawa. Minneapolis: Kar-Ben, 2013.

Pinkwater, Daniel Manus. *Beautiful Yetta: The Yiddish Chicken*. Illustrated by Jill Pinkwater. New York: Feiwel and Friends, 2010.

Rael, Elsa Okon. *When Zaydeh Danced on Eldridge Street*. Illustrated by Marjorie Priceman. New York: Simon & Schuster Books for Young Readers, 1997.

Schwartz, Howard. *Gathering Sparks*. Illustrated by Kristina Swarner. New York: Roaring Brook Press, 2010.

Shulevitz, Uri. *The Magician*. New York: Macmillan, 1985.

Singer, Isaac Bashevis. *Zlateh the Goat and Other Stories*. Illustrated by Maurice Sendak. Translated by Elizabeth Shub. New York: Harper & Row, 1966.

Sinykin, Sheri. *Zayde Comes to Live*. Illustrated by Kristina Swarner. Atlanta: Peachtree, 2012.

Taylor, Sydney. *All-of-a-Kind Family*. Westchester, IL: Follett, 1951.

Chapter 4

What Is Time?

Jewish Rites and Holidays through Jewish Children's Literature

Ms. Green brought a quilt from her home into her first-grade classroom and laid it on the rug where they had sharing time. She told the children, "Sit on the edge of the quilt." Then she took out *The Keeping Quilt* by Patricia Polacco and read it aloud. *The Keeping Quilt* tells the story of Anna (beginning as a young child) and her family and a quilt they made from old scraps of family clothing. They made the quilt after immigrating from Russia to the United States. The family kept the quilt, passing it down mother to daughter again and again. In each generation they used the quilt as a tablecloth on Shabbat, as a *chuppah* (a wedding canopy, under which people are married), as a blanket for welcoming babies into the world, and for comforting the ill.

When they finished reading the story, Ms. Green asked her students, "Why did they keep the quilt for so long? Why didn't they just buy a new one?" The students gave her all kinds of answers, but the answer she liked best was, "Because it was like family." "What do you mean, 'it was like family'?" she asked the child. The child responded, "Like it had been there and everybody knew the blanket; it was their special blanket." Ms. Green proceeded to ask, "Do you have anything in your home that is special like the quilt was special to Anna and her family? Maybe it is not a quilt or a blanket, maybe it is a cup or book or a scrapbook or a photograph or a toy." Each time a student gave an answer, Ms. Green asked, "What makes it special? What makes it family?"

The Keeping Quilt is a book that has both universal themes and is specifically Jewish. Through these uses of the quilt, we begin to understand the cycles of time that give meaning to people's lives. Over time, children grow, and their old clothes no longer fit; the old clothes are given new purposes—they become a quilt.

The quilt is used as a tablecloth to celebrate Shabbat, a Jewish holiday each week that begins Friday at sunset and lasts through Saturday sunset. Shabbat reminds us that being human is more than laboring; everyone has the right to relax, rest, and celebrate life and family (and for those who choose, to pray and study Torah). The quilt is also used for life-cycle events: children become adults, move away, marry, have their own families, people grow old and die, a new generation comes, and life continues. The quilt ties these life-cycle events together, one generation to the next, and reminds us all that we are part of something bigger than ourselves. These are difficult and complex ideas for young children; yet, it is exactly these ideas that intrigue them.

In this chapter, the use of Jewish children's literature about Jewish holidays and Jewish customs/rites is discussed. Although children's literature can help children understand the different practices that people of different cultures and religions have, more is going on in stories about life-span rites and holidays. For example, Jewish children's literature about rites and holidays poses many enduring questions that all children can explore. But first, it is important to know about the Jewish calendar.

THE JEWISH CALENDAR

Most of the world follows a Gregorian calendar (also called a Western, Christian, or civil calendar)

THE KEEPING QUILT

[A quilt is shared through four generations of the author's own immigrant Jewish family.]

I chose Patricia Polacco, author and illustrator of *The Keeping Quilt*, in a first-grade classroom. I have read this book aloud many times in first-grade classrooms, and it always elicits powerful and deep responses from students. I use this text as a tool to open the floor for students to make connections, ask questions, and reflect on the story. I ask as many open-ended questions as possible to get the students to share as much as possible. I then listen with a caring ear, to notice important themes, ideas, and wonderings that students are sharing with me. This sometimes also includes how students build connections with each other through their sharing.

The last time I used the book, the students noticed and connected with how the quilt was being passed down and used within Patricia's family. It was a cycle that kept "going and going and going." They thought that was neat. Students named the cycle, "wedding, baby, death, play, wedding" . . . and said it would repeat.

A lot of students shared connections to death in the book. They wanted to share about someone close to them who had passed away in their family. I tried to build off of their responses and encouraged them to share more, tell a special memory, or why that person was special to them. Even after the class discussion was "over," many students ran up to me and wanted to tell me about someone close to them who named after Pope Gregory XIII, who introduced it in October 1582. The Gregorian calendar arbitrarily set the length of months to 28, 30, or 31 days. Every fourth year an extra day is added to the yearly calendar (leap year) so that the seasons and the calendar remain correlated. The Jewish calendar is different. It is based on three astronomical phenomena independent of each other: the rotation of the Earth (a day); the revolution of the moon about the Earth (a month); and the revolution of the Earth about the sun (a year). Each week, Jews celebrate Shabbat from Friday at sundown through Saturday at sundown. Traditionally, observant Jews will not work, ride, or even turn lights off or on during Shabbat. They follow these traditions because they interpret the Torah as requiring them to do so and because they view these traditions as validating their humanity—that regardless of how wealthy or poor they are, they are not merely "beasts of burden." These traditions may pose challenges in how Jewish children and families might participate in the broader community.

In the book *Hannah's Way* by Linda Glaser, Hannah and her family are Orthodox Jews who have moved to a small town in Minnesota, where her family is one of the few Jews in this community. Hannah wants to attend a class picnic; however, the picnic is on Saturday, and her family will not

had passed. We decided that maybe the next book we would write in class would be a "special memories" book. They could choose to write about a special person in their life, whether living or deceased, and that would be a special way to capture those memories.

Renee Klein, first-grade teacher, public school, Ohio

HANNAH'S WAY

[Hannah and her family move to northern Minnesota, where she is the only Jewish person in the school. Her class is arranging rides to a picnic at a park on Saturday, but Hannah is unable to ride because of her family's observance of Shabbat.]

I read *Hannah's Way* by Linda Glaser and illustrated by Adam Gustavson with fifth-grade students. We read this book as a part of our classroom-book-a-day experience. Developed by a school librarian, the purpose of classroom-book-a-day is to read a picture book every day to build community through shared read-alouds.

Early in the school year, I talked with my students about the importance of representation, and central to my selection of texts is to share diverse texts so that my students both see characters who are like them and those who do not represent them.

After we finished reading, I asked my students what they thought about the book. Nancy said that the book would be good for teaching and encouraging empathy, referencing allow her to ride to the picnic. Orthodox Jews and many other Jews will not ride on Shabbat. They view doing so as violating the commandment to keep Shabbat holy and not to do work on Shabbat. Hannah is embarrassed to tell her teacher, Miss Harley, and classmates her reason for being unable to attend. Later, Hannah finally gets the courage to tell her teacher the reason. With this new information, Miss Harley asks for volunteers to walk with Hannah. All the children raise their hands to volunteer.

Hannah's Way highlights how very important it is for teachers to learn about children's home practices so all children will be included in all class activities. The challenge for teachers is to help all the Hannahs, whether or not they are Jewish, share their family's observances without feeling that they may be stigmatized or considered weird. Many Jews, however, don't practice like Hannah's family but will do some work on Shabbat, ride in a car or airplane, and turn on and off lights; nonetheless, Shabbat is special to them. It is a reminder of their connection to other Jews around the world and to Jews throughout history. It is also a reminder of their humanity and everyone else's humanity as well. Shabbat reminds them that they are part of something bigger than themselves.

the students volunteering to walk with Hannah. Diane added that a benefit of reading *Hannah's Way* is that students will learn about customs and traditions of Judaism. This prompted me to ask whether books about Jewish characters should be used in all classrooms, and their answer was a definitive "yes." They pointed out that no one in the class is Jewish.

It was here in our discussion that Alan asked if the author and illustrator of *Hannah's Way* are themselves Jewish. This was not something I had researched in advance, but I asked them why they were curious to know this. Alan's response was that they felt that a Jewish author not only would have firsthand knowledge about Judaism but may also relate to Hannah's concern that her classmates would not understand this aspect of her identity.

Allison Volz, fifth-grade teacher,
urban elementary school
in the Midwest

The yearly Jewish calendar consists of twelve lunar months that do not correspond to the months of the Gregorian calendar. Each month of the Jewish calendar begins when the first sliver of the new moon becomes visible after the dark of the moon. Every seventh year, an extra month is added to the yearly calendar so that the months associated with each season remain associated with that season. This is why Jewish holidays always seem to be on a different day of the year when looked at from the point of view of the Gregorian calendar.

One more "time" issue is important for teachers to know. When referring to historical events, people often use the abbreviation BC or AD, referring to Before Christ and Anno Domini (meaning "in the year of the Lord"). Many Jews will not use these terms and find them offensive because they require everyone, regardless of their religion, history, ethnicity, and culture, to employ a Christian framework for noting time. Instead, many Jews prefer to use BCE (before the common era) and CE (common era). The National Council of Teachers of English style guidelines call for the use of BCE and CE rather than BC and AD, respectively. For example, in the year 2023/2024, the Jewish year is 5784. Does this matter? Many Jews think so. It reminds Jews of their very long history and that they are part of something much bigger than themselves.

JEWISH CHILDREN'S LITERATURE AND HOLIDAYS

Many Jewish children's literature books are about Jewish holidays, too many for one chapter. So, this chapter focuses on select stories for a few holidays starting with Rosh Hashanah (the Jewish New Year) and Yom Kippur, followed by Sukkot, Hanukkah, Purim, and Passover. Many other holiday stories are listed in appendix A. Also discussed is Jewish children's literature about bar/bat mitzvah, a life-cycle event that only occurs once in a person's lifetime. In the last section of this chapter, select stories about Shabbat are discussed. Descriptions about each of these holidays are provided to give an understanding of how each story addresses aspects of the particular holiday. Teachers may want to integrate these Jewish holidays, and others, in the educational curriculum, not just to teach about Jewish customs, traditions, and stories regarding a particular holiday but to engage students in asking enduring questions of each child's relationship to themself and others in the world.

Rosh Hashanah and Yom Kippur

Unlike the secular New Year holiday on January 1, Rosh Hashanah—which is the Jewish New Year—is a solemn holiday followed ten days later by Yom Kippur, a holiday of prayer, reflection, and asking forgiveness of others and of God for the sins we have committed. These holidays are celebrated during the first ten days of Tishri, an autumn month of thirty days usually occurring in September–October on the Gregorian calendar.

Even Higher, originally written by I. L. Peretz and adapted by Eric A. Kimmel, tells the story of the rabbi of Nemirov, who would disappear during

Rosh Hashanah. This was very strange, as a rabbi should be in the synagogue praying during Rosh Hashanah. The Jews in the village believed that the rabbi of Nemirov disappears for a few days before Rosh Hashanah and visited heaven to beg and plead with God that each soul be inscribed in the book of life for the year.

A stranger from Lithuania decides to follow the rabbi to see where he actually goes. He finds that the rabbi doesn't go to heaven but puts on a disguise to chop and take wood to a sick elderly woman. The stranger is impressed by the rabbi's act of caring. When asked what he found out about where the rabbi goes—did he go to heaven to plead for their souls?—the stranger says that the rabbi goes "even higher" than heaven but does not reveal the rabbi's secret.

Were the rabbi's acts of kindness a miracle? Even higher than going to heaven to argue with God for the souls of the Jews in the village? Such enduring questions intrigue children: What are the miracles in their everyday lives? What about the acts of caring, kindness, and generosity they find in their families and in their communities? Are those miracles? What about the love they share with parents, siblings, and family? Is learning and teaching a miracle? Such questions, of course, have no definitive answers. Engaging in and struggling with such questions may prompt children to see differently things that they have taken for granted.

New Year at the Pier by April H. Wayland portrays how a family shows repentance through *Taslich*, a ceremony performed on the first day of Rosh Hashanah to cast off sins of the previous year by tossing breadcrumbs into flowing water. Rabbi Neil, who coordinates Tashlich on the pier, states, "Tashlich is the time we apologize for things we wish we hadn't done. Tashlich means to throw . . . away things we don't like or don't need. Tashlich is like cleaning your heart's closet. A new year, a clean heart." But is it enough to toss breadcrumbs into flowing water? What makes an apology an apology? What does it mean to have a clean heart?

What does it mean to observe high holy days whether you are Jewish or another religion when the rest of the world continues with their lives? Jews are often part of two worlds (the Jewish world and the non-Jewish world), and during these religious times difficult decisions must be made as to how one respects the holiday. This was the situation with Sandy Koufax, a Los Angeles Dodgers baseball player, a star pitcher, who chose to "sit out" the 1965 World Series game on Yom Kippur. David Adler was inspired by Sandy Koufax as he wrote *Yom Kippur Shortstop*.

In this book, Jacob, who never missed a Little League game in three years, now must decide whether he will play in the championship game, which is on Yom Kippur. His team is counting on him to play. Teachers might ask their students, "What would you do? Why?" But such questions need to be followed by asking, "How would you respond to someone who made a decision about playing that was different from what you and others thought was the right decision?" and "Should a baseball game be scheduled on an important holiday like Yom Kippur knowing the difficult decision that would create for Jewish ball players? What about scheduling a sports game on important holidays for people of other religions?"

Sukkot

Sukkot follows four days after Yom Kippur and is a harvest holiday. During this holiday people build a *sukkah*, similar to a homemade shed or lean-to covered with leafy branches. Building a sukkah commemorates the Jews building only temporary huts during their forty years of wandering in the desert after they escaped from slavery in Egypt until they entered the Promised Land. Many Jews became farmers when they reached the Promised Land. Fruit is often hung in the sukkah, and people eat there under the stars. The *esrog* (also called etrog), a fruit, is one of four species of plants pertinent to this holiday. In the story "The Esrog" by Sholom Aleichem, adapted by Aliza Shevrin in *Holiday Tales of Sholom Aleichem*, the esrog is said to have special powers.

The tale takes place in a Ukrainian Jewish community where a

YOM KIPPUR SHORTSTOP

[Jacob is Jewish. His little league baseball team is playing in the championship game, which is on Yom Kippur. Will he play?]

I read and reread the book focusing on different parts each time with my kindergarten–fifth graders, who have special education needs.

My students made connections to making difficult decisions in life. They talked about decisions they have had to make in their lives and that they were not simple decisions to make. Students came up with things that might help them decide what they should do. We talked about how Jacob, the main character, had to decide between celebrating a holiday that is very important to his family or missing the championship baseball game that his team had worked so hard for. We also talked about how he felt trying to make those decisions.

We also discussed how our friends and family and teammates should be understanding of different beliefs and cultures, even if our own cultures have different thoughts. We spent some time discussing what it would be like if our parents let us decide what to do and what we would have chosen. My students commented that they wished their parents would let them make more decisions, and we talked about why parents may not allow them to sometimes. I even asked the students if there was a holiday or something they would never miss for anything else in the world.

After we finished reading and discussing, I gave the students time to very poor man, Moshe Yankel, wishes to buy an esrog for his wife, Batya Beile, and son, Leibel, to enjoy for the upcoming Sukkot ceremony. Moshe is tricked into buying an esrog from Henzel, who assures him that this particular esrog is rare and special. Moshe takes the esrog home and places it in a protective place with instructions not to bother the esrog. It's very difficult for Leibel to stay away from the esrog, especially when he thinks the esrog is calling him to take a bite.

> write their ideas about the book. Fifth-grader Susan wrote, "I think that the story is trying to say pick family over a game or friends. Pick an important holiday over a game or friends because that is the right thing to do."
>
> Audrey Stafford, elementary intervention specialist, online academy, Ohio

When no one is looking, he bites the stem and then proceeds to try to put it back on with spit. Zalman, a carpenter who helps build the sukkah for Moshe's family, is invited to their ceremony. Zalman is invited to take the esrog out of its coveted place. When he takes out the esrog, Moshe notices that the stem is off and blames Zalman for his clumsiness. Leibel never acknowledges his actions.

Several enduring questions are posed here: Should Leibel admit his guilt even if the consequences for doing so are unpleasant? Why would anyone admit guilt if he might get away without anyone knowing that he—not someone else—is the guilty person? Does justice lie in getting caught, or does justice lie elsewhere? Is it ever fair for an innocent person to take responsibility for something he didn't do?

In *Shanghai Sukkah* by Heidi S. Hyde, ten-year-old Marcus finds himself with his family in Shanghai as they flee the Holocaust in Europe during the 1930s. Marcus is lonely and unhappy in this new place that is so different from his home in Berlin. He prepares to celebrate Sukkot by building a sukkah. Marcus doesn't expect this holiday to be much like the Sukkot holidays he has previously experienced, but he finds this celebration to be very special through a friendship he makes with Liang, a boy from Shanghai.

This story prompts important enduring questions: How do people—in this case, children—decide to help one another and be part of each other's lives? How can we be part of other people's lives, traditions, and holidays, and yet also be ourselves with our own lives, traditions, and holidays?

Another story of this holiday, which takes place in a more contemporary time, is *Tikvah Means Hope* by Patricia Polacco. Here the Roths, children Justine and Duane, and neighbors are cheerfully getting ready for Sukkot when suddenly catastrophe strikes. The catastrophe is the great Oakland fire that destroyed their town, burning more than three thousand houses and uprooting many families. After it is safe to return to the remains of their homes, they find that the sukkah they built is still standing and even Tikvah, the Roth's cat, is found and is safe. What does *tikvah* (Hebrew for "hope") mean? Are there miracles and hopes even in the midst of a catastrophe such as the Oakland firestorm? How can friendship among the people in the neighborhood, including Jews and others, be understood? What does their friendship mean about finding a community and place to celebrate beliefs in the midst of disaster?

Hanukkah (also spelled as Chanukah or Hanukah)

Mr. Tull wants his fourth-grade students to appreciate the many diverse cultures and religions in the United States and across the world. He has been thinking about which books he might use in December to help his students appreciate the great diversity of holidays. He has only one Jewish student in his class, Rifka, and the community has very few Jewish families. He worries that in the excitement around Christmas, his students will not be thoughtful about how their words and actions might make Rifka feel. Not knowing what might be a good Hanukkah book to read, he calls Rifka's parents. They are more than happy to share with Mr. Tull some of Rifka's favorite books, which Mr. Tull asks the school librarian to order for the school and for his classroom.

One of Rifka's favorite Hanukkah books was *A Parakeet Named Dreidel* by Isaac Bashevis Singer. During Hanukkah, a parakeet flies to the window of a Jewish family. It is cold outside, so the family removes the menorah and burning candles from the window and lets the parakeet into their house. The parakeet speaks a little Yiddish and plays with a dreidel, a special spinning top with four sides. A Hebrew letter is on each side: נ (N), ג (G), ה (H), and ש (SH), which stands for the Hebrew phrase *nes gadol hayah sham*, which means "a great miracle happened there."

Because the parakeet likes playing with the dreidel, they name the parakeet "Dreidel." The family falls in love with the parakeet but realize that he belongs to another family. They post signs and put a notice in the newspaper. No one comes to claim the parakeet, so they decide to keep Dreidel. They buy a cage for Dreidel, but when it comes time to put Dreidel in the cage, the family decides not to close the door or lock it, ever. Dreidel came during Hanukkah, a holiday celebrating freedom, and Dreidel loves his freedom to fly around the house. So, no locking Dreidel in a cage.

Many years later, one of the children in the family, David, goes away to university and tells his friends about the parakeet Dreidel. One of the students, Zelda, tells David that her family lost their parakeet about the same time and that, indeed, their parakeet spoke a little Yiddish. Also, they lived just a few streets from David's house (but they had not seen the posters or the newspaper notice). They had missed their parakeet ever since. David's family talks about the situation and debates whether they should give Dreidel back to his original owners. Not to worry: David and Zelda fall in love and decide to get married, and Dreidel goes to live with them.

After reading the story to his students, Mr. Tull asks them, "Let's pretend that David and Zelda did not get married, and the parakeet had to live with one family or the other. Would you give Dreidel back to the original family?" "Would you have locked Dreidel in a cage for fear he might escape, fly out the window and get lost, or worse, freeze in the cold weather?" "What difference does it make to have a pet, like a parakeet, in your family?" "Do you think it was just luck that David and Zelda bumped into each other at university? That they fell in love, married, and made a home for Dreidel?"

One reason why Jewish people celebrate Hanukkah is that after they had fought for their freedom, they went to the Temple to light a holy lamp. They only had oil for the lamp to burn just one day. But it lasted eight days—a miracle. So, Hanukkah is not only about freedom, but it is also about a miracle. Do you think it was a miracle that the parakeet just happened to fly

THE PARAKEET NAMED DREIDEL

[During a winter evening in Brooklyn, young David, Mama, and Papa are celebrating Hanukkah. They let in a parakeet that is sitting on their window ledge and find that it speaks Yiddish.]

My students and I read this book as a read-aloud, and we used a few "thinking routines" for the discussion. We started with "What do you see? What do you notice?" with the front cover, and many students excitedly noted that they saw a dreidel and a menorah. Their classmates nodded in agreement and recalled they had learned about dreidels and menorahs in music class when they studied and performed a song for Hanukkah. They were proud to make this connection and have background knowledge heading into the story. A few other students remembered a friend who was Jewish and had moved away. During the book, students had many questions about the Yiddish language and latkes.

When we finished the story, we wrote on an index card one question we still had and something we liked in the book. Responses varied from

- students wanting to know other Jewish languages, to
- did the family eventually get another parakeet? and
- how is a latke or potato pancake made?

My students were very engaged throughout and enjoyed the illustrations as well as the storyline.

Katie Konrad, third-grade teacher, public school, Ohio

into the window of that family? Do you think it was a miracle that Dreidel found a family that did not want to cage him? Do you think it is a miracle that people fall in love? That they even have love for parakeets and other pets? Is friendship a miracle? Is joy? Is learning?

Many Hanukkah books are about making *latkes*. Latkes are potato pancakes, fried in oil, and often eaten with sour cream and jam or applesauce. In many of these stories, lots of latkes are prepared. In Naomi Howland's *Latkes, Latkes, Good to Eat*, a magic frying pan makes latkes and will only stop when someone says, "a great miracle happened here." So many latkes were made that everyone had a feast and no one went hungry on Hanukkah. Is the only miracle in this story the miracle of the oil lasting for eight days in the Temple in Jerusalem? Or is there another miracle in this story? Is it a miracle that no one went hungry on that Hanukkah? What counts as a miracle?

Eric Kimmel tells a slightly different story of making latkes in *The Chanukkah Guest*. A bear wakes up in the middle of the winter and smells latkes being cooked. He enters the house where a ninety-seven-year-old woman with very poor eyesight and very poor hearing mistakes the bear for the rabbi. She had expected him to come with the rest of the town to eat her delicious latkes. The bear eats all of the latkes; and when the bear leaves, the woman gives the bear a scarf, still believing the bear is the rabbi.

When the rabbi and the people in the town finally do come to her house, they discover the mistake. They all laugh, and together they all make more latkes. There is a goodness, a dignity, and a generosity in the old woman and in the people of the town that is so much more important than the latkes. The story poses questions to children about the obligations we all have to those, like the bear, who are hungry and cold; and it poses questions about the obligations we have to work together to create joy and celebration.

Eating latkes on Hanukkah is an Eastern European Jewish tradition. However, the Jewish people are very diverse and live in every part of the world and have diverse traditions and foods. *The Queen of the Hanukkah Dosas* by Pamela Ehrenberg is a story about a family in which the mother is Indian and the father is Jewish. They incorporate Indian food into their celebration of Hanukkah. The making of *dosas*, like the making of latkes, is a way to remember that the oil for the Temple lamp lasted eight days when there was enough oil for only one day. The story involves a young boy and his little sister. The little sister loves to climb on everything and often causes trouble by doing so. The young boy is upset with his sister and her incessant climbing.

One day, during Hanukkah, when dosas are cooking on the stove, the family accidentally is locked outside the house. The only way into the house is through a very narrow opening in one window. Only the little sister is small enough to climb through the window, and her climbing ability saves the family. They come back into the house and all enjoy the dosas.

The story not only exposes children to diversity within the Jewish community but also poses enduring questions: Do we just dismiss some people in our lives and in our community because they are annoying or because they seem to cause trouble? What would it mean not to overlook them? How can we "see" them as valuable? As having strengths? How do we provide opportunities for all to use their strengths?

Purim

Queen Esther, retold by Tomie dePaola, is recounted from the biblical book of Esther. Esther, the heroine of the holiday, brings evil to justice during the fifth century BCE by saving the Jewish people in Persia from a devious plot by Haman, an adviser to the king. Haman has convinced King Ahasuerus to kill all the Jews. Esther's cousin, Mordechai, overhears this heinous plot and pleads with Esther to speak to her husband to save the Jews. King Ahasuerus does not know that Esther is Jewish. Esther risks her life by approaching the king and telling him of the plot to kill the Jewish people and herself, revealing her Jewish identity and opposing Haman.

The story of Esther can be used to ask a series of enduring questions: Why do some people feel that they have to hide their identity—as Esther did from the king—to be safe? Why was it not safe for Esther to reveal her identity and her religion? It takes a lot of courage to stand up to such evil as Haman's. What are our obligations to stand up to evil? What about King Ahasuerus? Should we hold him responsible for not realizing how evil Haman was? King Ahasuerus was so easily convinced by lies about the Jewish people; should we also hold him accountable for allowing Haman to spread lies and evil? King Ahasuerus did not have much respect for women and did not treat them equally. Is his treatment of women a problem? Should we consider that part of the problem? What about how King Ahasuerus treated the previous queen (whose name was Vashti)? Is that part of the problem?

An engaging book about the previous queen, Vashti, might be read along with books about Esther and Purim. In *Queen Vashti's Comfy Pants* by Leah Rachel Berkowiz, Queen Vashti refused to abandon her friends and dance for the king, who had become bored. She gave up living in the palace and all her riches so that she could live in her comfy pants. She wanted to enjoy being with her friends and decide for herself what to do.

The story also poses enduring questions that are important for all children to think about. Just because you might have power, like King Ahasuerus, does that mean it is righteous for you to demand that other people entertain and serve you? What about Queen Vashti's refusal to do what the king wanted? Is that a kind of power? What does it mean to respect other people?

Another story about Purim and what it means to be brave and stand up for being "different" is *The Purim Superhero* by Elisabeth Kushner, illustrated by Mike Byrne. Nate lives with his sister and two dads. One dad he refers to as Abba (dad in Hebrew) and the other as Daddy. Abba is waiting to hear the type of costume Nate wants him to sew for the Purim parade. This is a difficult decision for Nate because all of his friends are dressing up as superheroes, but Nate really wants to dress up as an alien. What will his friends think of him if he doesn't go along with their decision? Nate shares his dilemma with his family. Abba references Queen Esther's bravery and how she saved the Jews because she didn't hide her Jewish identity. Abba tells Nate that standing up for who you are, especially when you are different, may be difficult. However, standing up for who you are can make you stronger. What does it take to be brave? Do you both lose and gain something in order to be brave?

The Purim Superhero shows that Purim is also a joyful holiday regardless of the evil of Haman and how close the Jews in Persia came to being destroyed. Many Jews exchange gifts of food, donate to the poor, and eat *hamantaschen* (triangle-shaped cookies). In *Cakes and Miracles* by Barbara D. Goldin, a Jewish boy, Hershel, who is blind, wishes he could help bake hamantaschen pastries with his mother. By helping to bake, he and his mother will have more baked items to sell at the market to support themselves. However, his mother doesn't allow him to help, explaining that a person needs to see to knead and shape the dough.

One night an angel tells Hershel to visualize in his dreams what he wants to make. Hershel takes the message of this angel and when his mother is sleeping, he makes little cookies in different shapes with the dough. Hershel's mother is surprised.

This story raises enduring questions about the limitations we place on others. Hershel had to overcome the limited expectations that his mother and others had placed on him because of his blindness. Among the enduring questions this story helps us ask are: What limited expectations might we place on others, perhaps without even knowing that we are doing so? What limited expectations might we place on ourselves? How might we limit our dreams without even realizing that we are doing so? How might we overcome these limited expectations?

Many stories of Purim describe this celebration where people attend in costumes of Purim characters as well as today's characters. The celebration includes noisemakers such as groggers that are sounded when the name of Haman is spoken. *Sweet Tamales for Purim* by Barbara Bietz is a story of this celebration adapted from a true event in 1886 when the Hebrew Ladies

Benevolent Society of Tucson, Arizona, held a Purim Ball for the entire community. One of the joys of this story is that it shows the cultural diversity of Jewish people. Instead of hamantaschen, they make sweet tamales. This true story poses an important enduring question: What is a tradition? Is the tradition eating hamantaschen, or is the tradition something deeper, less tangible?

Passover/Pesach

Passover (also called Pesach) celebrates the freeing of the Jews from their enslavement in Egypt. The first night of Passover begins on the fifteenth day of the month of Nisan, typically in March or April of the Gregorian calendar. Some Jews celebrate Passover for seven days and others celebrate for eight days. The word *seder* means "order," but most Jews use the word *seder* to refer to a traditional meal held during Passover in which the story is told of the Jews' liberation from Egypt.

Many children's books tell the story of how Passover is a commemoration of God's liberation of the Jewish people from slavery in Egypt and their freedom as a nation under the leadership of Moses. This exodus is vividly told from a young enslaved Jewish girl's perspective in the story *The Longest Night: A Passover Story* by Laurel Snyder. This story describes (as told in the Torah) how God helped the Jews escape from slavery by inflicting ten plagues on their oppressors. One of the foods eaten during this holiday is *matzo*, flat unleavened bread representing the lack of time for the bread to rise as the Jews made their exodus. Matzo is also referred to as "bread of affliction," symbolizing both a lesson in humility and an act that enhances the appreciation of freedom.

The Passover seder is not just about the freedom from slavery of the Jews, but also about people who are still enslaved and need to be freed. What is our role and our obligation to support the freedom of people still enslaved? How can we have peace in the world without freedom for all? What is our role to help make peace and to help people who are enslaved be free? What does it mean to be enslaved? To be free? Is being enslaved or being free just about the body? Or is it also about the mind? About our relationships with others? About whom we love?

In the story "The Magician" written by I. L. Peretz (which can be found in *The Seven Good Years and Other Stories* adapted by Esther Hautzig), a magician comes to a town in Volynia in Eastern Europe a few days before Passover. (This story was briefly discussed in chapter 3.) He appears as a mysterious man dressed in ragged clothes, looking very poor but performing magic. He pulls turkeys from his boots and gold coins from the sole of his boot.

In the town lives Chaim-Yonah, who at one time was a prosperous lumber merchant but through misfortune had become penniless. He and his wife, Rivkah-Beilah, have no money for Passover preparations, and Chaim-Yonah refuses to ask for charity. On the first night of Passover, the magician comes to their door wanting to be a guest at their seder. They welcome the stranger into their home even though they have nothing. The guest enters their home, magically provides all the preparations and food for the seder, and then mysteriously leaves.

As discussed in chapter 3, the story of the magician has many retellings including Uri Shulevitz's *The Magician's Visit*, Barbara D. Goldin's *The Magician's Visit: A Passover Tale*, and *The Passover Guest* by Susan Kusel. The story of the magician requires children to ask, "Who is this person, this magician?" According to myth and tradition, the prophet Elijah, who lived in the ninth century BCE, travels around the world on Passover visiting every seder. His presence reminds Jews to have hope and keep working for fairness and justice. Often, a door is opened during the Passover seder and a wine glass is filled and placed on the table so that Elijah will have something to drink when he comes. In some families, children are told to watch the cup of wine carefully to see if Elijah comes and takes a sip.

Other stories during this holiday focus on the role of Elijah as a peacemaker. *Elijah's Door by* Leopold Strauss is a folktale of two families (the Galinskys and the Lippas) who live next door to each other and for years share seder together. Because of an unresolved disagreement, they no longer speak to or see each other. In fact, Papa Galinsky cut a new side door in his house so he can leave without seeing a Lippa. Each family has a child, David Lippa and Rachel Galinsky, who love each other and, when they grow up, they very much want to engage both families in their happiness.

With the help of their rabbi, the three—Rachel, David, and the rabbi—plan to have one seder with both families present. They are successful in doing so, and celebrating Passover together becomes a tradition. People throughout the community join the two families, and the Passover seder grows. This book poses many enduring questions: How do you live in a world where others have different viewpoints from your own? How do you overcome disagreements to move forward? What makes a disagreement so profound as to cause the two parties from moving forward? What is missing when disagreements aren't resolved? Is it possible to disagree with a person but still interact with that person on another level? Do you need miracles to occur—such as David and Rachel falling in love—for disagreements to be resolved?

BAR MITZVAH/BAT MITZVAH/B-MITZVAH

Children in their early years are already thinking about their future identities as being older, bigger, wiser, and assuming more responsibilities for themselves and their communities—locally and globally. Becoming an adult is often an individual journey, with the child beginning to make decisions as to the type of person they want to be in the world; their relationships with their peers, families, and other adults, and how they want to contribute to society. Many cultures chart paths to be taken and goals to be reached to assist in reaching this age of maturity, but in the end, it is about how the child takes up this journey.

According to Jewish law, at thirteen years old, Jewish children reach an important transition in their lives from leaving their childhood to becoming an adult (in some cases, this transition happens at twelve years old). This transition culminates in a ritual that has been called bar mitzvah (males), bat mitzvah (females), and b-mitzvah (gender neutral).

Many Jewish communities prepare the child for this event by studying at Hebrew school, attending Sabbath prayer services, and taking on a *tzedakah* (social justice) or community project. Tzedakah (righteousness) is considered more than charitable giving in the modern Western understanding of charity but is an ethical obligation.

In the children's novel *Turtle Boy* by M. Evan Wolkenstein, Will is a very shy boy with low self-esteem. He has one good friend. He is bullied at school partly because of the shape of his chin, which is shrinking due to micrognathia that requires extensive surgery. Will has difficulty finding a tzedakah project that is meaningful to him until his rabbi encourages him to develop a relationship with RJ, a boy hospitalized with a fatal illness.

RJ has a bucket list that he is unable to physically complete and calls upon Will to perform these activities from his list. Their relationship, although stressful at first, brings Will out of his shell as he tackles RJ's bucket list.

Turtle Boy raises important questions: Who is helping whom? Is Will helping RJ get his bucket list done, or is RJ helping Will gain confidence in himself and self-esteem? Or maybe "helping" is not the best word to describe what is happening between Will and RJ. Maybe it is not charity or helping at all, but friendship? Among the enduring questions that *Turtle Boy* poses: What does it mean to engage in helping others? Is it really just about doing for others? Or, as happens to Will, is the situation more complex? Is it more a relationship in which everyone benefits? What are our obligations to others who, like RJ, might be in difficult situations?

Understanding one's Jewish heritage becomes part of the preparations, whether through learning the blessings, Torah stories, or other Jewish history.

A tzedakah and community project that some children preparing for bar mitzvah/bat mitzvah/b-mitzvah might pursue is a "twinning project." Twinning projects are designed to help strengthen a person's identification with their Jewish heritage by having the student research the story of another person of similar age as themself, perhaps who has been through the Holocaust or lived during another historical time period.

The Diary of Laura's Twin by Kathy Kacer is an example of a twinning project. Here, Laura's rabbi arranges for her to meet a woman who has been through the Holocaust. The woman gives Laura a journal she wrote when she was similar in age to Laura. Laura does not realize that the diary was written by the woman she met. As she reads more about the person in the diary, Laura finds similarities between herself and this other girl. She imagines this girl within the particular time period and conditions. One of the enduring questions that a story like *Laura's Twin* poses is about our ability to see ourselves in others. What does it mean to have a "twin," to remove the separation of time and place among people?

Jewish children grow up in diverse family configurations. This includes children who are in families in which one of the parents is Jewish and the other is not. Some children in such families grow up with strong Jewish identities, whereas others do not. Tara, in *My Basmati Bat Mitzvah* by Paula J. Freedman, is a child from a dual heritage marriage, (i.e., her father is Jewish and born in the United States of European heritage; and her mother, who is of Indian heritage, converted to Judaism when she married). Tara is confronted with many perceptions from her peers regarding who is and is not a Jew. Who can have a bar mitzvah/bat mitzvah/b-mitzvah? How do you represent your multiple identities at this important event? Do you need to believe in God to have a bar mitzvah/bat mitzvah/b-mitzvah?

MY BASMATI BAT MITZVAH

[Twelve-year old Tara Feinstein, whose father is Jewish and whose Indian mother has converted to Judaism, explores her Jewish identity as she prepares for and experiences her bat mitzvah.]

As the school librarian at an independent day school, I worked with English teachers to create a list of books that represented a range of culturally diverse authors for a reading workshop unit. *My Basmati Bat Mitzvah* was one of the ten titles offered to students. Students enjoyed browsing through each of the books, and then they each selected two titles to read.

The teachers gave the students options for their long-term projects including writing a five-paragraph essay, creating a graphic novel based on the story, writing a series of social media posts on behalf of the characters, flipping the perspective in a written piece, or creating a work

For most Jews, each person must struggle with such questions.

In *My Basmati Bat Mitzvah*, Tara has to work out answers to such questions herself, although her rabbi, her peers, and family members support her in doing so. The culmination of bar mitzvah/bat mitzvah/b-mitzvah is a Jewish ceremony in which the child reads a portion of the Torah at Shabbat services. Often the young person talks about the meaning of this ceremony by explaining parts of her journey. At the heart of the ceremony are these questions: What is my relationship to the Jewish community? To Judaism? To Jewish history and Jewish memory? What does it mean to be Jewish? Such questions are similar to the enduring questions that all children might ask themselves: What is my relationship to my community? To the various communities to which I belong? To history? To my community's history? To America's history? To world history?

of art based on the text. Several students selected *My Basmati Bat Mitzvah* for their reading workshop project. In each case, the student opted for the five-paragraph essay.

This is written in the voice of Tara, the book's first-person narrator, and it is both educational and very funny. A special component of this book is a glossary of Hindi-Hebrew-Yiddish-English vocabulary. Recipes that combine Indian and Jewish culture are also included. The story provided connections for students to discuss pivotal moments in the characters' and their own lives and relate these to the grade-level themes of identity. Students were able to make connections to the world around them and to their own lives. One student who selected the book stated that while reading the book she asked her best friend, who was planning her bat mitzvah, about the process that goes into planning her bat mitzvah so she could better understand that part in the book.

Susan Polos, school librarian, independent school, Connecticut

SHABBAT

Well before the woodcock calls, when morning still looks like night, my mother rises. Moving silently over the earth floor, she lifts the bamboo pipe from the wall and kneels with it over the hearth. Again and again she blows through the pipe . . . until at last, her breath rekindles yesterday's embers. As the fire grows, my mother mixes teff flour with water and pours it on the iron griddle. Now our *injara*, our bread pancakes, are sizzling. We throw off our sheepskin covers and dress in our long *shammas* (robes). Father pours water from the gourd onto our outstretched hands. Around the *massob*, our table made of woven reeds, we eat our pancakes, washing them down with strong coffee.

Suddenly we hear it! The clang of the iron gong, the boom of the big drums
. . . The elders are moving through the village, reminding us that Sabbath, the
Day of Delight, begins at sundown.

This excerpt from *Day of Delight* by Maxine Rose Schur portrays how Jews who live in the high mountains of Ethiopia celebrate Shabbat. The story, narrated by a ten-year-old boy, is more than a Shabbat celebration; it is also a celebration of their lifestyle of farming, cooking, weaving, and growing up in this Ethiopian community.

Jews have lived in Ethiopia for more than two thousand years. These Jews call themselves Beta Israel, "House of Israel." The Jews in Ethiopia have maintained their independence for more than one thousand years in spite of religious persecution, enslavement, continuous massacres, and forced conversions. (For more information on Jews in Ethiopia, see https://www.cultural-survival.org/publications/cultural-survival-quarterly/plight-ethiopian-jews.)

Joseph Who Loved the Sabbath, retold by Marilyn Hirsh, is a tale about a man, Joseph, who works on a farm for a selfish and greedy boss named Sorab. Although Joseph works hard, he receives little money and never gets a raise. All the money Joseph earns is spent on making Shabbat a special day with items such as hallah, oil lamps (today candles), foods such as poultry and fish, a nice tablecloth, and good china. In addition, he wears a prayer shawl with fringes and robe. Sorab is haunted by a genie who appears in a dream. The genie tells Sorab that his house and land will go to Joseph. Sorab proceeds to sell all his properties in exchange for a ruby that he wears on his tall hat and goes out to sea to a land far away from Joseph. Sorab is swept into the sea by a storm and never seen again. One day Joseph buys a fish for Shabbat and finds the ruby in the fish. He buys Sorab's house and lands and invites all to share Shabbat with him. Would Sorab have been saved if he hadn't been so greedy? What do you sacrifice in order to have something you really want?

Each holiday and tradition brings memories of something bigger than ourselves, shared histories, and shared values. Holidays and traditions connect Jews through time all over the world. How one celebrates Jewish rites and holidays is not perceived as a separate place in time but passed from generation to generation. Although some traditions may remain relatively the same, they vary and evolve according to how each person wants and uses his resources to celebrate each event. They also vary as times change and people's understanding of everyone's humanity and dignity evolves. The stories discussed in this chapter and others that take up Jewish rites and holidays ask us all to think deeply about enduring questions as we realize the complexity and existence of being part of a multicultural and diverse world.

WORKS CITED

Children's Literature

Adler, David A. *Yom Kippur Shortstop.* Illustrated by Andre Ceolin. Millburn, NJ: Apples & Honey Press, 2017.

Aleichem, Sholom. *Holiday Tales of Sholom Aleichem.* Selected and translated by Aliza Shevrin. New York: Charles Scribner's Sons, 1979.

Berkowitz, Leah Rachel. *Queen Vashti's Comfy Pants.* Illustrated by Ruth Bennett. Millburn, NJ: Apples & Honey Press, 2021.

Bietz, Barbara. *Sweet Tamales for Purim.* Illustrated by John Kanzler. Atlanta: August House, 2020.

dePaola, Tomie. *Queen Esther.* New York: HarperCollins, 1986.

Ehrenberg, Pamela. *The Queen of the Hanukkah Dosas.* Illustrated by Anjan Sarkar. New York: Farrar, Straus & Giroux, 2017.

Freedman, Paula J. *My Basmati Bat Mitzvah.* New York: Abrams, 2015.

Glaser, Linda. *Hannah's Way.* Illustrated by Adam Gustavson. Minneapolis: Kar-Ben, 2012.

Goldin, Barbara Diamond. *Cakes and Miracles: A Purim Tale.* Illustrated by Erika Weihs. New York: Viking Penguin, 1991.

———. *The Magician's Visit.* Illustrated by Robert Andrew Parker. New York: Viking, 1993.

Hirsh, Marilyn. *Joseph Who Loved the Sabbath.* Illustrated by Devis Grebu. New York: Viking Kestrel, 1986.

Howland, Naomi. *Latkes, Latkes, Good to Eat: A Chanukah Story.* Boston: Clarion, 1999.

Hyde, Heidi Smith. *Shanghai Sukkah.* Illustrated by Jing Jing Tsong. Minneapolis: Kar-Ben, 2015.

Kacer, Kathy. *The Diary of Laura's Twin.* Victoria, BC: Orca, 2008.

Kimmel, Eric A. *The Chanukkah Guest.* Illustrated by Giora Karmi. New York: Holiday House, 1990.

———. *Even Higher.* Illustrated by Jill Weber. New York: Holiday House, 2009.

Kusel, Susan. *The Passover Guest.* Illustrated by Sean Rubin. New York: Holiday House, 2021.

Kushner, Elizabeth. *The Purim Superhero.* Illustrated by Mike Bryne. Minneapolis: Kar-Ben, 2013.

Peretz, I. L. "The Magician." In Esther Hautzig (translator), *The Seven Good Years and other Stories of I. L. Peretz*, 37–46. Illustrated by Deborah Kogan Ray. Philadelphia: Jewish Publication Society, 1984.

Polacco, Patricia. *The Keeping Quilt.* New York: Simon & Schuster Books for Young Readers, 1988.

———. *Tikvah Means Hope.* New York: Doubleday Books for Young Readers. 1994.

Schur, Maxine Rose. *Day of Delight: A Jewish Sabbath in Ethiopia.* Illustrated by Brian Pinkney. New York: Dial Books for Young Readers, 1994.

Shulevitz, Uri. *The Magician's Visit.* New York: Macmillan, 1985.

Singer, Isaac Bashevis. *A Parakeet Named Dreidel*. Illustrated by Suzanne Raphael Berkson. New York: Farrar, Straus & Giroux, 2015.

Snyder, Laurel. *The Longest Night: A Passover Story.* Illustrated by Catia Chien. New York: Schwartz & Wade, 2013.

Strauss, Linda Leopold. *The Elijah Door: A Passover Tale.* Illustrated by Alexi Natchev. New York: Holiday House, 2012.

Wayland, April Halprin. *New Year at the Pier: A Rosh Hashanah Story.* Illustrated by Stephane Jorisch. New York: Dial Books for Young Readers, 2009.

Wolkenstein, M. Evan. *Turtle Boy.* New York: Delacorte, 2020.

Chapter 5

What Is Wisdom and What Is Foolishness?

Humor and Jewish Literature for Children

In *The Rooster Prince of Breslov*, retold by Ann Redisch Stampler and illustrated by Eugene Yelchin, a young prince—just a boy growing up—starts acting like a rooster. He pecks at the ground like a rooster, walks around naked and bent over like a rooster, and crows like a rooster. No one knows why, and no one knows how to get him to stop acting like a rooster.

The king brings in all kinds of experts to help his son, the prince. But none is able to help. An old man approaches the king and offers to help. He joins the prince and starts acting like a rooster, too. When two mattresses are placed in the room, the old man—pretending to be an old rooster—asks the prince what they are. The prince says they are mattresses and that an old rooster might want to sleep on them instead of the ground. They both sleep on mattresses. The next day a loaf of bread is placed in the room, and the prince suggests that maybe a hungry old rooster could eat just a little of it. They both eat a little. Bit by bit, the old man—pretending to be an old rooster—helps the prince become a boy again (and to stop being a rooster). He does so by encouraging the prince to care about another person and to engage in good deeds.

When four-year-old Diane was first read the story, she asked, "Why does he want to be a rooster?" Why indeed? Why would anyone give up all of the lavish food, clothing, gifts, and privileges of a prince to be a rooster? Why would someone choose to sleep on a cold, hard floor and eat hard kernels of corn?

When Ms. Singer read the story to her first-grade classroom, she asked six-year-old Steven, "Why do you think the old man succeeded in helping the prince when the others failed?" He answered, "I don't know." It is a difficult question to answer. So often young children are given books that appear simplistic in their content, but they may not be used to questions that ask them to think deeply. Sometimes children view their teachers as having all the answers, so children see any question as a game of trying to guess the answer the teacher wants. They do not think for themselves, they do not explore possibilities, they do not think deeply. However, that doesn't mean they cannot think deeply, and with a little encouragement they enjoy doing so. With a little prompting from his teacher, Steven speculated, "Maybe he didn't want the old man to sleep on the floor."

The Rooster Prince of Breslov is a humorous story. Children often laugh as it is read and playact being roosters. But, like much of humorous Jewish children's literature, wisdom is behind all that humor. As the endnote in the book explains, the story is an old Yiddish folktale that, like so many Jewish children's stories, can be traced back to the stories told by Rabbi Nachman of Breslov (1772–1810).

The Rooster Prince of Breslov highlights two important aspects of being human: *rakhmones* (compassion for others) and *mitzvot* (good deeds). Rakhmones and mitzvot are not just nice things for a person to do, as the story shows; they are key parts of what makes us human (and not roosters). *The Rooster Prince of Breslov* opens conversations on enduring questions about what it means to be fully human (and not an animal). This is basically what Diane was asking when she asked, "Why does he want to be a rooster?" There is, of course, no one correct answer to what it means to be fully human and not a rooster, but it is a conversation worth having again and again with children, regardless of their age.

The Rooster Prince of Breslov is also a good story for teachers to discuss among themselves. The old man is a teacher. He was teaching the prince about being human, about rakhmones and mitzvot. A teacher can certainly tell a student about rakhmones and mitzvot and tell students what it means to be fully human; but as educators know, telling is not teaching, and it is not learning. Among the enduring questions that *The Rooster Prince of Breslov* poses is "How can teachers create the conditions for student learning, especially when that learning needs to run deep inside of the student?"

This chapter asks, "What is wisdom and what is foolishness?" Many of the books and stories discussed in this chapter are humorous, but not all of them are. Some of the stories help us all laugh at our foibles. Sometimes we are lazy, sometimes we gossip, sometimes we are arrogant. Laughter and humor help us recognize our faults. Although we will never be perfect, we can become better friends, family members, classmates, community members, and become kinder and more open to people who are different from us. Some of the stories discussed in this chapter ask children to question self-centeredness and greed.

An old Jewish saying is attributed to Rabbi Hillel: "If I am not for myself, who will be? If I am only for myself, what am I?" In part, this saying is about balancing one's own needs and the needs of others. But it can also be understood as reminding all of us that we exist in a world with others; that our lives are inseparable from the lives of others. If I am only for myself, am I human? Some of the stories discussed ask children to question the relationship of power and wisdom. Does being powerful or rich make one wise? The old man who helped the rooster prince was neither powerful nor rich, yet he was wise. The king who had power and the experts who had knowledge lacked the wisdom to help the rooster prince.

Because many of the stories discussed in this chapter are humorous, it may be useful to talk a bit about Jewish humor. Much of Jewish humor is the same as humor everywhere: making fun of the hypocrisies of the rich, powerful, and famous; looking at one's own foibles; and simply enjoying those absurdities of life that make it beautiful—such as four-year-old Shoshana placing spaghetti, peanut butter, hummus, and ice cream (her favorite foods) on a slice of challah and giving it to her mother as a present who, taking a bite, tells her how delicious the sandwich is.

But some Jewish humor comes from a long history of Jewish experience, much of which—but not all—is of persecution, poverty, disrespect, suffering hatred, being minoritized, ghettoized, murdered, discounted, and overlooked. How does one deal with such a history and such circumstances beyond crying, memorializing, and remembering? One answer to this question is, in part, by pointing out and remembering all that is wonderful about Jewish life, culture, and people; all of the accomplishments; and the sense of pride and richness of spirit a people develop by having survived such circumstances and indescribable pain. Another answer, in part, is by laughing at the world and at oneself—not the laughter of making fun of the world and oneself but the laughter of having survived the unsurvivable again. (If you are interested in further discussion of Jewish humor, see appendix A.)

THE WISDOM (AND FOOLISHNESS) OF CHELM

Before discussing how such stories might be used to engage children in conversation about enduring questions, two caveats are needed. First, sometimes it is enough just to read a story and laugh. Learning that reading can be fun and make you laugh is an important lesson. However, that leads to the second caveat. There is always the danger of laughing *at* people (particularly people of other ethnicities, races, geographies, etc.) and forming stereotypes. Whether one is teaching a classroom with many Jewish students, some, or none, it is important to consider carefully how students might take up stories of Chelm. If there is a danger that the children in your classroom might come away from reading or listening to a story of Chelm with negative views of

Jewish people or with stereotypes, then you should avoid such stories. Plenty of other stories within Jewish children's literature can be used to engage students in enduring questions.

When approached with humility, stories of foolishness—despite their humor—can often lead us to reflect on our own lives and the worlds in which we live. They can also help us appreciate and value clear thinking. Many cultures have similar humorous stories, often called "noodlehead" stories. Stories about the people of Chelm, discussed below, with all their foolishness, serve all these purposes and more. With a teacher's help, the stories can engage students in discussions of enduring questions.

In Jewish literature, the city of Chelm is an imagined city in which the people seem to be fools. (Poland actually has a city named Chelm, but it bears no resemblance to the city of Chelm in Jewish literature.) It is fun to read stories about Chelm to children. Sometimes the wisdom of Chelm is straightforward, hilarious, and silly, such as nailing matzo balls (soup dumplings made from matzo meal) to plates so that the matzo balls won't roll off. Children who have not heard such stories before often sit quietly at first wondering if they are allowed to laugh at the people of Chelm and how illogical they are. Then, when the children realize that they are supposed to laugh, they may shout out, "What? That's so stupid," and they giggle or laugh aloud. Not all of the Chelm stories easily lend themselves to engaging enduring questions. A few of the Chelm stories that do lend themselves to engaging enduring questions are discussed in this chapter.

In Eric Kimmel's *Right Side Up: Adventures in Chelm*, illustrated by Steve Brown, the title story concerns a slice of buttered bread that fell with the butter side up. Everyone knows, so the people in Chelm claim, that whenever you drop a slice of buttered bread, the butter side is the side that hits the ground. However, when Simon's mother threw a slice of buttered bread to Simon through the window as he was playing outside, the butter side landed up, wrong side down. This created a lot of stir in the town.

Rather than be happy that the butter side did not land down, the people of Chelm were upset that what they thought should happen did not happen. The town council met and discussed the matter for a long time. Finally, the town council came to this conclusion: Simon's mother had been in a hurry and had buttered the wrong side of the bread. They reasoned that this was why the butter side landed up when she threw it and Simon failed to catch it. So, they passed a law, bread must only be buttered on the right side and never the wrong side.

Of course, the real issue was the careless treatment of throwing a buttered slice of bread, but the town council could not see it. We can laugh at the town council—after all, a slice of bread has no right or wrong side. Whether the buttered side or nonbuttered side lands on the ground is a matter of chance. It is not predetermined or preordained, not a matter of right and wrong.

As important, why should there be such an uproar about such a trivial matter? Once students are encouraged to stand back from laughing at the people of Chelm, we can ask them, what is it about the town council and the people of Chelm that they feel the need to debate so long and ardently about such a trivial matter? What are they really concerned about? These are not easy questions to answer. Is it ego? Is it the desire (and the arrogance) to try to control chance or luck or nature? Do such things happen beyond Chelm?

Then, there's the story of "The Sign" (which can be found in *Kibitzers and Fools* by Simms Taback and another version in *Right Side Up: Adventures in Chelm* by Eric Kimmel). A fishmonger makes a sign for his shop so that he can advertise and people will come to his store to buy fish. As people come by the store, they give him advice about revising his sign. One tells him that he does not need to put his name on the sign because everyone knows his name. So, the fishmonger crosses out his name. Another passerby tells him that the sign does not need to say that fish are sold there because that is obvious. Another comments that he does not need the word *fish*. People already know what he is selling. Soon the fishmonger has crossed out all the words on his sign. His friend asks why he even bothers to have a sign because every word is crossed out. He tells his friend that he needs to advertise if he wants to have a successful business.

We laugh—but why do we laugh? The fishmonger works hard, and he provides a valuable service to the community. He gets advice from so many people, all of whom mean well. So where did it all go wrong? Should the fishmonger have ignored all the advice he was given? But how could he know what was good advice and what was bad advice? Did the fishmonger act foolishly by not understanding what would happen if he followed all the advice he was given? But how should he know how much advice to follow and how much to ignore? Was the fishmonger wrong to trust others' wisdom and not his own? If so, how can a person know when one's own wisdom should supersede another's? And should the focus be just on the fishmonger? What responsibilities and obligations do the people have who gave him advice?

One Chelm story is about a man named Schlemiel (whose name in Yiddish means an inept and clumsy person). Schlemiel tried to solve the problem of a Rosh Hashanah holiday with no honey. (The story is told by Valerie Estelle Frankel in *Chelm for the Holidays*.) Rosh Hashanah is the holiday of the Jewish New Year. It is tradition in Ashkenazi Jewish communities (Jewish communities with a heritage in Europe) to dip apples in honey and to bake honey cakes. But that particular year, Chelm had no honey.

Schlemiel had an idea. Nearby was a field of flowers and lots of bees busy with the flowers. Schlemiel thought that if he disguised himself as a flower, the bees would not sting him and he could get the bees' honey. He put flowers in his beard and draped a quilt decorated with flowers around himself. But the bees were not fooled. They swarmed at Schlemiel and tried to sting him. He ran to his home and shut the door before any of the bees could get in. Soon, there was a knock on the door. When the bees swarmed around Schlemiel and followed him to his house, other people in the town could then easily get the honey from beehives as all the bees had followed Schlemiel.

They thanked Schlemiel for distracting the bees and decided to do the same thing every year. Every year Schlemiel should dress up as a flower, distract the bees, and hopefully run home and shut the door before he got stung. Should Schlemiel take the credit for distracting the bees and thereby providing honey for the holiday? Should he agree to do it again next year? And every year thereafter? Schlemiel is making a sacrifice for the broader community. But when is such a sacrifice too much to ask of someone else? When should someone say that the sacrifice he is being asked to make for the broader community is too much? And what constitutes a sacrifice anyway? How can we know?

Many versions exist of the story about the attempt by the people of Chelm to capture the moon. One version is *Rachel Captures the Moon* by Richard Ungar (who adapted the story from Samuel Tenenbaum and illustrated it). In this version, the beauty of the moon dominates.

Because the moon does not always shine, the people of Chelm decided to capture the moon so that they could always see it. They tried many different ways to capture the moon. They built a high ladder, they tried to entice the moon to come to Earth by cooking wonderful food, sending the aromas toward the moon in the night sky. They knitted a warm blanket to wrap around the moon, and a fisherman tried to cast a net over the moon to capture it. None of these tactics worked. Then Rachel, a child, said that she could capture the moon with a barrel of rainwater. Sure enough, on a night with a full moon, the people of Chelm could see the moon in the barrel of rainwater. Quickly they put the lid on the barrel and captured the moon.

In another version, titled *The Sages of Chelm and the Moon* (by Shlomo Abas and illustrated by Omer Hoffmann) the emphasis is on the light the moon provides so that people can find their way in the dark. The people of Chelm decide to buy the moon and travel to an inn in a faraway village. The innkeeper filled a barrel with water and then told the Chelmites to look inside the barrel where they could see the moon (of course, only its reflection). The innkeeper put a lid on the barrel, and the Chelmites took it back to Chelm. When they opened the barrel, there was no moon. Perhaps the innkeeper had tricked them by taking the moon out of the barrel when they weren't looking.

In a third version (which can be found in *Right Side Up: Adventures in Chelm* by Eric Kimmel), the Chelmites try to entice the moon by filling a barrel with wonderful *borscht* soup and sour cream. They see the moon in the borscht and put a lid on the barrel. Later, when they go to check on the moon, they cannot find it. They speculate that the moon melted in the borscht.

We can laugh at the antics of the people of Chelm as they try to capture the uncapturable. Yet, at the same time we recognize the common human desire to capture and preserve beauty and light. We understand Rachel's joy at finally capturing the moon and its beauty, although we know that she has not done so. Is beauty something that people can capture and hold on to? Or is it inherently uncapturable? Is the wonder of beauty only in the moment, perhaps capturable in memories but not in itself? Is the effort to capture beauty a fool's errand, or is something noble in the attempt that is destined to fail?

EXPERIENCING THE SAME DIFFERENTLY

In the storybook *Lemuel the Fool* (by Myron Uhlberg and illustrated by Sonja Lamut), Lemuel decides to sail away from his village to find a wonderful city he believes exists over the horizon. As he sails, a storm knocks him down. When he awakens, he sails to what he believes is a new village. To his surprise, the new village looks exactly the same as his own village. (Children listening to and reading the story will know immediately that it is, indeed, the same city, and that Lemuel is a fool.) As Lemuel explores the "new" city, he finds a family just like his own family. He decides to leave the "new" village, sets sail, but soon falls asleep. When he wakes, he sees land and his own village. He can hardly contain his excitement and joy at being home. His wife, however, thinks he is a fool. Where else could he be but at home?

Why is Lemuel so happy at being home? We could imagine that he might have been quite disappointed. After all, he went on a long, difficult journey, only to arrive back at his own village. Why is he so happy to be home? What about his dream of finding the wonderful city over the horizon? Does it mean that he should no longer dream of wonderful places and just be satisfied with what he has? And what does he have? He has to work very hard every day and, even so, he has just enough to get by. Shouldn't he be allowed to have dreams? Shouldn't he be allowed to pursue those dreams? What dreams should he be allowed to have? Is he a fool for pursuing those dreams? Who gets to tell him which dreams he should have and whether to pursue them? It is fun to laugh at Lemuel and his foolish navigation skills and his inability to recognize the "new" village as being his own village. Yet, in a sense this fool has gained some wisdom, although perhaps he is unaware of that. What is the wisdom he has gained?

Margot Zemach's *It Could Always Be Worse* has many versions. For example, one version is "An Overcrowded House" in *My Grandmother's Stories: A Collection of Jewish Folk Tales* by Adèle Geras and illustrated by Anita Lobel; another version is *Such a Library!* by Jill Ross Nadler and illustrated by Esther van den Berg.

In Zemach's version, a poor man and his family are unhappy with their small house. The poor man complains to the rabbi, who tells him to bring the chickens, the rooster, and the geese inside the house. Things get worse, and the rabbi tells him to bring in the goat, then the cow. When the poor man cannot stand it anymore, the rabbi then tells him to take all the animals out of the house. Finally, the poor man and his family are able to sleep peacefully. They tell the rabbi their house is so roomy and a pleasure.

When read to children, they laugh and giggle each time another animal is brought into the house. Some of them know from the beginning what the "game" is. The laughter aside, there are some serious questions to discuss. Nothing has really changed for the poor man and his family. Just like Lemuel, they end up the same as they were. The only thing that has changed is how the poor man and his family now view their situation. Is perception that malleable? Is perception that powerful? What if the situation were worse? What if the children were hungry? Not starving, just hungry all the time from not having enough food. Would it make things better to take away what little food the children had so that afterwards they would perceive the situation differently? Even if they perceive the situation differently, their health would nonetheless be jeopardized.

The man in *It Could Always Be Worse* is a poor man. Is the rabbi really suggesting to him that he should accept his poverty? Alternatively, given that the economic situation is not likely to change, should the poor man and his family just be angry and disgruntled all the time because their house is so crowded? Once children get beyond the laughter, there are serious questions to explore.

TRICKSTER STORIES

The cover of *The Clever Little Tailor* first attracted six-year-old Max's interest. The cover illustration shows a man hiding behind a tree, holding a knife, waiting to attack the unsuspecting driver of a horse-drawn wagon. Max wonders, "Who is he? What is he going to do? Is he going to kill the driver?" *The Clever Little Tailor* by Solomon Simon, translated by David Forman with illustrations by Yehuda Blum, is a bilingual English–Yiddish collection of stories about Shnayderl, which in Yiddish means little tailor. Max knew a bit about Yiddish—his grandfather spoke Yiddish. Max knew that, like Hebrew, Yiddish books opened right to left (just the opposite of English books); but all he wanted to know was what happened. He wanted the story read to him.

In the first story, titled "The Robber Hargim," a rich merchant is unable to ship his merchandise to market. Each time he sends a wagon of merchandise through the woods to market, the robber Hargim stops the wagon, steals the merchandise, and kills the wagon driver. The rich merchant is in despair, and everyone but Shnayderl is afraid to drive the wagon. Shnayderl says he has nothing to lose. He is already poor, and if he doesn't find work, he will die of hunger anyway. So, he is willing to take the risk. However, he wants the wagon loaded so full that the horses would not be able to run. Shnayderl wants the merchandise tied down with wire and not string.

Max could not guess why Shnayderl wanted the wagon loaded and tied that way. But he laughed and whooped when Shnayderl tricked the robber and was able to deliver the merchandise to market. Two more times Shnayderl drove the wagon for the rich merchant, each time tricking the robber Hargim in a different way. Max was astonished each time by Shnayderl's trick. Max was so engrossed in the story and in each trick that he could not wait for the second story, titled "Shnayderl Fools a Band of Robbers." So, he read it himself and then had to tell everybody about how Shnayderl tricked the whole band of robbers.

Max was so caught up in Shnayderl's trickery that he had forgotten until he was asked about it the desperation that had motivated Shnayderl to take the risk in the first place. Was it right that a rich person, the merchant, should have poor people risk their lives so that he could stay rich or become even richer? Yes, Shnayderl did get paid well for driving the wagon and tricking the robber Hargim, but even so, was it fair for Schnayderl to have to risk his life? Max began to brainstorm other ways that the wagon could have been driven without Shnayderl or others needing to risk their lives. The brainstorming Max did was a clear indication that he believed that the situation wasn't fair.

In many children's stories, the woods are often a dangerous place. For Max, and for many children, the woods represent all those hidden fears they have of unnamed and vague powerful, dangerous forces that lie just outside the boundaries of their known family, school, and community world. Shnayderl's successful trickery is also their victory over those unnamed dangerous places.

In the story "Gold in a Hole," Shnayderl was traveling home from another adventure when he came to the estate of a rich person who had built a high wall all around it. Next to the wall was a stranger crying. The stranger had lost his money. The stranger had been traveling to the big city to purchase merchandise and other goods that shop owners and others in his town needed. They had all given the stranger money to purchase those items. The night before, the stranger had decided that going to an inn with so much money was dangerous. Someone at the inn was sure to notice that he had a lot of money and would either rob him or kill him to get the money. So, the stranger had decided to hide the money.

When the stranger came to the wall around the estate, he decided that next to the wall would be a good place to hide the money. He looked around to ensure that no one was looking and then dug a hole and placed two thousand ducats (units of money) in the hole. He went to the inn, had a good night's sleep, but when he returned in the morning, the money was gone.

Shnayderl listened to the stranger's story, saw a very small crack in the wall, and speculated that the rich person who owned the estate had seen the stranger bury the money and had taken it. Shnayderl made a plan. He told the stranger to go to the house of the rich estate owner and ask him for advice about where to hide an additional five thousand ducats. The stranger needed to tell the rich man that he had not gone back to the hole to see if the two thousand ducats were still there. Shnayderl told the stranger to ask for advice from the rich man about whether it would be a good idea to hide the additional five thousand ducats in the same place as he had hidden the original two thousand ducats.

The stranger did exactly what Schnayderl advised. The rich man advised the stranger to place the new five thousand ducats in the same hole as the original two thousand ducats.

The rich man schemed. He would put the original two thousand ducats back in the hole so that when the stranger came to bury the new five thousand ducats, the stranger would believe the hole to be a safe place. The rich man predicted that the stranger would put the new five thousand ducats in the hole. Then the rich man planned to later come and take it all.

So, the rich man put the two thousand ducats he had stolen back in the hole and waited for the stranger to come back to the hole. Soon enough, the stranger came back to the hole, but instead of leaving five thousand ducats—which, of course, he did not have—he took the original two thousand ducats that the rich man had put back hoping to further trick the stranger. Shnayderl's plan had tricked the rich man, and the stranger had gotten back his stolen two thousand ducats.

Max had to think carefully about the trick that Shnayderl and the stranger had played on the rich man. Shnayderl used the rich man's greed against himself. But was the rich man a thief? True, he did not threaten people with a knife the way the robber Hargim did, but the rich man did know that the money belonged to the stranger, not to himself. If he is a thief, shouldn't he be arrested? Is it enough that the stranger got his two thousand ducats back? Why is the robber Hargim arrested and brought to trial, whereas the rich man with the estate is no worse off than he was before? And why is this rich man so greedy? The rich man is already very wealthy; is it sinful for him to want even more, especially when getting more would create misery for others? If getting more when you are already rich is sinful, does it matter whether you get more legally or illegally?

Should Shnayderl's cleverness be considered wisdom? Shnayderl was not a learned person the way a rabbi or a professor is; nonetheless, was he wise? Clearly, wisdom is unrelated to power or wealth. Yes, Shnayderl did get paid for helping others solve their problems, but he did not become wealthy or powerful. Should wisdom lead to wealth and power? Rich and powerful people hired Shnayderl to use his wisdom to solve their problems. Does this mean that wisdom can be bought? What do we make of the fact that throughout the stories of the clever little tailor, all Shnayderl wants for himself is to go back to his family and not be hungry? Is this wisdom?

At the end of the collection of stories, Shnayderl asks the prince for whom he had solved a problem for permission to go back to his wife and children. The prince agrees and offers to send soldiers with Shnayderl to honor him. Shnayderl declines the soldiers and the pomp and circumstance. If he travels with soldiers, people will believe that he has gold, and a gang of robbers will attack them. If he goes alone, no one will attack him because he is only a poor tailor. Is that wisdom? Maybe, but maybe someone or some group might just attack because he is a poor tailor. In such a world, what is wisdom?

Hershel of Ostropol is the hero of many trickster stories. But he doesn't look much like a hero. He's poor; wears old, disheveled clothes; and travels from one place to another and doesn't seem to ever settle down (although in some stories he has a wife). He is what is called a *luftmench*, an airhead—but he really isn't as empty-headed as he might first appear. And that, of course, is the point.

In one of the stories about Hershel, he has been on a long journey and is returning home on foot to Ostropol, as told is in the *Adventures of Hershel of Ostropol* by Eric Kimmel and illustrated by Trina Schart Hyman. Hershel has had nothing to eat, and he has no money. He stops at an inn and asks for something to eat. The innkeeper and his wife tell Hershel that they have nothing to give him; they are all out of food.

It is a lie. They just do not want to give Hershel food for free. He is welcome to sleep in the barn, but they will give him no food. Hershel responds to them. He tells them that if he is not fed, then he will do what his father had done. Although Hershel does not tell them what his father did (at least not until the end of the story), the innkeeper and his wife worry that Hershel might do something to harm them. So, they give Hershel plenty of food, and Hershel eats until he can eat no more. Hershel finishes eating and is well satisfied. What did Hershel's father do? He did nothing; Hershel's father just went hungry.

We could say that Hershel tricked the innkeeper and his wife into giving him free food. Such a trick suggests that Hershel is not a luftmench but a clever person. The story could be left at this simple level and thoroughly enjoyed. After all, how many times have each of us been in a situation in which someone with resources or power could be helpful but refuses to do so, refuses to be generous and charitable? Maybe it is not an innkeeper; perhaps it is a wealthy person, the government, a big corporation, an administrator, an insurance company, or other. If only we could be as clever as Hershel. But this story is not simply about cleverness and overcoming obstacles.

How should we view Hershel's cleverness? Although he never said he would harm the innkeeper and his wife, Herschel was perceived to be threatening them. Is it a lie even if the words themselves are not untrue? Was Hershel lying? What constitutes the truth—what is said, or how what we say is perceived by others? Is it moral to deliberately deceive people (even if our words are not explicitly untrue) when our circumstances are such that basic needs are not being met through no fault of our own and in the face of great inequity? Are morality and ethics situational and dependent on context, or do situation and context not matter to what is moral and ethical? When children read or listen to such a story, we can ask them, "Do you think that it was OK for Hershel to mislead the innkeeper and his wife?" Regardless of how they answer, we need to help them understand the complications of any answer to such an enduring question.

Beyond the question of whether Hershel's deception was ethical, this story evokes another enduring question: How is it that some people have no food and have to beg for a meal whereas others, such as the innkeeper, have plenty of food but refuse to share? Many teachers keep food in their classroom cupboards because they know that some of their students' families struggle to put food on the table. We wonder how we can live in a society that is so wealthy but debates whether to fund healthy breakfast programs for young children. This is one of the enduring questions to raise with students; not just, "Why are there so many hungry people?" but as important, "How can we address such widespread hunger?" Are the solutions to such a problem just cleverness, or something more systematic? Is there an answer to such questions, or do we just try to do the best we can, knowing that it will never be enough? These are, of course, very difficult questions for young children to consider; yet, they can begin to struggle with them, especially when guided in such discussions by a caring teacher.

For Jews, caring for others, whether family or strangers, is not a discretionary act, something you do if you feel like it. Feeding others who are hungry—whether it is hunger for food, for love, for shelter, for safety, for freedom, for family—is an obligation, a mitzvah that Jews are required to perform. Of course, not just Jewish people have such an obligation, but people from a broad range of communities.

To understand Jewish children's literature, including Hershel of Ostropol stories, it helps to recognize that such obligations are ever-present. At the same time, it is important to recognize that such obligations are complex. A person could give away his every penny and still not make much of a dent in the number of hungry children and families. Should one give money to individuals who are hungry, or work for broader solutions? If so, what? In some classrooms, teachers actively engage their students in food drives and contributing to food banks. Is this enough? None of these questions is truly answerable; and yet, in pursuing such questions children can begin to navigate how they might act ethically and morally, how they might engage in what Jews call *tikkun olam*, healing the world.

The book *Hershel and the Hanukkah Goblins* by Eric Kimmel is a trickster story that can be used at Hanukkah time. On the surface, the book is about Hershel of Ostropol, who comes across a town that has not lit even one Hanukkah candle. The town is dark. Hershel learns that goblins have entered the town and are making it impossible for the town to celebrate Hanukkah. If they light a candle, a goblin blows it out. If they cook a *latke* (a potato pancake), a goblin throws it on the floor.

Hershel decides to help the town and outwit the goblins. He enters the old synagogue and lights a candle. A goblin confronts him and threatens to blow out the candle. Hershel tells him that if he interferes, Hershel will crush him like a stone. Hershel then takes a soft-boiled egg, which the goblin thinks is a stone, and squeezes it until the yolk squirts out and the rest crumbles. The goblin becomes so scared of Hershel's strength that the goblin flees. Each night another goblin comes, and Hershel outwits it. Finally, on the last night of Hanukkah, the king of the goblins comes. Hershel outwits him by telling him that he needs light to see how big and scary the goblin is. Thus, Hershel lights each candle of the menorah and tricks the king of the goblins into allowing the whole menorah to be lit. Defeated, all of the goblins leave the town, and the people there get to light their menorahs and celebrate Hanukkah.

This story is about more than just clever trickery. Was it a miracle that Hershel just happened to come upon this town when the goblins were causing trouble? Were the people in the town afraid of the goblins? Was Hershel?

Why or why not? What does it mean to be afraid? Each goblin seemed to have a bad trait or flaw such as greed, gluttony, vanity, and love of power. How was Hershel able to defeat the goblins? What do we learn from Hershel?

Bone Button Borscht (by Aubrey Davis and illustrated by Dušan Petričić) is a version of the story that many people know as *Stone Soup* (see *Stone Soup* by Marcia Brown). Many cultures have a version of this story. It can be an insightful lesson to have children read various versions of the story and ask questions about the differences.

In *Bone Button Borscht*, a beggar was walking during a cold winter day and arrives at a village. He goes from house to house seeking shelter and food, but he is turned away from every house. The people themselves are poor and barely able to feed themselves, never mind sharing with a poor stranger. The beggar finally comes to the synagogue where he finds shelter but no food. He pulls five buttons off his coat and tells the *shamas* (the caretaker of the synagogue) that if he had one more button, he could make a soup for the whole town, a nice borscht soup. The shamas goes to the town tailor to get a button. He tells the tailor and others that the beggar will make soup out of the buttons—a miracle. As he is making the soup, the beggar tells the townspeople

HERSHEL AND THE HANUKKAH GOBLINS AND THE CHANUKKAH GUEST

[In *Hershel and the Hanukkah Goblins*, Hershel approaches a village on the first night of Hanukkah, but not a single candle is lit. There are goblins. In *The Chanukkah Guest*, Bubba Brayna, who is almost blind and deaf, makes the best latkes. On Hanukkah, she cooks latkes for the rabbi. When she hears a pounding at the door, she lets in her guest. It is a bear that she confuses for the rabbi.]

I read two stories to my preschoolers, who knew little of Jewish culture. First, I read *The Chanukkah Guest*. I invited children to share what they knew about Hanukkah. One child stated, "Hanukkah is lighting candles on a menorah" followed by a child asking, "What's a menorah?" The discussion prepared the children for the vocabulary in the book. The children asked questions including, "Why is she calling the bear a rabbi?" and "What is a rabbi?" When the bear eats the latkes, the children wanted to make their own latkes. The following day, we made latkes. The children enjoyed the humor in the story and making latkes.

Then, I read *Hershel and the Hanukkah Goblins*. At first, the children were intimidated by the cover photo of the goblins. The children enjoyed Hershel's trickery to make the goblins leave the town. The children made connections between the pictures, the story, and *The Chanukkah Guest*. For example, one child stated, "He's lighting a bit by bit that the soup could use some pickle juice, some garlic, some carrots, onions, beans, and so forth. So, bit by bit the soup gets made, and everyone in town finally has a good meal.

As the beggar leaves, he gathers his buttons. The townspeople are alarmed. They tell him that they will starve without the buttons; the beggar tells them that he will freeze if he cannot button his coat. So, the townspeople make a trade. They give the beggar fancy brass buttons for the ordinary bone buttons the beggar had used to make soup. They never see the beggar again.

menorah!" We then created our own goblins. We placed a diagram on chart paper of different parts of a goblin (eyes, nose, horns, etc.) and aligned them to match a number on a six-sided die. Each child rolled a large die and then came to the easel and added to the group goblin. Then, they made their own goblins.

Lily Blackburn, preschool teacher, public school, Ohio

The townspeople seem foolish. They do not realize that the soup is not really made from buttons. It is through their collective efforts and their cooperation with each other that they are all able to be fed. Although they do work together, it is not clear that they understand that their survival depends on working together. The beggar tricked them. He got them to give him food even though they would not do so at first, even though they thought they did not have any food to share.

An enduring question to ask, then, is did the townspeople change? Did they learn anything about the importance of working together, or did they simply get one nice meal and go back to their isolated ways of living? Did the beggar have an obligation to point out to the townspeople that, indeed, the buttons had not really made the soup? Did he have an obligation to point out that no miracle happened? What does it take for people to realize that sometimes—maybe even a lot of times—problems only are solved if people work together?

The beggar leaves having traded ordinary buttons for fancy brass buttons, tricking the people again. Was that honest? Did they deserve to be tricked? After all, they would not give the beggar shelter in their homes or provide him a meal (the beggar could only find shelter in the synagogue). A Jewish legend is about Elijah the prophet, who shows up often as a beggar (or an outcast of some type) to see how people treat those most in need. In stories about Elijah, often some miracle or magic occurs as Elijah both teaches and promotes justice. Was the beggar in *Bone Button Borscht* Elijah? Even if he wasn't Elijah, should they have treated the beggar as if he was or could have been Elijah? In our own lives, homes, and communities, what might it mean to treat a beggar as if the beggar was Elijah?

Chapter 5

WISDOM AS CARING

After the very first page of *The Yiddish Fish* (written and illustrated by Santiago Cohen), five-year-old Sam finds a talking fish that speaks Yiddish. Sam had come across talking animals before but not one that spoke Yiddish (all of the Yiddish in the book is accompanied by English translation). The fish was about to be chopped up by Rob Costello, the fishmonger, when the fish spoke aloud in Yiddish. Although Rob did not understand Yiddish, he could not kill a talking fish. Rob told his boss about the talking fish. His boss spoke Yiddish. The boss thought the fish sounded like his Aunt Louise.

They could not kill a Yiddish-speaking fish, but the fish did not know that. So, scared of what the men might do, the fish jumped back into the barrel of fish from which it came. Neither Rob nor his boss knew which fish in the barrel was the talking fish, so they decided to throw all the fish back into the lake from which they came. After they did so, they thought they heard the fish laughing and then singing. Rob and his boss went home and wondered whether the fish had talked, or whether they had just imagined it.

When Sam was asked whether the men had imagined it, or whether the fish talked, Sam began to argue with himself. First, he said, no. It was a talking fish. Then, he said, they might have imagined the fish talked. Then, he said that maybe the fish talked, and maybe they imagined the fish were laughing and singing. Clearly, he was having fun wondering whether the fish talked, or whether they just imagined it. In a hushed, serious tone, in the manner of an actor telling the audience an aside, Sam confides, "Fish don't actually talk; this is just in the book."

Sam is asking questions about perception and knowing. Did Rob and his boss really hear the fish talk? Was it really the boss's Aunt Louise? Did the fish really laugh and sing? Or was it all imagined? How might we know? What difference does it make if it was really so or just imagined? Are there things in our lives that we presume to be real but that might, instead, just be imagined? Beyond the surface of the story lie questions about the relationship of the imagined and the actual. Rob and his boss acted in a caring and ethical manner to what might just be something they imagined. Their caring and ethical actions were not imagined, even if the talking fish was. And what about the story itself? As Sam noted, "fish don't actually talk; this is just in the book"—it is just imagined. But what was just imagined prompted Sam to struggle with the relationship between the imagined story world and the actual world.

Another question prompted by struggling with the relationship of the story world and the actual world in *The Yiddish Fish* is "What should be the relationship between people and animals?" Many children's stories raise this enduring question. In *The Carp in the Bathtub* (by Barbara Cohen, illustrated by Joan Halpern)—discussed in the introduction—the children try to save a fish by hiding it. However, their parents insist—and the children come to understand—that the family does not have the money to let the carp go. They would go hungry. So, the carp is killed and turned into gefilte fish.

Should the fishmonger have done the same with the talking fish? Or maybe the carp should have been let free, and the family should have gone hungry? Or maybe both stories are ethically correct? Even if one decides that it is ethical to eat fish and other animals—as most people in the United States do—the question still is about how people should treat animals, part of the rationale for kosher laws. Although not all Jews keep kosher—follow all of the Jewish laws about meals and eating—many do. One set of kosher laws requires that animals be slaughtered in ways that are not painful. Another set of laws requires that dairy products not be mixed with meat products. Underlying this kosher law is the idea that it is cruel to cook a lamb, for example, in its mother's milk. Of course, neither the lamb nor its mother is able to appreciate the symbolism of separating meat and dairy, so such kosher laws can be understood as being more about people and how people should relate to animals.

In *A Sack Full of Feathers*, retold by Debby Waldman and illustrated by Cindy Revell, a young boy, Yankel, loved to tell stories about other people. Mostly his stories were gossip and half-truths. Yankel told a story about the baker who mistook salt for sugar and ruined all his sweet bakery goods. Some who heard Yankel's story decided not to go to the bakery. Unfortunately, Yankel only heard part of the story before he started spreading the gossip. The baker caught the error, corrected the mistake, and made delicious baked goods for everyone to enjoy.

Then, there is the story Yankel told about two women in the store who fought over a piece of cloth they both wanted. Unfortunately, Yankel only saw part of what happened and, therefore, his story was only half true. The two women apologized to each other and decided to share the cloth. Nonetheless, Yankel's gossip had already caused damage to their reputations.

Yankel saw two people kissing. He believed that one of them was already engaged to another person, so Yankel started spreading gossip about them. Of course, Yankel had only part of the story. In fact, the person who was engaged was no longer engaged, and the two people Yankel saw were in love with each other and planned to marry.

The rabbi saw Yankel running around spreading gossip and decided to give him a job. He gave Yankel a bag of feathers and told him to place one feather on each doorstep in the village. Although he did not understand why, Yankel did the job. When he was done, he returned to the rabbi, who gave Yankel another task. He was to retrieve the feathers he had left on the doorsteps and put them back in the bag. Yankel tried to retrieve the feathers, but by the time he got to each doorstep, the feathers were gone. He tried all day to retrieve the feathers but was unable to retrieve even one of them. The rabbi told Yankel that stories are just like the feathers: once told, you cannot get them back, and you cannot control where they go. You also need to make sure that the stories you tell are your own stories.

At a simple level, *A Sack Full of Feathers* is a didactic story of why gossiping is wrong. But so much more is going on, so many enduring questions to ask. Why did the rabbi just not punish Yankel for gossiping? What has Yankel learned? Is there a difference between adhering to a rule—such as do not gossip—and the wisdom to not gossip? Is there a connection between wisdom and caring? Is there a connection between storytelling and caring? The rabbi tells Yankel to tell his own stories. Yankel seems to have learned this lesson because he will tell the story of a boy with a sackful of feathers. But, what does it mean to tell your own story? Are some stories yours and also belong to others? Being a good storyteller is one thing, but being a wise storyteller might be something different. What is that difference? What does it mean to be a wise storyteller?

The Generous Fish by Jacqueline Jules, illustrated by Frances Tyrrell, is based on two Jewish tales, a folktale called "Cast Your Bread Upon the Waters" (see Ellen Frankel's *The Classic Tales*) and I. L. Peretz's story "The Revelation." In this story, a young boy named Reuven, standing on the shore, sees a golden fish. Remembering his father's words, Reuven shares some of his bread with the fish. The fish asks Reuven to play with him in the water. They have great fun.

One day Reuven hugs the fish too hard and a golden scale comes off. The fish is not upset because his scales will grow back. Reuven takes the scale, which is made of gold, to town, and everybody is excited and wants scales for themselves. The fish is generous, gives away too many of his golden scales, and becomes tired and weak. Reuven becomes worried about the fish. When the townspeople come down to the shore, Reuven believes that they have come to take the last scale from the fish; instead, they have come to help the fish by bringing honey and soup. Over time, the fish's scales grew back, and the fish is again able to play in the waves. Reuven hugs the fish but gently, so that no scales will fall off.

One could say, all's well that ends well. The fish is healthy, Reuven is happy, and the townspeople get some gold, even if not all the gold they wanted. Yet, the story begs to have disturbing and enduring questions asked: Did Reuven and the townspeople misuse and even abuse the fish? Is it acceptable just to take from the fish or from any other animal? Even if a fish or a person offers generously, is it always moral to take from them? How can a person (or a town) balance its needs with a concern for animals and the environment? When the townspeople came to help the fish become healthy, were they motivated by greed and the desire for more gold scales, or did they have more noble goals? Does it matter whether they had noble goals and a desire to protect fish, other animals, and the environment, or is the fact that they came and helped nurse the fish back to health enough, regardless of their motivation? What relationship do we have as human beings to the other creatures in the world?

THE ARROGANCE OF WISDOM IS NO WISDOM

The Wooden Sword by Ann Redisch Stampler and illustrated by Carol Liddiment retells the story of an Afghani shah who sneaks out of his palace in disguise to find out more about the ordinary people in his country. He meets a poor Jewish shoemaker who seems too happy. The shoemaker believes that things will work out for him and his family. One way or another he will always find a way to feed, house, and clothe his family. The shah decides to test the shoemaker's optimism and his faith that everything will turn out as it should.

The shah outlaws shoemaking, so the poor Jewish shoemaker will have no livelihood. So, the shoemaker becomes a water carrier and sells water throughout the city and makes enough money to buy food for his family. The shah then outlaws water carrying. The shoemaker becomes a woodcutter and thereby provides for his family. Frustrated by the resilience of the poor Jewish shoemaker, the shah then orders all woodcutters to become soldiers in his Royal Guard.

The poor Jewish shoemaker becomes a member of the Royal Guard and after a day of service asks the leader of the Royal Guard for his pay. The leader of the Royal Guard tells him that they only get paid at the end of the month. The poor Jewish shoemaker will have no money to buy food for his family for a month, and they will starve. So, the poor Jewish shoemaker decides to sell the shiny silver sword he received as a member of the Royal Guard for enough money to feed his family for the month. He makes a wooden sword to replace the silver one that he sold, hoping that no one will notice the difference.

All is well until the shah—still in disguise—hears what the shoemaker has done. He orders the leader of the Royal Guard to have the shoemaker cut off the head of a thief. The poor Jewish shoemaker does not want to cut off anyone's head, including that of a thief. On the other hand, if he refuses to obey orders, he might be punished. The Jewish shoemaker prays aloud so that everyone can hear. He prays to God that if the thief's life should be spared, his sword should be turned into wood. He pulls out his sword, which everyone can see is made of wood. The thief's life is spared. The shah removes his disguise and appoints the Jewish shoemaker one of his advisers.

We can cheer at the outcome of the story. The poor Jewish shoemaker has survived the shah's tests and is better off than he was. But as we stand back from the story, many enduring questions can be asked and explored with children. The poor Jewish shoemaker attributes his continued ability to provide for his family to his faith, but each time he is tested, his own perseverance, cleverness, and willingness to do whatever is necessary make it possible for him to provide for his family. How might we understand his continued ability to provide for his family? And what about those people—other shoemakers, water carriers, woodcutters, and soldiers—who are not as clever or as lucky as the Jewish shoemaker? Do they deserve to starve? And what about the shah? It seems cruel to put a poor Jewish shoemaker through so many tests. Even one test would seem cruel. Is the shah cruel? Does his rewarding the poor Jewish shoemaker at the end make up for the pain that his tests caused?

How should we understand the poor Jewish shoemaker's pulling out his wooden sword? Everyone except for the shoemaker and the shah believes that a miracle happened. Does the shoemaker have an obligation to tell them the truth, or should he let them believe in miracles? And what about the order to cut off the head of the thief? Maybe the thief needed to feed his family and had no other choice; if so, should people not have *rakhmones* (compassion for others) for the thief? The shah has so much money and so much power; is it fair that he has so much when people struggle just to feed their families?

"The Loaves in the Ark" is a story from Jane Yolen and Heidi Stemple's *Jewish Fairy Tale Feast: A Literary Cookbook*, illustrated by Sima Elizabeth Shefrin. It includes recipes for *latkes* (potato pancakes), honey cake, chicken soup, and *challah* (a special Jewish bread), among many more traditional Jewish foods. The recipes are fun to make with children, although probably too much for doing with a classroom of hungry children.

The story that accompanies the challah recipe tells about a Marrano husband and wife who traveled from Portugal to the city of Safed in what was then Ottoman Palestine. Marranos were Jews of Hispanic heritage who had been forced to adopt Christianity under threat of death but who practiced Judaism in secret. They are also called *conversos*, and they traveled to many parts of the world including Mexico and Latin America, where they also practiced Judaism in secret. In Safed, Marranos could live openly as Jews but—as was true of many Marranos—their knowledge of Jewish customs, traditions, and laws was not as thorough as they wanted it to be. One day the couple heard about a special bread—shewbread—that Jews used to leave in the Temple as an offering to God. It is not clear exactly what kind of bread shewbread was except that it was a special bread with fine flour and made with great care—perhaps it was like challah. The Marrano couple decided that they would bake shewbread and leave it at the Holy Ark in the synagogue in Safed as an offering to God. They carefully baked the shewbread and left it at the base of the Holy Ark. They felt a great deal of joy in making the bread and offering it.

The caretaker of the synagogue was a poor man with a family. He found the shewbread at the base of the Holy Ark and believed that God had provided it for his family. He believed it was a miracle. The Marrano couple came back to the Holy Ark, saw that the shewbread was gone, and believed that God had received their shewbread. It was a miracle. Week after week for months, the Marrano couple left the bread, and the caretaker found it and enjoyed it with his family. Then, one day, just before Shabbat evening, the rabbi of the Safed synagogue caught the Marrano couple leaving the bread. The rabbi castigated them; did they believe that God had a mouth like people have? He told the Marrano couple that they were shaming the Torah and God. At that very moment the caretaker arrived, and the rabbi castigated him as well. The rabbi told him he was a sinner.

At that same moment, a messenger arrived with a letter from a more senior and esteemed rabbi. The message said that the rabbi who castigated the Marrano couple and the caretaker would die the next day. When the rabbi inquired as to why, he was told that he had deprived God of a great pleasure of the offering of shewbread as well as depriving God of the pleasure that the bread had gone to a family that had so little; moreover, he had humiliated the Marrano couple and the caretaker.

The story of the Marrano couple and the shewbread is similar to *Bagels from Benny* (see chapter 3) and "The Disappearing Challah" (a story in Valerie Estelle Frankel's story collection, *Chelm for the Holidays*), although this story has a much harsher and somewhat shocking ending. Does the rabbi really deserve to die because he spoke so arrogantly to the Marrano couple and the caretaker? Beyond that question is what is wisdom, and who is wise? The rabbi has a lot of knowledge, is well educated, and viewed by ordinary people in the community as wise—wise enough that he is often asked to solve their problems. But does he exhibit wisdom in how he responds to the Marrano couple and the caretaker? What would be wisdom in that situation? And what would be wisdom in response to the rabbi's castigation of the Marrano couple and the caretaker? The Marrano couple baked the shewbread and left it at the base of the Holy Ark. They thought that God ate the bread—a miracle. They had no idea that the caretaker was taking the bread home to his family. The caretaker thought it was a miracle that God was providing the bread. Are they fools? Or, is there at least some degree of wisdom in what they have done?

WISDOM, FOOLISHNESS, AND HUMOR

Here is a shortened version of an old, well-known Jewish joke. A Jewish beggar knocks on the door of the house of Rothschild, the well-known wealthy Jewish family. The beggar is let into the house and approaches Lord Rothschild. The beggar asks Rothschild for a thousand dollars. Stunned, Rothschild tells the beggar "that is not the way to beg." To which the beggar responds, "With all due respect, I don't tell you how to manage a financial empire; you don't tell me how to beg." We laugh at this joke because it violates all of the assumed, unspoken norms of the relationship of rich and poor. Yes, rich people do give to charity, but they do not give a beggar a thousand dollars. Beggars need to ask for reasonable sums or, better yet, not ask at all and gratefully receive whatever is given. Beggars need to stay in their place. In the joke, the beggar makes his position the equivalent of Rothschild, raising all sorts of questions about the assumptions we hold about the place of wealthy people such as the Rothschilds, poor people such as beggars, and their hierarchical relationship to each other.

When we laugh at this joke—as when we laugh while reading *The Rooster Prince of Breslov*, the stories of the people of Chelm, and so many other humorous Jewish stories—we are really laughing at ourselves, at the unspoken assumptions we hold. If we are lucky enough to be able to talk about the story after reading it, the laughter will lead to wisdom: the wisdom of questioning assumptions and hierarchies.

The people of Chelm believe themselves to be wise. We laugh at their foolishness and how they mistake it for wisdom. In *The Clever Little Tailor*, rich and powerful people lack the wisdom to solve their own problems. They rely on Shnayderl, a poor tailor whose ambition is simply to live with his family and not suffer from hunger. Wisdom lies close to caring; as we see in *The Generous Fish*, wisdom is as likely found in a child as in an adult. Although certainly study and learning are important and to be valued, they should not be confused with wisdom. The Marrano couple in "The Disappearing Challah" sought knowledge of Jewish learning and Jewish traditions, whereas the rabbi who had such knowledge lacked the wisdom to understand *rakhmones* (compassion for others) and the miracles of ordinary, everyday life and its happenstances. About miracles, Nobel Peace Prize winner Elie Wiesel (112) writes,

> As a Jew, I believed in miracles. Our survival is just that. But according to the Talmud, miracles ceased with the destruction of the Temple. Since then, miracles of another sort, daily and ordinary, occur before our eyes. I speak to someone who understands what I say—isn't that a miracle? I love someone who loves me—isn't that a miracle? Any encounter involves the miraculous. We find it also in the connection between the event and the story of that event. And in the hidden meaning of that story. (145)

Wisdom and humor are these kinds of miracles.

WORKS CITED

Children's Literature

Abas, Shlomo. *The Sages of Chelm and the Moon.* Illustrated by Omer Hoffman. Translated by Gilah Kahn-Hoffman. Yorkshire, England: Green Bean Books, 2019.

Brown, Marcia. *Stone Soup.* New York: Charles Scribner's Sons, 1947.

Cohen, Barbara. *The Carp in the Bathtub.* Illustrated by Joan Halpern. New York: Lothrop Lee & Shepard, 1972.

Cohen, Santiago. *The Yiddish Fish.* New York: Sky Pony Press, 2014.

Davis, Aubrey. *Bone Button Borscht.* Illustrated by Dušan Petričić. Toronto: Kids Can Press. 1996.

Frankel, Valerie Estelle. *Chelm for the Holidays.* Illustrated by Sonja Wimmer. Minneapolis: Kar-Ben, 2019.

Geras, Adèle. *My Grandmother's Stories: A Collection of Jewish Folk Tales.* Illustrated by Anita Lobel. New York: Knopf Books for Young Readers, 2003.

Jules, Jacqueline. *The Generous Fish.* Illustrated by Frances Tyrrell. Bloomington, IN: Wisdom Tales, 2020.

Kimmel, Eric A. *Adventures of Hershel of Ostropol.* Illustrated by Trina Schart Hyman. New York: Holiday House, 1998.

———. *Hershel and the Hanukkah Goblins.* Illustrated by Trina Schart Hyman. New York: Holiday House, 1989.

———. *Right Side Up: Adventures in Chelm.* Illustrated by Steve Brown. Millburn, NJ: Apples & Honey Press, 2019.

Nadler, Jill Ross. *Such a Library!* Illustrated by Esther van den Berg. Seattle: Intergalactic Afikoman, 2020.

Peretz, I. L. "Revelation or, The Story of the Billy Goat." In R. Wisse, ed., *The I. L. Peretz Reader*, 212–17. New Haven, CT: Yale University Press, 2013.

Simon, Solomon. *The Clever Little Tailor.* Illustrated by Yehuda Blum. Translated by David Forman. New York: Kinder-Loshn Publications, 2021.

Stampler, Ann Redisch. *The Rooster Prince of Breslov.* Illustrated by Eugene Yelchin. Boston: Clarion, 2010.

———. *The Wooden Sword.* Illustrated by Carol Liddiment. Park Ridge, IL: Albert Whitman, 2012.

Taback, Simms. *Kibitzers and Fools: Tales My Zayda Told Me.* New York: Viking, 2005.

Uhlberg, Myron. *Lemuel the Fool.* Illustrated by Sonja Lamut. Atlanta: Peachtree, 2001.

Ungar, Richard. *Rachel Captures the Moon.* Toronto: Tundra, 2001.

Waldman, Debby. *A Sack Full of Feathers.* Illustrated by Cindy Revell. Victoria, BC, Canada: Orca, 2006.

Yolen, Jane, and Heidi E. Y. Stemple. "The Loaves in the Ark." *Jewish Fairy Tale Feasts: A Literary Cookbook.* Illustrated by Sima Elizabeth Shefrin. Northampton, MA: Crocodile, 2013.

Zemach, Margot. *It Could Always Be Worse.* New York: Farrar, Straus & Giroux, 1976.

References

Frankel, E. *The Classic Tales: 4,000 Years of Jewish Lore.* Northvale, NJ: Jason Aronson, 1989.

Wiesel, E. *The Forgotten.* New York: Schocken Books, 1992.

Chapter 6

What Is Evil? How Might We Respond to Evil?

Jewish Children's Literature, Anti-Semitism, and the Holocaust

Eliana, a third-grade student, had been reading *Brundibar* by Tony Kushner, illustrated by Maurice Sendak. *Brundibar* is the story of two children whose mother is ill. The doctor tells the children they need to get milk for her if she is to get well. The children go to town, where they see many people with money buying all sorts of wonderful things. The children find the milkman and ask him for milk. But he will not give them milk unless they pay him. They have no money and do not know how to get any money. They see Brundibar, an oddly dressed man, in the market square playing a music box and singing a song (a song they view as awful). People give him money for his singing. They decide to do the same, but no one will give them money because Brundibar is singing louder. They try to scare Brundibar by acting like bears, but Brundibar is not fooled and states that children are worse than bears. He expels them from the market square.

They are sad about not being able to earn money to buy milk for their mother. Some talking animals advise them to get help from other children. They follow this advice, and three hundred children join them. They all go to the market square, sing a song, and all the people give them money for their singing. Brundibar is upset, tries to take their money, but all the children and adults chase him out of town. Everyone cheers, and the children now have money for milk. However, Brundibar leaves a note saying that he will be back.

The story of Brundibar is only given in part through the words. The pictures add depth and meaning not explicitly found in the words. In the illustrations, some Jews, such as the doctor, are wearing yellow stars (as the Nazis had required of Jews). Jewish stars are on some of the buildings, and background writing is associated with concentration and death camps. Other subtleties in the illustrations also reference the Holocaust. Readers who recognize the references interpret the story of Brundibar differently than those who do not. Eliana, eight-years-old, did not.

Being one of two Jewish children in her whole school, Eliana is already aware of anti-Semitism, having experienced it from other students, from adults, and unfortunately from some teachers and educational administrators. Although she knows about something called the Holocaust, she does not have much awareness of it, its horrors, or its nightmares. When asked about the story, Eliana talked about how mean and selfish Brundibar was and that if people are determined, a bully can be defeated.

When asked if it was a Jewish story, she said that she had noticed the Jewish stars on some of the buildings and the yellow Jewish stars on some of the people. She thought they were awards and medals that some of the Jewish people were wearing proudly (of course, they were not awards and medals). Eliana liked the story and thought that other children would like it, too. When Eliana was asked if Brundibar was evil, at first, she said, "No." She explained, "Well, I don't think he was evil. He wasn't nice, either. He was just very selfish, greedy, and selfish." When she was asked about the note Brundibar wrote at the end of the story that he would be back, Eliana said that the note means that "there's more to the story—keep you imagining."

As much as we would like to protect our children, part of growing up is recognizing the evil that exists in the world and that, as much as we would wish it otherwise, it's in our lives, too. Eliana is growing up, and her parents and teachers are carefully guiding her and, similarly, other children, to address that evil. As an eight-year-old, Eliana's response to *Brundibar* is just fine. She is using both her own experiences and her experiences as a reader to interpret the book. She enjoyed discussing the story and thinking about whether Brundibar was evil.

She may read *Brundibar* again when she is eleven or twelve, then maybe again in high school, perhaps even at the university. She'll understand more with each reading. If her parents and teachers guide her well, as she grows, she will recognize the references to the Holocaust, and it will make a difference in her interpretation of the story. Perhaps more important, as she reads and rereads stories such as *Brundibar*, she will continue to

BRUNDIBAR

[Two children with a sick mother rush to town for milk to make her better. Their attempt to earn money to purchase milk is thwarted by a bullying, hollering grinder, Brundibar, who tyrannizes the town square.]

I decided to read the book to my sixth graders during our social emotional learning (SEL) period. We've had some bullying issues in class, and I thought reading and discussing Brundibar would allow us time to review bullying behaviors, the role grapple with these questions: What is evil? How might we address it, especially, if like Brundibar, evil always comes back?

In this chapter, we discuss Jewish children's literature that engages children in asking, "What is evil? How might we respond to evil?" As parents, grandparents, teachers, and teacher educators, it hurts us to have to write this chapter. Like other parents and teachers, we want to protect our children—especially our young children—from evil. We are reluctant to tell them about the evil in the world. We want them to believe in a world that is inherently a good place. We are fearful that if we tell them about the evil in the world and the terror, pain, and death it causes, our children will have nightmares.

As much as we wish it were otherwise, few children make it through elementary school without confronting or having to address evil of some kind. It is better and healthier for children to be guided by thoughtful, caring teachers in discussing the questions of "What is evil?" and "How might we respond to evil?" than for children to have to explore such questions by themselves, especially if they have been victims of evil.

For Jews, good and evil have no governing dogma. Jewish philosophers, scholars, poets, writers, authors, and rabbis have debated questions about evil and how it should be addressed. For Jews, life

of bystanders, and the importance of standing up to bullies in groups, not alone. We discussed the following questions:

- Why might a person be friendly toward a bully or do things to please a bully?
- Do you think people who behave in these ways help a bully gain what he wants?
- Why don't people stand together and oppose a bully?
- If new bullies would replace Brundibar, what behaviors do people need to use more often to stop bullies?

I did not tell my students that the book was based on Hitler or Nazi Germany until we had discussed these questions. Once we discussed the origins of the book and opera, students were better able to understand the ideas and characters in the book.

The book approaches bullying differently from many other children's books on bullies and allowed for a much deeper discussion of behaviors, bystanders, and the fear that keeps people from standing up to bullies. The only difficult part of reading this book to an entire class is that the pictures and captions are pretty detailed, and I don't think kids get the full effect of the illustrations while I'm walking around reading and showing them the pictures briefly. It would be much more impactful if they each had a copy or the book projected onto a screen.

Tammy Dalling, sixth-grade teacher, public school, Montana

is viewed as inherently good; similarly, so is the world. If life, people, and the world are inherently good, how then can people understand evil and suffering, and what might we do to address it? Jewish children's literature provides one tool for discussing questions about evil and how it might be addressed.

This chapter is divided into two sections. The first section focuses on Jewish children's literature about anti-Semitism other than the Holocaust. The second section discusses Jewish children's literature about the Holocaust. Given the large number of children's literature books on the Holocaust—and the complexity of the issues involved in using such books in the elementary classroom—this second section is long. Even so, space did not allow including all of the books that teachers and students might find useful in exploring "What is evil?" and "How might we respond to evil?"

WHAT IS EVIL? CHILDREN'S LITERATURE AND ANTI-SEMITISM OTHER THAN THE HOLOCAUST

A Ceiling Made of Eggshells by Gail Carson Levine tells the story of Loma, a young Jewish girl, and her family in Spain in the late 1480s and early 1490s. She is seven years old at the beginning of the book, sixteen at the end. She and her family live in the Jewish ghetto. They suffer through the Black Death, and several members of her family die. They also suffer from vile lies and violence from the Christian community and from the Christian Church.

For some children and adults, it will be difficult to read about the evil that members of the Christian community and church committed against Jews: their endless efforts to convert Jews, and the threats made if Jews did not convert. Loma travels around Spain with her grandfather, a wise and wealthy man who uses his wisdom, experience, and money to save Jews and Jewish communities. Loma is kidnapped by Christians so that they can convert her to Christianity against her will. They are only stopped from doing so because Loma's grandfather pays to have her released.

Because her grandfather is well-known, the king and queen of Spain meet with him. He brings Loma with him. The grandfather gives the king and queen money for their wars and for their luxury. Their daughter, the princess, becomes fond of Loma but only because she wants Loma to convert to Christianity. Eventually, the king and queen expel from Spain all the Jews who refuse to convert. If they do not convert or leave, they will be executed.

A Ceiling Made of Eggshells shows the constant danger and violence that Jews in late-fifteenth-century Spain faced, even as they tried to live a normal life—making meals, praying, learning, playing games, children growing up, and adults trying to make a livelihood. The novel also shows what it was like to be a young woman in those times: arranged marriages, married and having children as early as age twelve, and being confined mostly to the home. Loma is an exception as she travels with her grandfather and attends events usually reserved for men.

A Ceiling Made of Eggshells is a long book—but from the very beginning it engrosses the reader. One is always asking, "How will Loma and her grandfather address the evil that faces them? How will they extricate themselves from the difficult and dangerous situations in which they find themselves?" The book could be used within a small reading group so that students could discuss each chapter as they read it; or it could be a recommended reading, especially for students who are avid readers. A helpful author's note is included at the end, along with a useful glossary. Students who are unfamiliar with Jewish kosher laws (dietary restrictions) may benefit from learning about kosher laws before reading.

Because the story is told from the perspective of Loma, a young girl trying to understand the evil that is being done to her, her family, and to other Jews, the reader is confronted again and again with the question, "Why are people doing so much evil?" The Christian people who are doing so much evil do not believe that they are doing evil; they believe that by forcing Jews to convert, they are "saving" them from hell. They believe they are doing good even as they torture, rob, and kill Jews. How can this be? How can it be confronted and stopped? In our own lives, could we be doing evil and think it good? How would we know?

The attacks on Jews, such as those described in *A Ceiling Made of Eggshells*, have led Jews to fantasize about a golem that might protect them. A golem is a person-like creature made from mud and then brought to life by a rabbi through mystical powers to defend the Jews from violent anti-Semitic attacks.

The story and illustrations in David Wisniewski's (author and illustrator) book *Golem* are riveting. The book, which has emotionally powerful and engaging illustrations, won a Caldecott Award. It is not just that children can spend many minutes searching in the cut-paper illustrations; it is also that the illustrations explode out at them, grabbing their minds, emotions, and their wonderment.

The story that Wisniewski tells is the traditional golem story. The enemies of the Jewish people create lies about them to incite violence and cruelty against them. Certainly, this is evil—to attack and murder a people based on lies, stereotypes, and scapegoating. But this is where the question of evil gets complex. Does the evil lie in the people who formed a mob and violently attacked Jews based on lies, or does it lie in those who told the lies and turned the Jews into scapegoats? Or perhaps the evil lies in the governments and rulers who forced the Jews to live in ghettos and segregated communities and made laws forbidding them to use weapons; and a legal system that provided Jews with no protection from such hatred?

Maybe all of them are engaged in evil—the rulers, the liars, and the people in the mobs? But does engaging in an evil act make a person evil? Or just ignorant? Shouldn't they know better? Is the person who deliberately tells a lie that they believe will result in violence against innocent people more evil than the person who, out of ignorance, believes the lie? Are there degrees of evil? After all, if based on a lie, a person commits an act of violence and harms or murders someone else, it matters little to the murdered person and his family whether it was done out of evil intent or ignorance. So, does that mean that ignorance is a form of evil?

To protect the Jews, the chief rabbi of Prague created a golem, a giant of living clay brought to life by *kabbalah* (mystical teachings). A golem could only be created and controlled by a *tzaddik*, a righteous person. The rabbi is a righteous person and fears for the safety of the Jews. So, he uses spells from kabbalah to give life to the pile of clay that had been shaped into the figure of a giant man. When the rabbi brings life to the golem, howling wind and torrential rain and lightning follow. Those with the rabbi grab each other in terror. The climate for bringing life to the golem is scary, as perhaps it should be. Is this righteous? Or is it evil? Yes, the threat to Jewish lives is real and imminent, but even so, is the creation of life in this way ethical or evil? Even the golem wonders.

The rabbi tells the golem that he is to guard the ghetto, catch the people trying to plant false evidence against the Jews, and bring them unharmed to the authorities. During the day, the golem is to be a servant in the synagogue. These seem like reasonable tasks, but the rabbi seems to have complete control. The golem has no choice in what he is to do. Perhaps this is acceptable; after all, the golem is not a real human being. Yet, the golem seems to have the very human quality of wanting to live, and he can appreciate the beauty of sunrise, the scent of a rose, the flight of a bird. He pleads for his life but is turned back to clay by the rabbi.

Is it ethical or is it evil for a person—even a rabbi—to create a life solely for the purpose of protection? Is it ethical or is it evil to control another's life, even a golem's life, so absolutely? Indeed, the mob did attack the Jews in the ghetto, and only because the golem defended them did they survive. The golem killed many in the mob before it retreated. How should we view the killings by the golem? Are those killings a good thing? Or were they a necessary evil? Is there such a thing as a necessary evil?

The emperor of the country becomes scared of the golem and asks the rabbi if the golem would be used to enslave the country. The rabbi tells the emperor that a people—the Jewish people—who celebrate the end of their own slavery do not want to enslave others, and that the golem is only for defense. What shall we make of the emperor? Is the emperor a good person or an evil person? The emperor did nothing to stop the mobs when they told lies about the Jews or when they attacked the Jews. He doesn't even refer to the Jewish people as citizens of the country. The emperor only guarantees the safety of the Jews so that the rabbi will get rid of the golem. Is it evil that the emperor acts only out of fear?

Because the emperor promised to protect the Jews, the rabbi must destroy the golem. The golem doesn't want to be returned to clay and pleads with the rabbi. Nonetheless, the rabbi returns him to clay. Was that a righteous act? An evil act? Somewhere in between? Maybe destroying the golem was a necessary evil? How can peace be achieved and people of different cultures, backgrounds, and religions learn to respect, appreciate, and learn to live with each other if people are afraid of each other?

Golemito by Ilan Stavans and illustrated by Teresa Villegas is set in a Jewish school in Mexico City. The author puts himself in the story as a young boy. The story is about bullying. Sammy, Ilan's best friend, is constantly bullied by two larger children. Sammy is a genius at science whereas Ilan loves languages, especially Nahuatl (the language of original Mexicans before the Spanish conquistadors arrived). Ilan also loves the poetry of Nezahualcoyotl, the Aztec ruler who was a poet and a philosopher and who led his army to victory over the army of a rival city-state.

After Sammy is threatened yet again by the bullies, Sammy asks Ilan to tell him the story of the golem. Ilan does so. Then, Sammy tells Ilan that he will create a golem to protect himself from the bullies. Ilan tells Sammy that he doesn't need a golem; he just needs courage. Ilan then recites a poem from Nezahualcoyotl about courage.

The next day Sammy goes to school with his latest creation, a small golem who looks like an Aztec warrior—a *golemito*. The golemito defends Sammy from the bullies. The golemito begins to grow and becomes huge and scary. The only way that Sammy can put the golemito to sleep forever is to recite Nahuatl poetry from a book that Ilan had given him. He recites the poetry over and over to the golemito. Although Sammy is not fond of poetry, he admits to Ilan that he really likes a line in the poem by Nezahualcoyotl, "Within myself I discover this."

Enduring questions can be discussed about whether it was wise for Sammy to create a golemito. Although the golemito did defend Sammy from the bullies, the way the golemito did so was by scaring the bullies with potential violence. Is it always wise to confront violence with more violence? Can we confront violence and the power that accompanies violence in other ways?

Were the bullies evil? Where were Sammy's teachers and friends who might have stood with him against the bullies and stopped them? Perhaps if they had helped Sammy, he would not have needed to create a golemito. Is helping someone in need a responsibility we all have? If so, when we do not help someone in need, are we partly to blame for whatever evil happens? Was the golemito evil? Was Sammy evil for creating the golemito? Also, consider the question whether Sammy has the right to destroy the golemito. Yes, Sammy did create the golemito and did give it life, but does creating something and giving it life give someone the right to destroy it?

This story also asks an interesting, probing question about poetry. Poetry and learning languages, such as Nahuatl, matter to Ilan but not to Sammy—at least not at the beginning. Sammy likes science and making inventions. Ilan says that he and Sammy complement each other. How is it that science and poetry/learning languages are complementary? How is it that poetry could put the golemito to sleep? How is it that words are as powerful as the violence of the golemito? One particular line in the poem Sammy repeated again and again resonated with him: "Within myself I discover this." What does that mean? Ilan had told Sammy that he did not need the golemito; he needed courage. How does a poem give one courage?

GOLEM

[In this retelling, a golem—a giant shaped of clay—is brought to life to protect the Jews of Prague from anti-Semitic attacks, violence, and treachery.]

I recently read *Golem* illustrated and written by David Wisniewski to my fifth-grade classes in our first class of the new trimester. The focus of this trimester is on how immigration shaped the cultural and racial landscape of the United States.

The story gave my students an insight into the religious persecution some who chose to immigrate experienced in their homelands and reminded them to be grateful for everyday happenings, the sun rising and setting, as it is in these moments that we truly appreciate life. Wisniewski's writing has great depth to it, and having Jewish knowledge can open the text to understand Jewish traditions and beliefs that much more. That said, students with little to no knowledge take so much away from the book. "It taught me to be grateful for the little things," shared Ellen. "Life is precious and it has to be protected," said John. "People will lie and stereotype others, and that leads to violence," explained Ann. "Why are some groups always targeted by others?" asked Rick. "The golem appreciated the little things; he wanted to live beyond the reason he was made," said Mickey.

It is an excellent book for explaining the blood lie/libel that has been used for centuries to persecute Jews. It is also a phenomenal book to discuss the difference between

Barbara Rogasky's version of *The Golem*, illustrated by Trina Schart Hyman, is a chapter book in which each chapter tells a different story. One humorous story is about the rabbi's wife who asked the golem to fetch water and fill a basin. The golem does so, but because no one tells him to stop, he continues to fetch water and pour it into the basin until it overflows and nearly floods the whole town.

justice and vengeance. If time permits, students could create their own collages mimicking Wisniewski's papercut illustrations to depict times when people stood up against discrimination and persecution.

Liz Paige, ethics and culture classes, private independent school, Utah

Rogasky's version also contains the story of babies secretly switched at birth by a well-intentioned midwife that nearly results unknowingly in the marriage of a brother and sister. The story raises important questions about when and whether people should intervene in others' lives, even if well-intentioned. But these two chapters aside, Rogasky's version of *The Golem* focuses on the murderous threat of the "blood lie."

The blood lie is the falsehood that for Passover (also called Pesach), Jews kill a Christian child and use the child's blood to bake *matzo* (the unleavened bread that Jews eat during Pesach). As outrageous and unbelievable as this lie is, not only did people believe it, but some still do. Some Christians and some governments have used the blood lie as an excuse to attack and murder Jews.

Many of the enduring questions that were shared in discussing David Wisniewski's version of *The Golem* earlier in this chapter can also be asked in reading Rogasky's version. Perhaps because Rogasky's version is a chapter book and is clearly intended for an older audience (children in grades 5 and above), the blood lie is a haunting evil presence throughout the book. It reappears again and again. Time after time, the rabbi and the golem uncover and stop people from planting false evidence of the blood lie and fomenting violence against Jews. It is as if the blood lie cannot be killed. This is a haunting situation, and it leads to enduring questions such as why does hate survive? Why do outrageous and dangerous lies survive when they make no sense to begin with, and they are proven to be false? Why do people so easily believe such lies, and why is it so difficult to get them to recognize them as lethal falsehoods? Of course, such lies are told about other groups as well and are just as dangerous, intractable, and evil. The same enduring questions need to be asked about those lies.

The blood lie was often used to initiate a pogrom. A pogrom is an "organized massacre aimed at the destruction or annihilation of a body or class of people, especially one conducted against Jewish people" (*Oxford English*

Dictionary). The term *pogrom* usually refers to violence in Russia, Poland, and other Eastern European countries; an organized, officially tolerated attack on any community or group. Although the definition of pogrom notes that one can be conducted against any group or community, pogroms predominantly were attacks against Jewish communities, often rural Jewish communities. Russia and many Eastern European countries had a series of pogroms. Some were organized by governments, others conducted by mobs that the governments encouraged. The pogroms of 1648–1649 and 1881–1882 were especially violent, murderous, and widespread, although they were not the only or last pogroms. In 1903 another especially violent and widespread pogrom—the Kishinev pogrom—was organized by government authorities then in the Russian empire.

Some scholars suggest that pogroms were a way for governments to distract from how terrible and oppressive government officials were, using Jews as scapegoats. Others point to the isolation of Jews, laws limiting where Jews could live, how they could make a living, and treatment of them as if they were subhuman. But how does one explain such evil? How does one help children recognize evil and address it without becoming overwhelmed and traumatized?

Broken Song by Kathryn Lasky is a story about fifteen-year-old Reuven Bloom and his family, who live in a small Russian Jewish village (which in Yiddish is called a *shtetl*). Reuven loves music and is a virtuoso on the violin. His best friend, Muttle, is a genius at religious studies and has memorized most of the Torah and Talmud. Reuven is not very good at religious studies. One day the tsar's army comes to their village looking to force Jewish boys and men to serve in the Russian army. While looking, they often destroy and rob. Reuven is able to hide, but Muttle is taken, and Reuven fears he will never see Muttle again. Unfortunately, the tsar's army comes back looking for any Jewish youth they had overlooked. Reuven hides in a small storage hole under the floor. The soldiers ransack the house and murder his father, mother, and young sister. One of the soldiers takes Reuven's violin.

When he comes out of the storage hole, he finds that his baby sister, Rachel, has miraculously been saved. He takes Rachel and leaves, trying to make his way to the city of Vilna (in what is now Lithuania), where he believes that they will be safe. The journey is dangerous, and several times they are almost caught. When Reuven and Rachel arrive in Vilna, Reuven joins the Bund, an organization of Jewish resistance to pogroms. Reuven sends Rachel to America with the wife of an older friend to keep her safe. He feels that he must stay and fight. He becomes very good at sabotage, although what he does is very dangerous.

At one point, he sees the Russian soldier who has his stolen violin. Reuven stalks the soldier, corners him, and places a knife against the soldier's throat, ready to kill him. Even though this was one of the soldiers who had murdered his family, Reuven walks away, taking the violin with him. He decides to immigrate to the United States, where he is reunited with Rachel. He is able to pursue his violin music and eventually becomes a member of the New York Philharmonic Orchestra.

Broken Song is a heart-wrenching book that is also scary. Although Reuven and Rachel survive, there is no escape for the rest of his family or for anyone else in his Jewish shtetl. Reuven loses his parents, his younger sister, and is separated from his best friend and also from his baby sister. As a member of the Bund, he fights against those soldiers who murder and cause so much destruction. Reuven feels great anger and wants revenge. It is difficult not to view the tsar's soldiers as evil. But are they evil? Are they solely responsible for the evil they do? What about the government that told lies about the Jews? Should the soldiers have known better than to believe those lies? When should soldiers disobey orders? What about the priests and other religious leaders who called Jews "Christ killers" and supported the pogroms? Are they evil? Is it evil for Reuven to want revenge? Is it evil for him to get revenge, to kill those who killed his family and other Jewish families? Even if it is not evil for him to seek revenge, what does seeking revenge do to Reuven or anyone else seeking revenge? How can such evil as the pogroms be confronted?

A Boy of Old Prague by Sulamith Ish-Kishor, illustrated by Ben Shahn, tells the story of a Christian boy, Tomás, in the mid-sixteenth century. The story is told from Tomás's perspective. Tomás is a peasant, a serf, extremely poor, and uneducated. He works for a noble, and he and his family are on the lowest rung of society. Tomás never has enough to eat, a decent place to sleep, or decent clothes to wear. He has to work all day, every day. He rarely gets to go home to see his mother and father.

One day he hears that his mother is very ill, so he decides to sneak away from his job and steals a chicken so that his mother will have something to eat. He is caught. Rather than hanging him, the noble gives him to a Jewish businessman to whom the noble owed money. The Jewish man lives in the ghetto where all of the Jews in Prague were forced to live. Tomás had huge fears about the Jews as he has heard all sorts of anti-Semitic lies about them. He assumes that he will be murdered and that his blood will be used by the Jews to make bread.

However, Tomás is treated well. He has a decent place to sleep, good food to eat, and nice clothes to wear. He has work to do, but he does not have to work on the Sabbath. Over time he learns that the lies, myths, and outrageous things he had been told about the Jews are untrue. He makes friends and comes to respect the people for whom he works.

He tells the Jewish businessman that his mother is ill and that he wants to visit her. He is allowed to do so and even given food to take to her. On his way back to the ghetto, Tomás finds that a mob is attacking the Jews in the ghetto. The mob has made a bonfire of Jewish bodies. The house in which Tomás had worked has been destroyed. There is no sign of the Jewish businessman for whom he had worked or of the businessman's family and friends. He realizes that he had love for them—and this realization surprises him. Only a short time before he would have thought it impossible for him to love Jewish people. Tomás has changed. What he had previously viewed as evil turned out not to be so. Indeed, it was just the opposite.

Before Tomás changed, was he evil? He had engaged in anti-Semitic activities—but was he evil or just ignorant? Can ignorance be evil? Tomás admired the noble for whom he worked. Yet, that nobleman and his assistants engaged in all kinds of cruel acts. They used lies to incite violence against Jews. Shouldn't Tomás have known better? Or do we give him a pass because he was uneducated, and his views were the same as those of everyone around him? But what about the fact that he had seen cruelty and ridicule against Jews and did not care? Is it ever the case that, like Tomás, we thought that something was evil only to learn that we were wrong? What does it take to change? To overcome our prejudices (just as Tomás had to overcome his prejudices)?

CHILDREN'S LITERATURE AND THE HOLOCAUST

On a cold Autumn morning, eleven-year-old Arnold—the only Jewish child in his classroom and one of only a handful in the school—was sitting next to the window on the school bus when his friend reached across and drew a swastika in the frost on the windowpane. When Arnold got to school, another child drew a swastika on his notebook, another on his chair, and later that day he was pushed down the stairs to the laughter of children around him. This true event did not happen in the 1930s in Germany but recently in the heartland of the United States. After reporting the events to his parents and then to the principal, the principal told him that he must be mistaken as they did not have bad children in their school. A teacher told Arnold and his parents that it was not a swastika that the children had drawn but a Navajo symbol (compounding anti-Semitism with racism against Indigenous people).

Such incidents are not isolated. By the time Jewish children are in the later elementary-school grades, most have experienced multiple incidents of anti-Semitism, and most are aware of the Holocaust and its symbols. There is a straight line between the blood lie, pogroms, the Holocaust, and more recent events such as white supremacists in Charlottesville shouting, "Jews will not replace us" and the murders at the Tree of Life synagogue in Pittsburgh. That said, along with their non-Jewish peers, even some Jewish students often lack knowledge about the Holocaust and, perhaps more important, need supportive contexts for processing the evil of the Holocaust and its legacy.

For those unfamiliar with the Holocaust, it was the systematic policy and action by the German government that Adolf Hitler and the Nazi party controlled to destroy and murder all Jews and all aspects of Jewish culture and life in Germany, in Europe, and beyond. As Nazi Germany took over other European nations, the Holocaust extended to those nations. It is important to note that not just government officials and soldiers committed acts of violence against Jews, but ordinary citizens as well. The Holocaust built on nearly two thousand years of anti-Semitism and pogroms. Nearly six million Jews were murdered, and Jewish communities throughout Europe were destroyed. The Holocaust occurred between 1938 and 1945.

Excellent resources are available from the U.S. Holocaust Memorial Museum, the Montreal Holocaust Museum, Facing History and Ourselves, and other respectable institutions for teachers and students to learn about the Holocaust. Teaching about the Holocaust, although important and necessary, is difficult because the extent and nature of the horror is unimaginable and traumatic. Before teaching students about the Holocaust, teachers should educate themselves about it and about which pedagogical strategies are effective and which are counterproductive. Of course, other events exist in human history whose horror is similarly unimaginable and traumatic. Students need to learn about these events as well. Only by learning about the Holocaust and similar events, guided by thoughtful, knowledgeable, and caring teachers, can we hope not to repeat them.

In general, experts say that education about the Holocaust itself should begin for children around age ten; education that prepares children to learn about the Holocaust should begin earlier—even in preschool. But such a guideline may not apply to your specific situation. You must think about the students you have, about the school community, and about yourself (about your preparedness to talk with your students about the Holocaust, anti-Semitism, and other evils). As a teacher, it is important to realize that many Jewish children, even preschool children, will have already experienced anti-Semitic acts such as Arnold experienced. Perhaps they do not understand such acts or place them in an appropriate context. They may even blame themselves, believing that something is wrong with them.

Unfortunately, many acts of anti-Semitism against young Jewish children are committed by other young children. They, too, may not understand what they are saying and doing—they may be only mirroring their families or other adults, or sadly, experimenting with the power of hate. Nonetheless, the pain they cause is real, and the damage they do to others and to themselves is also real. Even if none of your children have experienced or committed acts of anti-Semitism, no young child can avoid the news reports and images of anti-Semitic acts of violence and murder that are ubiquitous in mass media and popular culture.

One of the best ways to learn about the Holocaust and how to teach about it using Jewish children's literature is through resources such as the U.S. Holocaust Memorial Museum (https://www.ushmm.org/teach/fundamentals/guidelines-for-teaching-the-holocaust) and the Montreal Holocaust Museum (https://museeholocauste.ca/en/resources-training/5-tips-teach-history-holocaust-elementary-school/). They provide excellent guidelines, discussions, and resources for teaching about the Holocaust and about anti-Semitism more generally. Some of their guidelines are in Table 6.1.

Reading and discussing Jewish children's literature addressing evils such as the Holocaust need to be accompanied by a history that can provide an accurate and truthful context. Teaching about the Holocaust and using Holocaust children's literature can be challenging, especially when teaching elementary children. How can one teach about what is incomprehensible and unimaginable? Even well-intentioned teachers can make problematic instructional choices or provide inaccurate information. The information provided by sources like the U.S. Holocaust Memorial Museum, the Montreal Holocaust Museum, and similar respected sources can be helpful in designing instruction that is effective, high quality, and engages children in appropriate ways.

Table 6.1. A Partial List of Guidelines from the U.S. Holocaust Memorial Museum and the Montreal Holocaust Museum

• Be prepared to define the term *Holocaust*.	• Respect the sensitivity and cognitive skills of students.
• Make clear that the Holocaust was not inevitable.	• Use personal stories to humanize history, develop empathy among students, and understand the complexity and diversity of experiences related to the Holocaust.
• Avoid simple answers to complex questions.	
• Strive for precision of language.	• Provide context and a variety of supports.
• Strive to balance the perspectives that inform your study of the Holocaust.	• Allow your students to express their emotions.
• Avoid comparisons of pain.	• Convey a message of hope and a better world.
• Avoid romanticizing history.	
• Contextualize the history.	
• Translate statistics into people.	
• Make responsible pedagogical choices.	

USING JEWISH CHILDREN'S LITERATURE TO INITIATE CONVERSATIONS ABOUT THE HOLOCAUST

Even when we are well-informed, it is still difficult to initiate conversations with children about the Holocaust. A genre of Holocaust literature portrays just this dilemma. In *Grandpa's Third Drawer*, written and illustrated by Judy Tal Kopelman and originally published in Hebrew, a young child, Uri, wonders what is in a locked drawer in his grandfather's desk. He knows that he is forbidden to open that drawer. However, he finds the key and opens it when, at that moment, his grandfather enters the room. Uri's grandfather is angry and yells at Uri. The grandfather sees that he has scared Uri, calms down, hugs Uri, and apologizes.

Then the grandfather tells Uri the story behind the things in the drawer: the yellow star Jews were forced to wear to mark them as outcasts; being driven out of his home; about the doll made of rags his mother made for his sister, because rags were all they had; and about being hungry all the time. He also tells Uri about the dominoes he made by hand from scraps of wood and that he and his sister would play with them for hours, getting just a bit of happiness as they played. Then Uri's grandfather tells him about being separated from the others in his family, from his sister and his parents who were taken to a concentration camp. He was taken to a work camp. He never saw his sister or his parents again. Then, Uri's grandfather cries. They stay up late, and Uri asks his grandfather many questions. They play dominoes using those same wooden pieces. Uri ends the book by saying that he never knew that his grandfather was such a brave kid or what he had been through—and that now he loves him even more.

Anyone—Jewish or not—who is a grandparent or who has had a grandparent will find this a heart-wrenching book to read as well as a book full of love. Children may have those same emotions listening to it or reading it. Before engaging children in asking enduring questions, it is important to help them understand the emotions they are feeling and validate those emotions. Teachers may find that the emotions their students have will change and evolve as they read such a book. It is important to take the time to help them understand the emotions they are having.

At the end of the story, Uri says that he now loves his grandfather even more. Why even more? Why did the grandfather keep all those objects from that horrible and terrifying time? Why didn't the grandfather want Uri to find out what was in the drawer? Once Uri opened the drawer and saw the items, why did the grandfather decide to then tell Uri about the items and about what happened? Did Uri change after learning about the items in the drawer and the story behind them? When Uri grows up and becomes a grandfather himself, should he save the items that were in his grandfather's drawer? Should Uri tell his own grandchildren about them?

WHAT IS EVIL? ESCAPING FROM THE HOLOCAUST

The plight of families during the Holocaust is the subject of Kathy Kacer's *Shanghai Escape*, a biographical account of the members of the Toufar family and their flight from Austria to China in 1938, where they lived for ten years. Historically, from 1937 through 1939, about twenty thousand Jews from Germany and Austria escaped the Nazis by traveling to Shanghai. Kacer's story begins with Lily, a four-year-old girl, her parents, grandmother, uncle, and aunt, all of whom are preparing to leave Vienna on the eve of what became known as Kristallnacht.

Kristallnacht refers to the Night of Broken Glass, which occurred on November 9 and 10, 1938. Kristallnacht was a series of pogroms that the Nazis initiated against the Jews in Germany. Jews were violently attacked, Jews were murdered, Jewish homes were ransacked, Jewish shops were vandalized, and tens of thousands of Jews were taken to concentration camps. The "broken glass" refers to the breaking of the store windows of Jewish shops. Although the Nazis initiated Kristallnacht, many other Germans also participated. More information about Kristallnacht can be found at the U.S. Holocaust Memorial Museum, https://www.ushmm.org/collections/bibliography/kristallnacht. An excellent video on Kristallnacht produced by Facing History and Ourselves can be found at https://www.facinghistory.org/resource-library/video/kristallnacht-november-1938-pogroms.

After a friend of the family alerts the father to the impending violence and helps them arrange for passage out of Vienna, the family begins the approximately eight-thousand-mile journey to Shanghai. Once there, they have a relatively safe life for a few years. The older members of the family find work, and Lily enters school.

However, their safety is shattered when the Japanese, who support Hitler, take over Shanghai. At that point, the Jews must move to the Chinese ghetto within the city. Living conditions in the ghetto are worse, and information about the wider war is demoralizing. One night, the family members sit together discussing a new threat to their survival—namely, their removal to Japanese prison camps. Lily's father then speaks to all of them in a strong, clear voice that whatever happens, the family will stay together. Despite the heated discussion that had preceded this proclamation, no one objects to the father's decision. They take the pledge to stay together very seriously.

It may be difficult to appreciate how hard it was to make this decision. Both immediately before and during the Holocaust, many Jewish families sought to save their children by sending them to safety in another country. Sometimes, organizations and other countries would allow children but not adults to emigrate. Although the decision to separate was heart-wrenching and painful, parents often believed that the separation was the only way to save their children—and their children's lives needed to be prioritized over the pain the separation would cause. Surviving was a kind of resistance.

When Lily's family decides not to separate regardless of what happens, they are making a very painful decision. They know they are putting all their lives at risk. Just having to think about such a decision must be painful. Why would a family make such a decision? What leads countries such as Germany and Japan to engage in such evils as murdering unimaginably large numbers of people? What if they had murdered only a few people because they were Jews; would that have made it better? Less evil?

The Journey That Saved Curious George: The True Wartime Escape of Margret and H. A. Rey by Louise Borden and illustrated by Allan Drummond tells the story of the authors of the Curious George books as they escaped from the Nazi takeover of Europe during World War II. Margret and H. A. Rey were German Jews who literally bicycled to safety. Many elementary school children will have read one or more of the Curious George books.

Curious George, a monkey, is always getting into trouble, and the man in the yellow hat is always coming to his rescue. The Curious George books are fun to read and filled with love and friendship; many children have fond memories of reading those books by themselves or with parents during bedtime story reading. So, reading about the escape of Margret and H. A. Rey may be a bit more personal to those children than reading about people to whom they are unconnected.

The book does not discuss or refer to the horrors of the Holocaust or the genocide of Jews—it is assumed that readers will bring that knowledge to the reading. The book does mention that Margret and Hans Rey were Jewish, but it is not emphasized; it is a context that readers need to bring to the text. In one scene in the book, Margret and Hans Rey are on a train, and an official searches their briefcase. Perhaps he suspected them of being spies or otherwise dangerous people. What he found were drafts of a Curious George story (at that time, Curious George was called Fi Fi). The official laughed and approved their passage; so, in a sense, Curious George helped Margret and Hans Rey escape.

Of course, the loss of lives is primary. Margret and Hans Rey could easily have been murdered by the Nazis. Had that happened, the world would not have had Curious George and all of those moments when children laughed at Curious George's antics. This, too, is the cost of evil. We can all be sad and horrified by those who were murdered while, at the same time, celebrating those who did escape. These are complex emotions to hold simultaneously, and it is important to help students explore these emotions.

Children—or, for that matter, anyone—can become stuck in fear and anger in response to the evil of the Holocaust, which makes it all the more important to celebrate and have joy in those few instances when people did escape, when they did overcome. How can we have hope in the face of such evil? Why is it important to have hope? How can we recognize, respect, and mourn all those who did not escape while still celebrating those who did? The Talmud says that to have saved a single life is as if one has saved the world. What does that mean? What does such a saying imply for how we feel and what our obligations are for all those lives we did not and were not able to save?

WHAT IS EVIL? RESCUING JEWS

A particular genre of Holocaust literature for young readers can be labeled "rescue" books. In these books, someone who is not Jewish helps someone who is Jewish escape or hide from the Nazis and death. Often, the saved Jews are children.

One such rescue book is *Hidden*, a graphic novel by Loïc Dauvillier and illustrated by Marc Lizano. Elsa is a young Jewish child in France during its occupation by the Nazis. We see how she is expelled from school because she is Jewish, how she must wear a yellow Jewish star, and how she and her family have to go into hiding. During their escape, Elsa's parents decide that it is safer if they separate from Elsa and let another family hide her. They are worried that they are likely to be caught, and they do not want their daughter to be caught. Separation is hard, and they remain separated for a long time. Elsa's father fights with the resistance. Her mother is taken to a concentration camp.

Eventually, they are all reunited, although the war has taken a toll on all of them. Much of the story is told through the graphics, especially the horror, the fear, the anxiety, and the love and relief. Some things are difficult to understand in the events in this book: How can the teachers and children who had known Elsa turn against her and treat her so terribly? Are they evil? It must have been very hard for Elsa's parents to leave her with others. Why would other people—people who are not Jewish—agree to take care of someone else's child, especially when doing so would put their own lives in jeopardy? What obligations do we have to provide safety for others? What risks should we take to do so?

The Grand Mosque of Paris: A Story of How Muslims Rescued Jews during the Holocaust by Karen Gray Ruelle and Deborah Durland DeSaix tells the true story of Muslims in Paris and elsewhere risking their lives to save Jews. The book gives a lot of detail but is told in a way that fifth and sixth graders should be able to read it independently. Under the leadership of the rector of the Grand Mosque of Paris, Si Kaddour Benghabrit, the mosque provided temporary shelter and a hiding place for Jews who were then moved to safe places where they could stay for longer periods of time. Both children and adults were hidden in the mosque.

Occasionally, the Nazis would search the mosque, but through various brave tricks, the rector of the mosque was able to prevent the Nazis from finding anyone. The book describes many ways that the Muslim community of Paris saved the lives of Jews and others and resisted the Nazi occupation. All too often people overlook what Muslims did to save Jewish lives. All too often in the United States, we see a stereotype of Muslims and Jews as enemies when, in fact, Muslims and Jews have often lived in harmony and in mutual respect. For Muslim, Jewish, and other students, an important question to ask is whether this book changed their views of Muslims and Jews? If so, why? Sometimes different religions seem to be in conflict with each other. People of one religion make terrible comments about people of another. Why? How can people of different religions live in peace with one another? What might people take from their religions that would encourage them to help others even if it meant risking their own lives?

Another rescue book is *The Secret of the Village Fool* by Rebecca Upjohn, illustrated by Renné Benoit. The story is based on true events. Anton is the village fool. Everyone laughs at him because he is different. He doesn't eat meat, he talks to plants and animals, he wears patched clothes, he thanks the sun for growing his plants, and he cannot read. Anton is not Jewish, yet when a neighbor says nasty and evil things about Jews, Anton confronts him.

When the Nazis invade their Polish town and begin to round up Jewish men and boys, Anton visits his Jewish neighbors who have two boys. He gives them girls' clothes so that the boys can disguise themselves. The disguises work; however, they know that the Nazis will come looking for them. So, Anton hides the whole family in his carefully hidden cellar. They have little food, and it is dangerous. The Nazis believe Anton is hiding Jews and arrest him, but they cannot find the Jewish family he is hiding. They survive.

We can explore enduring questions using *The Secret of the Village Fool*. Why weren't there more Antons? Everyone thought Anton was a fool and uneducated, but he was brave and confronted hate, murder, and anti-Semitism. Is there no relationship between education and being brave and confronting evil? What kind of education would help us be brave and recognize and confront evil, murder, and genocide?

Irene Watts's *Seeking Refuge*, illustrated by Kathryn Shoemaker, is a graphic novel that tells a story of eleven-year-old Marianne, who is transported by train from Germany to England in 1938 as part of what is called the Kindertransport. *Seeking Refuge* received the 2017 Vine Award for Canadian Jewish Literature. The Kindertransport was an organized effort by private aid organizations in Britain to transport children from Germany and German-annexed areas to Britain. The British government allowed Jewish children under age seventeen to come to Britain, but payment for their care had to be guaranteed by private organizations and individuals. Parents could not accompany their children. The drawings are pencil sketches in black and white, giving the book a gray, sober tone.

Marianne does not have an easy time in Britain, which showed little tolerance for her. The adults who are supposed to care for her are often mean, treating her like a servant rather than a child. Some want to make her their own child (when, in fact, she has a mother in Germany), and some want to convert her to Christianity. Some adults try to protect her and find places for her to live that will respect her as a Jew and as having parents. Eventually, Marianne is reunited with her mother.

Seeking Refuge is important because it reminds us that the outcomes of immigration and operations such as the Kindertransport—although necessary—were not happy ones. Children suffered. Their families suffered. They had to make wrenching, heartbreaking decisions. *Seeking Refuge* requires us to ask difficult questions: Why were so many adults so mean to the Jewish children who sought refuge in England through the Kindertransport? To Jewish people who immigrated in general? Why did Britain not let their parents come? Why did they try to convert the children? How does a child get over such trauma? Does anyone ever really get over that trauma? Does the evil that the Nazis did and would have done to the children justify how the children were treated? As human beings, what do we owe those who are forced to immigrate to where we live?

WHAT IS EVIL? HIDING AND SURVIVING

The Island on Bird Street by Uri Orlev, winner of many awards including the Hans Christian Andersen Award, tells the story of twelve-year-old Alex, who hid by himself, alone, for more than a year in a dilapidated house in the Warsaw ghetto. The book begins with Alex and his father living in that ghetto. Alex's mother had already been taken by the Nazis.

Life is hard. Alex and his father have various strategies to survive. Nonetheless, Alex and his father are rounded up by the Nazis and taken for a selection—those selected to go to the right go to a work camp; those selected to go to the left are taken to a death camp. Children such as Alex are almost always sent to the left. Alex had to run in order not to be selected; he had to leave his father. Alex had to hide. He had to find shelter, food, water, and a way to survive the Nazis' constant searching for the few Jews left hiding in the Warsaw ghetto.

The book is told from Alex's perspective. He misses his father. He needs to hide near the place where he and his father had agreed to meet when his father would be able to return. He meets others; some are helpful, others are not. In one scene Alex has to shoot and kill a German soldier who was about to kill a Jew who had been escaping from one of the searches the Nazis conducted.

In another scene, Alex is able to see across the wall that separates the ghetto from the rest of the city. He can see the life they have and wants to be part of it, being able to play, eat a warm roll, go to school, and have friends. Alex finds a way to sneak out of the ghetto and his hiding place and interacts with some of the people and the children outside the ghetto. He tries to be normal, to enjoy playing football with other children, but those moments cannot last, and they are risky. Another child identifies him as a Jew, so Alex must retreat back into his hiding place in the ghetto. After more than a year, his father returns, finds Alex, and they escape to the woods to join the partisans.

What happens to Alex, his father, and his mother is evil. How can people commit such evil? How do they not see it as evil? Perhaps the greatest fear a child can have is the loss of his parents. For Alex, this loss is compounded by not having anyone else in his life. He is alone, scared, and worried that he will never see his father again. Being alone is hard. Why? What does it say about us as human beings that we find it hard to be alone for a long period of time? Although it is hard to be alone, many people spend a lot of time alone. What obligations do we have to those people?

Alex must make some hard, painful decisions. Deciding to kill the German soldier—even though necessary to keep that soldier from murdering a Jewish man just trying to survive—was a wrenching decision. When, if ever, is it acceptable to kill another person? Alex must rely on his own abilities and cunning to survive. Is survival enough? Some people would argue that the act of surviving the Holocaust is in itself enough, an act of resistance; it might even be considered a miracle. Is it? Is it enough? Having survived, what obligations does Alex (and anyone else who survives) have to those who did not survive? To others who did survive? To future generations?

Jane Yolen's *The Devil's Arithmetic* is the story of thirteen-year-old Hannah, who lives in a contemporary suburb of New York City. Hannah and her family travel to Passover seder at her grandparents' home. Hannah does not want to go—it is boring, and she does not like the way her older relatives act. She does not like that everything is about remembering. Her grandfather and grandmother are survivors of the Holocaust, having lost many family members. Hannah's grandfather has a number tattooed on his arm. Hannah does not understand the number. When she was younger, she took a pen and wrote a number on her own arm and showed it to her grandfather. He became very upset. Hannah washed it off but still did not understand. The Nazis tattooed numbers on the arms of Jewish concentration camp prisoners.

During a ritual in the Passover seder, the door of the home is opened to allow the prophet Elijah to enter if he happens to be nearby. Hannah opens the door, steps out into the hallway, and is magically transported back in time and place to a small village in Poland in 1942, a few days before Passover. Hannah is no longer Hannah but Chaya (her Hebrew name). Nazis arrive in the shtetl. Chaya tries to warn her family and the people in the village of the danger, but they do not believe her. Chaya, the family, and others are rounded up, stuffed and locked into boxcars on a train, and taken to a concentration camp. Chaya enters the camp, learns the daily routine, suffers through the meager food rations and living conditions, goes through a "choosing" (in which some Jews are chosen for death and some for work), and sees people die all around her, including a young boy she had been taking care of. She sees people executed just because they were Jews.

One day the guards come to select three more Jews for death. They need to fill their quota. One of the women they select is a ten-year-old friend of Chaya's. As they march out, Chaya tells Rivka to hand over her headscarf and then run. She does. Chaya ties the headscarf around her head and takes Rivka's place as the three are marched to their deaths.

At that moment, Hannah finds herself back at the Passover seder in contemporary times. Her family is yelling at her to come back to the table and shut the door. She does so. She sees the number on her Aunt Eva's arm and stares at it. Aunt Eva touches Hannah's hand and tells her that when she was in the concentration camps, her name was Rivka. Hannah tells her, "I remember. I remember."

Jane Yolen is a master storyteller, as *The Devil's Arithmetic* can be read at many levels of sophistication, insight, and maturity. On one level is the plot in which, unlike so many other Holocaust stories, the protagonist—Chaya—does not survive. Chaya is brave and saves Rivka's life. Should she have done that, sacrifice her life for another? Of course, Hannah is not murdered, as she returns to the contemporary Passover seder. So, what really did happen? Was it all just in her mind? Hannah seems to know things that she learned from having been magically transported in time and space. So, was she, indeed, transported back in time and space? What does all of this mean?

At most Passover seders, as Jews retell the story of the Exodus from Egypt, they repeat a phrase that Moses said to the Jewish people, as recorded in the Torah, that can be translated as, "It is because of what God did for me when I went out of Egypt." For Jews, it is as if we ourselves were freed, not just Jews a long time ago. To remember is to collapse time and space; this is what happened to Hannah. If we take this version of "remembering" seriously, what might that mean for how we see history? How we see ourselves? How we see others and their histories? Although we only get a brief glimpse of Hannah after she "comes back," it does seem like she has changed. How has she changed? How might we change if we treated remembering as collapsing the distance between us and those we are remembering?

JANUSZ KORCZAK AND EDUCATION

Earlier, the question was posed, "What kind of education would help us be brave and recognize and confront evil, murder, and genocide?" This question leads to discussion of the Polish Jewish educator Janusz Korczak and his relationship with his students. We have placed discussion of the books about Korczak here because he is most famous for staying with his students when they were taken to a death camp by the Nazis. However, we could have discussed the books about his life in chapter 3, "What Is Love?"

Many books have been written about Janusz Korczak, including *Janusz Korczak's Children* by Gloria Spielman, illustrated by Matthew Archambault; *A Hero and the Holocaust: The Story of Janusz Korczak* by David Adler, illustrated by Bill Farnsworth; and *Mister Doctor: Janusz Korczak and the Orphans of the Warsaw Ghetto* by Irène Cohen-Janca, illustrated by Maurizio A. C. Quarello.

Janusz Korczak was the pen name of Henryk Goldszmidt. He became a doctor, and he wrote stories about the poor people of Poland, which made him famous. He became the director of the orphanage for Jewish children. His educational theories were revolutionary, especially for his time. The school embraced democracy. It had "courts" run by the children; and even adults, including Korczak, could be brought before the court for breaking a rule. It had a weekly newspaper to which everyone contributed. Children were treated as deep thinkers, poets, and philosophers; and they were cared for and listened to. Korczak wrote several children's books including *King Matt the First* (in which a child becomes king).

When the Nazis occupied Warsaw, they ordered Jews to wear a yellow star. Janusz Korczak refused. He was twice arrested for not wearing a yellow star. When all the Jews were forced into the ghetto, Korczak led the children into the ghetto and set up their school there. Despite very difficult times, Korczak did what he could for the children, but eventually the Nazis came for the children. Although he could have saved his own life, he refused to leave the children. They were all taken to Treblinka (a Nazi death camp) and murdered. How should we understand Korczak's staying with his students when it was certain they would be murdered and that if he stayed with them, he would be murdered, too? Why did he not save his own life? Although we can learn a lot about education from his teaching techniques, can we learn something from his commitment to the students?

WHAT IS EVIL? JEWISH RESISTANCE AGAINST THE HOLOCAUST

A dangerous myth circulates not only among non-Jews but some Jews as well: Jews did not resist and fight back against the Nazis. This myth is an anti-Semitic justification for the Holocaust and the murder of nearly six million Jews. Jews did fight back, and heroically.

Many Jews and some non-Jews know about the efforts of Hannah Szenes (also spelled Senesh). Szenes was a young woman who loved poetry and at the time was living in Palestine. Although she could have remained safe in Palestine, she became a member of a Jewish resistance group that parachuted into Czechoslovakia to help organize resistance to the Nazis. She was captured and executed. Many books about Hannah Szenes exist, but few are for preschool and elementary-school children. One book for children, *Hannah Szenes: A Song of Light*, is by Maxine Rose Schur. Although Hannah Szenes's story is an important one, the Jewish resistance was broad, deep, and courageous.

Doreen Rappaport's book *Beyond Courage: The Untold Story of the Jewish Resistance during the Holocaust* provides a series of narrative descriptions of Jewish resistance during the Holocaust that are at an accessible reading level for children in grades 5 and 6. Children can read one chapter at a time and discuss it. One chapter is about Jewish resistance in Berlin, another about resistance in Paris, one set in Greece, and in the Jewish ghettos in Warsaw, Theresienstadt, and Vilna (now Vilnius). Chapters on Jewish uprisings in the camps—in transit camps, in forced labor camps, and in concentration and death camps—are also included. The book includes maps and photographs, including some of armed Jewish partisans.

Perhaps the most famous Jewish uprising was in the Warsaw ghetto. The chapter on the Warsaw ghetto uprising begins with twenty-three-year-old Mordechai Anielwicz, who helped to organize a Jewish fighting group there. They tried to buy weapons from the Polish underground, which refused to share as saving Jewish lives was not one of their priorities. Young women and men helped smuggle what guns they could find into the ghetto. They prepared to fight the Nazis building hidden, fortified bunkers—even though they knew they could not defeat the Nazis.

On the first night of Passover, April 18, 1943, the uprising began. At first, the Jewish resistance fighters had success and forced the Nazis to retreat. When the Nazis came back, the Jewish resistance fighters had moved to another part of the ghetto. After three days of the uprising, the Nazis decided to set the entire ghetto on fire. They set fire to the buildings, street by street, but even so, the fighting continued. Not until May 16, 1943—nearly a month after the beginning of the uprising—could the Nazis claim that they had defeated the uprising. Some Jewish resistance fighters had sneaked out of the ghetto through the sewers, many had been killed, a few were able to hide, and some killed themselves rather than surrender.

The photographs of the people prevent the chapter from being just a story. It is a hard chapter to read, as are many of the chapters in *Beyond Courage*, and young people need teachers to help them think about the events and people portrayed. The Jewish resistance fighters knew that they had little chance of success or even surviving. Why fight back rather than try to save themselves by escaping and hiding? Mordechai Anielwicz, one leader of the uprising, was outside of the ghetto and came back to help organize the uprising. Why would he do that? For Jews, life matters. Even the life of a single individual matters. The preservation of life supersedes most other things. Even so, are some things so important they are worth risking one's life? Where is hope?

In *Uncle Misha's Partisans* by Yuri Shul, a young boy, Motele, joins Uncle Misha's partisans, a group of Jewish resistance fighters. Disguised as a non-Jewish boy, he plays the violin for Nazi soldiers and gathers information for Uncle Misha's partisans. He also uses his disguise to blow up Nazi buildings. Based on actual events, the novel shows us Motele's thoughts and feelings. He not only shows courage, even though he is sometimes afraid, but he also shows anger and vengeance.

Similar in many ways to *Uncle Misha's Partisans* is Judy Batalion's *The Light of Days: The Untold Story of Women Resistance Fighters in Hitler's Ghettos*. (The book has two versions, one for young readers and one for adults.) Jewish women, no less than Jewish men, were part of the resistance to the Nazis' genocide. The stories of the mostly young women who engaged in a broad range of resistance activities—spying, bombing, shooting, organizing escapes of Jews, and much more—show their bravery, leadership, and sacrifice. We learn of their struggles to get the few weapons they could gather so that they could fight back.

In addition to telling what happened, the stories also show the feelings and emotions of the young resistance women and those with whom they worked and tried to protect. Without becoming sentimental, the stories show us their fears, anxieties, doubts, traumas, dreams, desires, and hopes—we get to see them as young people just like ourselves. The book includes photographs of some of the resistance fighters, and the author's notes at the end describe the research conducted about the women resistance fighters.

Where does the bravery of young people such as Motele and the young women in *The Light of Days* come from? Why would someone put their own life at risk and sacrifice their life for others? When is such risk and sacrifice necessary, and when is it foolishness? When we read about the stories of resistance fighters, should we view them as different and distant, or should we see ourselves in them?

FINAL THOUGHTS—JEWISH CHILDREN'S LITERATURE AND THE QUESTION "WHAT IS EVIL?"

As teachers and parents, we all struggle with questions about evil. Why is there so much evil in the world? How can we confront that evil? We struggle with these questions throughout our lives. We know that our children and students look to us for answers, but we have no answers to give them. How can we explain to them why evil happens? How do we explain wars? Hatred? Slavery? Genocide? All we can give them are opportunities to explore such questions. Teachers can use Jewish children's literature to prompt and enrich discussions of the question "What is evil?" Of course, as we discuss in chapter 8, many high-quality books of children's literature from other cultures can also enrich the exploration of enduring questions.

The contribution of Jewish children's literature to exploring the enduring question of "What is evil?" comes in part from Jewish history, experience, and culture, and in part from Jewish philosophy and ethics. Memory, remembering, and witnessing—in which time and place are collapsed, removing the separation between ourselves and those who came before—along with courage and sacrifice are core elements in the exploration of enduring questions such as "What is evil?" and "How might we respond to evil?"

WORKS CITED

Children's Literature

Adler, David A. *A Hero and the Holocaust: The Story of Janusz Korczak and His Children*. Illustrated by Bill Farnsworth. New York: Holiday House, 2002.

Batalion, Judy. *The Light of Days Young Readers' Edition: The Untold Story of Women Resistance Fighters in Hitler's Ghettos*. New York: HarperCollins, 2021.

Borden, Louise. *The Journey That Saved Curious George: The True Wartime Escape of Margret and H. A. Rey*. Illustrated by Allan Drummond. New York: Houghton Mifflin Harcourt, 2005.

Cohen-Janka, Irène. *Mister Doctor: Janusz Korczak and the Orphans of the Warsaw Ghetto*. Illustrated by Maurizio A. C. Quarello. Toronto: Annick Press, 2015.

Dauvillier, Loïc. *Hidden*. Illustrated by Marc Lizano. New York: First Second, 2014.

Ish-Kishor, Sulamith. *A Boy of Old Prague*. Illustrated by Ben Shahn. New York: Pantheon, 1963.

Kacer, Kathy. *Shanghai Escape*. Toronto, ON: Second Story Press, 2013.

Kopelman, Judy Tal. *Grandpa's Third Drawer: Unlocking Holocaust Memories*. Philadelphia: Jewish Publication Society, 2014.

Korczak, Janusz. *King Matt the First*. Translated by Richard Lourie. New York: Farrar, Straus & Giroux, 1986.

Kushner, Tony. *Brundibar*. Illustrated by Maurice Sendak. New York: Hyperion Books for Children, 2003.

Lasky, Kathryn. *Broken Song*. New York: Viking, 2005.

Levine, Gail Carson. *A Ceiling Made of Eggshells*. New York: HarperCollins, 2020.

Orlev, Uri. *The Island on Bird Street*. Translated by Hillel Halkin. Boston: Houghton Mifflin, 1983.

Rappaport, Doreen. *Beyond Courage: The Untold Story of Jewish Resistance during the Holocaust*. Somerville, MA: Candlewick, 2012.

Rogasky, Barbara. *The Golem*. Illustrated by Trina Schart Hyman. New York: Holiday House, 1996.

Ruelle, Karen Gray, and Deborah Durland DeSaix. *The Grand Mosque of Paris: A Story of How Muslims Rescued Jews during the Holocaust*. New York: Holiday House, 2010.

Schur, Maxine Rose. *Hannah Szenes: A Song of Light*. Philadelphia: Jewish Publication Society, 1985.

Shul, Yuri. *Uncle Misha's Partisans*. New York: Four Winds, 1973.

Spielman, Gloria. *Janusz Korczak's Children*. Illustrated by Matthew Archambault. Minneapolis: Kar-Ben, 2007.

Stavans, Ilan. *Golemito*. Illustrated by Teresa Villegas. Montgomery, AL: NewSouth Books, 2013.

Upjohn, Rebecca. *The Secret of the Village Fool*. Illustrated by Renné Benoit. Toronto: Second Story Press, 2012.

Watts, Irene N. *Seeking Refuge*. Illustrated by Kathryn E. Shoemaker. Vancouver, BC: Tradewind Books, 2017.

Wisniewski, David. *Golem.* New York: Clarion, 1996.
Yolen, Jane. *The Devil's Arithmetic.* New York: Viking-Kestrel, 1987.

References

Oxford English Dictionary. Pogrom. Retrieved April 26, 2022, from https://www-oed-com.proxy.ohiolink.edu:9100/view/Entry/146571?rskey=ySRnWZ&result=1#eid.

Facing History and Ourselves has excellent resources on anti-Semitism, the Holocaust, genocide, and the teaching of history, https://www.facinghistory.org.

The Montreal Holocaust Museum, https://museeholocauste.ca/en/resources-training/5-tips-teach-history-holocaust-elementary-school/.

The U.S. Holocaust Memorial Museum, https://www.ushmm.org/teach/fundamentals/guidelines-for-teaching-the-holocaust.

Chapter 7

What Is Justice?

What Is a Righteous Person to Do? Jewish Children's Literature and the Pursuit of Tikkun Olam

Gathering Sparks is a heartwarming intergenerational story that beautifully introduces young children to the Jewish concept of *tikkun olam*, repairing the world. In *Gathering Sparks* by Howard Schwartz and illustrated by Kristina Swarner (which is also discussed in chapter 3), a grandfather retells his granddaughter the teaching of the sixteenth-century Rabbi Isaac Luria about collecting sparks of light from shattered vessels sent by God. When someone performs a kind or righteous deed, a spark is released and makes the world a better place.

The concept of tikkun olam calls on each individual to contribute to the common good and repair the world. It is a hopeful concept, looking forward to a better future—an ideal world where peace and prosperity exist for everyone. Repairing the world and making it a better place take many forms, from simple acts of personal charity to public acts dealing with societal issues. Children themselves have the potential to be agents of change, empowered to do deeds that demonstrate care and compassion for others and that make the world a better place.

Another essential concept in Judaism is justice, as written in Deuteronomy 16:20: "Justice, justice shall you pursue." The Torah includes numerous references to seeking justice and the responsibility to act justly. In the Hebrew Bible, the prophet Amos says, "Let justice roll down like waters and righteousness like a mighty stream." Jews have a responsibility to seek justice for all people and the world. These concepts are expressed in the Hebrew words *tzedek* (justice) and *tzaddik* (a righteous person). Related to these concepts is the teaching from the Talmud that if you save a single life, it is as if you have saved the entire world.

This chapter discusses Jewish children's literature with themes of social justice, righteousness, and repairing the world. The books include both fiction and nonfiction that describe how people, real and imagined, adults and children, practice tikkun olam and the pursuit of justice, sometimes in the wider world or other times within their own community.

Several award-winning novels explore themes related to justice and righteousness. In Anne Blankman's *The Blackbird Girls*, Valentina Kaplan and Oksana Savchenko are fifth-grade neighbors. However, they are not friends because Oksana has learned anti-Semitism from her father and is mean to Valentina. It is 1986, and the nuclear disaster of Chernobyl forms the backdrop for this novel. When an accident occurs at the nuclear power plant, everyone must evacuate Chernobyl and, for a variety of reasons, both girls are sent to Leningrad, where Valentina's estranged Jewish grandmother, Rita, lives.

Told from the perspective of Valentina with alternating flashbacks of her grandmother's life in 1941 during World War II, the book shows how true friendship can develop in the most unlikely circumstances. When the secret of Oksana's abusive childhood is revealed, Rita fulfills the Jewish Talmudic teaching that if you save a life, it is as if you saved the entire world.

This multilayered book prompts enduring questions: How does Rita demonstrate that she is a righteous person? How can you seek

THE BLACKBIRD GIRLS

[It's 1986, in Ukraine, where Oksana and Valentina, fifth graders who are foes, are thrown together following the Chernobyl nuclear power plant explosion, which kills both of their fathers.]

I read *The Blackbird Girls* before sharing it with my class, and I had my doubts that it would capture their imaginations. I couldn't have been more wrong. Today, we finished reading the author's note at the end, and nineteen of my twenty-three students gave it a five-star review. My school is white, upper-middle-class suburban (two Indian students, two African American students, nineteen white students).

In the story, Oksana suffers terrible abuse at the hands of the people she loves most and learns that family is more than just about blood. She learns that her father was wrong about the Jewish people. Valentina learns that everyone's truth is not what it appears on the outside, and people hide the things that hurt them the most.

My students followed their stories and had deep conversations about how a father can be so awful to his own child. Their eyes were opened to the idea that not everyone has a loving and caring home.

We also discussed the treatment of Jewish people in the Soviet Union and other countries. I have one Jewish student. When I would read sections in which there was blatant racism, the other students in my class would look at him to see his reaction. He handled this with such justice for a friend? If you might be endangering yourself, do you still have the responsibility to seek justice? How does Valentina show courage?

The novel *Linked* by Gordon Korman is set in a small, contemporary Colorado town where Dana is the only Jewish girl in middle school. Her family has recently moved to town so that her parents can work on an archaeological dig sponsored by a university. When a swastika is painted on a school wall, school officials try to apprehend the culprit. As swastikas continue to appear throughout the school, the students want to take some kind of action.

grace. We would debrief after each of these passages. My students were adamant that this way of thinking is not acceptable.

We wrapped up our discussion by making slides with pictures that represent each of our cultures. There is quite a bit of overlap in our classroom, but this is giving us a window into each other's lives.

Dakota Lowelle,
fifth-grade teacher,
public school, South Carolina

Inspired by the Tennessee school that collected six million paper clips to commemorate the six million Jews that Hitler and the Nazis killed, the students decide to make a paper chain with six million paper links. During this time, the most popular boy in the seventh grade, Lincoln, learns of his Jewish heritage and decides he wants a bar mitzvah. He and Dana become friends as she helps him learn how to be Jewish and prepare for his bar mitzvah. A surprise ending reveals the culprit and the success of the paper chain.

This book will resonate with students with its humor, suspense, and many surprises. It also fosters many enduring questions: In what ways does this book represent tikkun olam? Why do you think it was so important to Lincoln to discover his Jewish heritage? In what ways has Lincoln changed? What causes people to change? How does Lincoln prove to be a righteous person? Should someone have to prove to be righteous, or should you just be righteous and behave in a righteous way? Why was it important for the students to demonstrate their remembrance of the Holocaust tangibly? If someone does an unjust act out of ignorance, is it the same as doing it deliberately? What motivated the students to paint the swastikas? If their motivation was different, does that change how we view their actions?

Another novel in which the anti-Semitic act of painting a swastika occurs is *No Vacancy* by Tziporah Cohen. This book explores the question of what is a righteous act. If you do something that would be considered "wrong," but your intentions are righteous, is that a righteous act? When Miriam's family moves from Manhattan to a small town in the Finger Lakes region of New York, Miriam must adjust to living in the rundown motel her family has bought. As the only Jewish family in this small town, Miriam befriends Kate, a Catholic girl her age whose grandparents own the diner next door to the motel.

Business is very slow for both the motel and the diner, so the girls devise a scheme to bring more visitors to town to save both the motel and the diner from bankruptcy. Their scheme is a success, and business is booming for both establishments. The only wrinkle in their plan is its deception—the girls have carved a cross on the movie screen of the long-closed drive-in theater under what could be perceived as a woman's face. People believe this is a vision of the Virgin Mary and flock to the town to see it and pray. The conclusion of the book reflects the righteousness of the girls and the people of the town after a swastika is painted on the motel's sign. Were the girls wrong to carve the cross on the movie screen, which was an act of vandalism? The girls kept their act a secret; was their deception justified? Their act did result in the success of the motel and the diner. Does a righteous intention justify a non-righteous act? How did the townspeople act in a righteous way?

Interfaith friendship also forms the basis of *A Place at the Table*, a collaboratively written novel by Jewish author Laura Shovan and Muslim author Saadia Faruqi. Good deeds to repair the world are prevalent throughout this book as middle school students Sara, who is Muslim, and Elizabeth, who is Jewish, learn to understand and respect each other's religions and learn to stand against bigotry. Due to her family's financial difficulties, Sara must leave the small Muslim school that she has attended for the large public middle school. An after-school cooking class that Sara's mother teaches forms the initial basis for Sara's friendship with Elizabeth.

Told in alternating chapters from Sara's and Elizabeth's perspectives, readers learn of both girls' family troubles, their desire to win a cooking contest to support their families, and the consequences of poor decision making, even if the decision is for the right reason.

The novel prompts many enduring questions: Why do you think Elizabeth doesn't defend Sara the first time she is the victim of name-calling? If we witness an unjust act that surprises us, is it unjust if we don't react immediately? Later, Elizabeth does confront the girl who name-calls Sara. Why does she change? How has Elizabeth become a righteous person? What assumptions do people make about those who are different from themselves? The students in the cooking class made assumptions about Sara and her mother. What causes them to change their ideas? How do all the students in the cooking class eventually demonstrate righteousness? Why does it sometimes take time to do the just thing and act in a righteous way? In what ways can people overcome bigotry and racism?

CHILDREN'S LITERATURE AND JEWISH INVOLVEMENT IN THE CIVIL RIGHTS MOVEMENT

When Ms. Lewis began the study of the civil rights movement with her fourth-grade class, she shared a personal story. In 1964, Ms. Lewis was a teenager. During this summer, called Freedom Summer in the civil rights movement, volunteers from around the United States traveled to Mississippi to assist African Americans in registering to vote. Efforts to prevent African Americans from voting persisted in Mississippi. It was often dangerous for African Americans to register to vote and to vote. The rabbi of her synagogue, Rabbi Arthur J. Lelyveld, was one of the volunteers who came to Mississippi to assist in registering voters. He was beaten with a tire iron by individuals opposed to Black voting rights and suffered a concussion.

Ms. Lewis asked her class, "Why do you think the rabbi decided to travel to Mississippi to help register Black voters? Because the rabbi knew there would be danger, did he make a wise decision? Why might people decide to do something even if danger is possible?" Ms. Lewis then told her class that many Jews were active in the civil rights movement. For example, Charles McDew was a leader in the Student Nonviolent Coordinating Committee and in the voter registration effort (see *Tell the Story* by Charles McDew). McDew was an African American Jew. Three young men, Andrew Goodman, Michael Schwerner, and James Earl Chaney, who were helping with voter registration, were murdered by white supremacists in Philadelphia, Mississippi, in 1964. Goodman and Schwerner were Jewish; Chaney was African American. (Information about Rabbi Lelyveld, Andrew Goodman, Michael Schwerner, and Earl Chaney can be found in *Freedom Summer: The 1964 Struggle for Civil Rights in Mississippi* by Susan Goldman Rubin.)

Ms. Lewis then read aloud two picture books about other rabbis who had a strong commitment to social justice. *The Rabbi and the Reverend* by Audrey Ades with illustrations by Chiara Fedele is subtitled *Joachim Prinz, Martin Luther King Jr., and Their Fight against Silence*. Rabbi Prinz was born in Germany, and when Hitler came to power, Rabbi Prinz spoke out against the injustices against the Jews. He was arrested for speaking out against these laws and exiled from Germany. When he came to America, Rabbi Prinz found that African Americans were experiencing the same kind of injustices that he suffered in Germany. Just as he had spoken out in Germany, Rabbi Prinz spoke out against these injustices in America. Martin Luther King Jr. heard about this rabbi, and they became friends. Rabbi Prinz stood with Dr. King at the 1963 March on Washington and spoke there, emphasizing the importance of not remaining silent against injustice.

Another rabbi who became friends with Martin Luther King Jr. was Rabbi Abraham Joshua Heschel. Like Rabbi Prinz, Rabbi Heschel came to the United States shortly before the Nazis invaded his homeland of Poland. Richard Michelson's *As Good as Anybody: Martin Luther King, Jr., and Abraham Joshua Heschel's Amazing March toward Freedom*, with illustrations by Raul Colón, contains a brief biography of each man. Both were committed to freedom and justice. In 1965, Rabbi Heschel marched with Dr. King from Selma to Montgomery.

These two books lead to enduring questions: Why did Rabbi Prinz believe so strongly that you can't remain silent in the face of injustice? How did the treatment that both rabbis experienced in Europe influence their beliefs? Why did they turn their personal beliefs into action? Is it enough to believe in justice and freedom without taking action to ensure that everyone has it? How did the rabbis fulfill the teaching of tikkun olam?

SMALL ACTS TO REPAIR THE WORLD

Several books describe ways that individuals, not necessarily famous or well known, have done small acts to repair the world and shown themselves to be righteous. In the fictional picture book *A Scarf for Keiko* by Ann Malaspina and illustrated by Merrilee Liddiard, Sam, who is Jewish, lives next door to Keiko, who is Japanese American, in the Boyle Heights neighborhood of Los Angeles. The families of Sam and Keiko are friends. The United States has entered World War II, anti-Japanese sentiment is running high, and Keiko is the victim of name-calling. Sam's friends discourage him from talking to Keiko or being her friend. Sam is concerned about the unfair treatment she is experiencing.

When Sam learns that Keiko's family is being sent to a Japanese internment camp, he wants to do something for her. Because his class has been knitting scarves for the soldiers, he decides to knit a scarf for her and send it to her at the camp. An author's note includes archival photos and an explanation of the removal of Americans of Japanese heritage living on the West Coast to internment camps. Even though Sam is young, he knows that the treatment of his friend Keiko is unfair.

This book prompts a series of enduring questions: Giving Keiko a scarf may seem like a trivial action, but is it, indeed, trivial? Sam cannot change what the government is doing by himself. In such cases, what does it mean to take action for justice? Keiko was a friend of Sam's. Does someone have to be a friend before we should act to ensure that they and others are treated justly? Do we have a responsibility to help others?

Eliza David, a real person who admired Charles Dickens, is the focus of the informational picture book *Dear Mr. Dickens* by Nancy Churnin and illustrated by Bethany Standcliffe. Eliza, who is Jewish, reads *Oliver Twist*, written by Charles Dickens, with dismay at how the Jewish character Fagin is portrayed as "dishonest, selfish, cruel and ugly." Dickens repeatedly refers to Fagin as the Jew. So, Eliza writes Dickens a letter expressing her concern that the book depicts Fagin as if his behavior reflects all Jews. When she is not satisfied with Dickens's response to her letter, she writes to him again.

In a later novel, *Our Mutual Friend*, Dickens writes a positive portrayal of another Jewish character. Eliza writes again to Dickens, thanking him for this positive portrayal. In future reprintings of *Oliver Twist*, Dickens changes the reference to Fagin as the Jew and uses his name to better describe that Fagin is one individual and not a representative of all Jews.

An author's note provides more background and information about this true incident. What motivated Eliza to take this action? Why did she continue to write to Dickens? Eliza was Jewish. Does one have to be Jewish to write to an author to get him to change how he represents Jews? Similarly, does one have to be of the same religious or ethnic or racial group to get someone of renown to change their publicly expressed prejudices? What responsibility does each of us have to ensure that our expressions do not contain hateful, prejudiced words? Eliza's actions may seem small. Nonetheless, how can one person's small actions make an impact on justice and fair treatment? Is it possible for small actions to have a large impact? How?

Another individual whose small actions resulted in a large impact was Aaron Lansky. When Aaron Lansky began to rescue old Yiddish books, he never imagined that his Yiddish Book Center in Amherst, Massachusetts, would become a leading resource for Yiddish language, literature, and learning. Since 1980, Lansky and his staff have rescued more than one million books from locations around the world. The story of Aaron Lansky's quest to rescue Yiddish books is told in *The Book Rescuer: How a Mensch from Massachusetts Saved Yiddish Literature for Generations to Come* by Sue Macy and illustrated by Stacy Innerst. The subtitle of the book describes Lansky as a *mensch*, which literally means person but is often used to refer to a person of integrity and righteousness.

The book shows how a young boy, interested in his grandmother's life in Eastern Europe before her immigration to America, began collecting Yiddish books so that the heritage of Yiddish-speaking Jews would be preserved. His story is an example of how one person perceived and responded to an injustice. During the Holocaust, the Nazis tried to destroy Jewish life, culture, literature, and language. After the Holocaust, in America and elsewhere, when elderly Yiddish-speaking Jews died, many of their Yiddish books were being thrown away. Saving those books helped preserve the culture, language, and literature of Ashkenazi Jews. In effect, Aaron Lansky engaged in acts of justice to prevent the loss of an important part of Jewish history and literature. He found a way to overcome a historical injustice.

The book includes an afterword by Aaron Lansky, notes by the author and illustrator, a glossary of Yiddish words and expressions, information about the Yiddish Book Center, and source notes. Students can learn about the Yiddish Book Center and discuss why Lansky became so determined to find and collect these books.

Why is it important to preserve a heritage? How did Lansky's behavior show that he was seeking justice for the language and literature of his heritage? Why are language and literature important parts of one's identity?

The lifelong friendship of the famous Jewish scientist Albert Einstein and the famous African American singer Marian Anderson began with small acts of righteousness. Their friendship is described in *The Singer and the Scientist* by Lisa Rose. Early in her career, in 1937, Marian Anderson performed at the McCarter Theatre in Princeton, New Jersey. Einstein attended the concert and was mesmerized by Anderson's voice. When Einstein learned that she was prevented from spending the night at the hotel because it was segregated, he invited her to stay at his home. Later, Marian Anderson was invited by First Lady Eleanor Roosevelt to sing at the Lincoln Memorial, and she became very famous. An author's note provides further background to the story and explains that Einstein was involved in organizations that worked against racism.

Children may wonder what segregation is, why it was tolerated, and how we might respond to segregation. Why would a singer be invited to perform a concert and not be allowed to stay at the city's hotel? What responsibility did the theater's owner have to arrange appropriate accommodations for Marian Anderson? The theater owner seems to think of Marian Anderson as only a performer and not as a human being. How can it be that some people cannot see other people as human but only as performers or only as workers? Why did Einstein invite Marian Anderson to stay at his home? How do you think Einstein's experience in Nazi Germany and the burning of his books influenced his action? At the end of the book, when Marian Anderson has become famous and is invited back to sing at the McCarter Theatre, the same theater owner treats her with great respect. Why do you think his treatment of Anderson has changed?

SEEKING JUSTICE THROUGH ART

Two famous Jewish artists known for their commitment to social justice are the subject of two biographies for children. Ben Shahn, who immigrated as a child from Lithuania to the United States, was famous for his story paintings featuring oppressed people. His life is described in the picture book biography *The People's Painter: How Ben Shahn Fought for Justice with Art* by Cynthia Levinson and illustrated by Evan Turk. This biography of Shahn traces his development as an artist who wanted his art to portray stories of real people who experienced hardships.

Beginning with the Depression until his death in 1969, his artwork brought social issues to the wider public and raised awareness of poor working conditions, poverty, unfair treatment of minoritized people, and other issues. The book's back matter includes both an author's note and an illustrator's note, a time line, bibliography, and source notes. Why was justice so important to Shahn? How did he use his artistic talent to repair the world? Does creating art—a picture, music, a sculpture, etc.—constitute an act of social justice, or should the artist be doing something else? When is art making social change?

Ezra Jack Keats, the son of Polish Jewish immigrants, gained prominence as a beloved illustrator of children's books. He created Peter in *The Snowy Day*, considered the first mainstream children's picture book that featured an African American child as the main character. The book won the Caldecott Medal and even prompted *The Snowy Day* postage stamp, with four different scenes of the character of Peter available.

A tribute is paid to Keats in *A Poem for Peter: The Story of Ezra Jack Keats and the Creation of The Snowy Day* by Andrea Davis Pinkney and illustrated by Lou Fancher and Steve Johnson. In this biography, children learn that Ezra Jack Keats was born Jacob Ezra Katz but changed his name as an adult due to anti-Semitism. During this time period, people with Jewish-sounding names were discriminated against in employment. Readers understand that he grew up in poverty and that his dreams of art school vanished when his father died suddenly a day before his high-school graduation.

The inspiration for Peter's character came from *Life* magazine photographs of an African American child. But it would be twenty years after saving this photo that Peter would spring to life. The book's back matter includes more information on "Ezra's Legacy" and "Keats, the Collage Poet." *The Snowy Day* is considered to have broken the color barrier in children's books and continues to be the most checked-out book in all categories at the New York Public Library (New York Public Library, 2020).

The Snowy Day was the first book that Keats both wrote and illustrated. Featuring an African American child as the main character caused controversy when the book was published. An oft-repeated statement is that "Art . . . is not a mirror, but a hammer: it does not reflect, it shapes [reality]" (originally from Trotsky, 1925, 137). Why did Keats decide to feature a Black child as the main character in *The Snowy Day*? How did Keats's book shape society? What kind of courage does it take to produce a work of art that shapes society? How did Keats and *The Snowy Day* contribute to repairing the world? Whenever someone creates art—whether visual, music, written, or other—he is taking a risk. Why do we think this risk is worth taking? How is art a way to shape reality and promote social justice?

REAL PEOPLE WHO MADE A DIFFERENCE

Several biographies of real people portray how they have practiced tikkun olam. Julius Rosenwald, the son of German Jewish immigrants and president of a major department store chain—Sears, Roebuck, and Company, befriended Booker T. Washington, a leading African American educator in the late nineteenth and early twentieth centuries. Rosenwald donated millions of dollars to build schools for African American children in the segregated South. With his assistance, 5,357 schools were built in fifteen southern states.

Marian Wright Edelman, founder and president emerita of the Children's Defense Fund, wrote a tribute to the Rosenwald schools in her online message to supporters in 2021. "As students start a new school year, this is a chance to honor the legacy of a group of schools that educated hundreds of thousands of Black children . . . by 1928 one in three rural Black school children in the South attended a Rosenwald school." Maya Angelou and Representative John Lewis are both alumni of Rosenwald schools. In addition, the Rosenwald Fund also supported Howard University and provided financial aid to African American students to pursue higher education.

Two children's books describe the difference that one person, Julius Rosenwald, can make in so many lives. *Schools of Hope: How Julius Rosenwald Helped Change*

SCHOOLS OF HOPE: HOW JULIUS ROSENWALD HELPED CHANGE AFRICAN AMERICAN EDUCATION

[In the early 1900s, Rosenwald, president of Sears, Roebuck and Company and a philanthropist, funded well-designed and well-equipped schools for many African Americans in the South.]

The text was fairly high for 9- to 10-year-old readers, so I chose to incorporate selections from the book as a read-aloud. I paired the book with a couple of video selections and Carole Boston Weatherford's picture book, *Dear Mr. Rosenwald*. Together, these resources illustrated a real-life story of *tikkun olam*—repair of the world—one of our school's values.

Students used questioning as a strategy to deepen their comprehension of the text. Some of the more meaningful questions students asked included: "Why were Rosenwald's

African American Education by Norman H. Finkelstein provides an informative account of Julius Rosenwald and the schools he helped to build. It is illustrated with archival photographs and images. The book explains that Rosenwald's desire to help others was influenced by Rabbi Emil Hirsch of Temple Sinai, who was committed to social justice. Rosenwald worked with Booker T. Washington and staff at Tuskegee Institute to begin a school-building project. Local communities would commit to raise funds and build the schools, with significant financial support from Rosenwald. The book describes the history of the schools, how they were built, and their impact on people's lives. The book's back matter includes source notes, a bibliography, and websites. Readers gain additional information from the captioned illustrations.

schools still segregated?" "Why did Rosenwald not want his Rosenwald Fund to go on forever?" "What were some of the teachings of Rabbi Emil Hirsch that influenced Rosenwald's social justice work?"

Beyond understanding Julius Rosenwald's philanthropic work, the book also inspired conversations about school and communities in general. It was inspiring to hear about the amount of community involvement that went into creating each Rosenwald school and how the Rosenwald schools brought more prosperity to the larger community. Through effort and community fund-raising, the Rosenwald schools were a true grassroots endeavor. This message of coming together, taking initiative, and dreaming big was a powerful message for students.

Maggie McCormick,
fourth-grade teacher,
private independent school, Utah

In the fictionalized picture book *Dear Mr. Rosenwald* by Carole Boston Weatherford and illustrated by R. Gregory Christie, the story of a Rosenwald school is told from the first-person perspective of a young, unnamed Black girl. It's 1921, and she attends a one-room school in the South. Her family earns a living by sharecropping. She learns that her church will be donating land to build a new school supported with funds from a man named Julius Rosenwald. The community, both Black and white, will also need to raise money for the school. In 1922 the White Oak School is completed, and the narrator writes a thank-you note to Mr. Rosenwald. An author's note provides additional factual information about the Rosenwald schools.

These books prompt many enduring questions: Why would one man contribute his fortune to help others? The book points out that many schools hung a portrait of Julius Rosenwald, though he preferred not to have his name identified with the buildings. Why did Rosenwald not want his name associated with the buildings? If you had a vast fortune, how would you spend it? How might you repair the world? What obligations to others do each of us have if we are lucky enough to be successful in our lives or if we become rich or are able to live in a nice and safe neighborhood? Are acts of tikkun olam acts of charity or acts of obligation? Are they *mitzvot*-like, commandments and obligations, or just whims of being nice? Why (and how) would providing educational opportunities be an act of justice?

Another Jewish philanthropist, Judah Touro, who lived in the 1800s, gave away his fortune in secret. His life is described in a fictionalized biography, *Judah Touro Didn't Want to Be Famous* by Audrey Ades with illustrations by Vivien Mildenberger. Judah set sail from Boston to New Orleans in 1801. There, he became a very successful shopkeeper and became very wealthy. After a serious injury in the War of 1812, Judah thought about why his life had been spared. He wondered what God had planned for him and decided to donate his fortune to making New Orleans a better city. He bought the freedom of enslaved Africans and funded hospitals, orphanages, schools, libraries, a synagogue for the growing Jewish population, and other things to benefit the people of the city. He did all of this secretly, because he didn't want to be famous.

Many of the enduring questions to ask about Judah Touro are similar to those for Julius Rosenwald. An additional important question is why Judah wanted his donations to be anonymous. Why might someone not want to be famous? How did Judah's buying the freedom of enslaved Africans and his donations help to repair the world?

What motivates someone to pursue a career in medical research and find a cure for polio? Children learn about Jonas Salk, who developed the polio vaccine, in *The Polio Pioneer: Dr. Jonas Salk and the Polio Vaccine* by Linda Elovitz Marshall. Born to Jewish immigrants, as a child Dr. Salk immersed himself in books. He wanted to have a career that would benefit others. When he finished medical school, Jonas collaborated with Dr. Thomas Francis to develop the vaccine against influenza (the flu). During this time, polio was affecting people of all ages including President Franklin Roosevelt. Jonas dedicated himself to finding a vaccine to prevent polio. He had many setbacks in his research. However, he eventually succeeded and found a vaccine for polio. To increase worldwide distribution, he refused profits from the vaccine. Today, polio has been almost completely eradicated. Dr. Salk was committed to helping people stay healthy. His work certainly reflected tikkun olam, repairing the world.

The conclusion of the book presents a challenge to readers on how they might make a difference in the world. This picture book biography, with a lengthy author's note, prompts enduring questions: Why do people dedicate their lives to helping others? Even if the task is challenging with setbacks, what motivates people to continue their work and never give up? Dr. Salk's polio vaccine had a worldwide impact, clearly repairing the world. Do you think he anticipated such results when he began his work? In what ways can children also use their talents and skills to make a difference in people's lives?

Jewish women have made prominent differences in the lives of others. Clara Lemlich's story is told in the picture book biography *Brave Girl: Clara and the Shirtwaist Makers' Strike of 1909* by Michelle Markel, with illustrations by Melissa Sweet. An immigrant to New York, Clara, like so many other immigrant girls, is hired in the garment industry. Hundreds of girls work with Clara at sewing machines in a locked factory. At the end of her shift, Clara attends night school. When working conditions become too deplorable, Clara leads the women on walkouts. She is fired, arrested, and beaten, but she never gives up. Union leaders meet to decide what to do throughout the city's garment factories. Clara shouts in Yiddish that they should strike, and thus begins the famous women's garment workers' strike of 1909.

The strike of women, some as young as twelve years old, garners attention of college girls and wealthy women who raise money and even picket with them. When the strike ends, the workweek is shortened, salaries are increased, and unions are formed. An afterword provides more

BRAVE GIRL: CLARA AND THE SHIRTWAIST MAKERS' STRIKE OF 1909

[During the 1890s, Clara arrives in America and supports her family by working long hours sewing in a factory for low wages. Clara leads the largest strike of women workers in U.S. history. A true story.]

I am a learning specialist at a Christian School. Ideals of social justice and "Seek first to understand rather than be understood," as well as "Love your neighbor as yourself" (Matthew 22:39), are core ideals that are imbedded in daily lessons for our learners. *Brave Girl* supports our respect for the Jewish people through a study of their history and culture each year within the curriculum.

I used *Brave Girl* to help address the essential question, "Why do people immigrate to new places?" I paired *Brave Girl* with *A Castle on Hester Street* and extended our essential question to "How would you feel if you had to flee your home, such as many of our new friends entering our country, our community, and even our school?" While reading the text, I stopped and modeled, "I think, I feel, I wonder" questions, encouraging students to write their responses, turn and talk, and share with the group.

Responses included: "Wow! I think Clara is so strong because she worked to help her family!" "Those guys were bullies!!" "I feel sad for Clara and her family because she STILL was hurt because she loved God!" "I wonder what she thought about America; it did not seem to factual information about the garment industry. A bibliography is included. (Clara's story is also part of the book *She Persisted: 13 American Women Who Changed the World* by Chelsea Clinton.)

One can't help but be inspired by this immigrant girl and her commitment to seek justice and better working conditions for hundreds of women employed in the garment industry. Even after she was beaten, Clara never gave up.

Brave Girl prompts a series of questions: Why did Clara "persist"? When we see injustice around us, what can we do to help? Why did the owners of the factories insist on such deplorable working conditions? Even if it is legal, is it ethical to hire teenage girls or children to work in a factory for low wages? What obligations do employers have to employees? Just because you might own a store or a factory or a business, do you get to establish working conditions and pay people whatever you want, or do you have a deeper obligation to treat your employees with respect? Should employees have the right to join a union and have collective bargaining?

get better for her!" "Hey! This is like Martin King; we talked about him today; he walked for people, too!" "I feel bad because our [Jewish] friends are still not treated nice . . . they were being bombed last summer, we prayed for them at church." "I wonder how Clara got to be so brave?"

All of these responses showed these young hearts seeking justice for all and gave another opportunity to discuss how we can be difference makers with new friends immigrating to America.

Stephanie K. Whitfield,
Independent learning specialist,
private religious school, Texas

Another Jewish woman who sought justice is Ruth Bader Ginsburg, the first Jewish woman to serve on the United States Supreme Court and a crusader for justice. Many biographies for children have been written about her. These include *Ruth Bader Ginsburg: The Case of R. B. G. vs. Inequality* by Jonah Winters and illustrated by Stacy Innerst; *I Dissent: Ruth Bader Ginsburg Makes Her Mark* by Debbie Levy and illustrated by Elizabeth Baddeley; *No Truth without Ruth: The Life of Ruth Bader Ginsburg* by Kathleen Krull and illustrated by Nancy Zhang; and *Ruth Objects: The Life of Ruth Bader Ginsburg* by Doreen Rappaport and illustrated by Eric Velasquez.

Born to immigrant parents, Ruth was influenced by her mother's desire for her not to be hindered because other people thought girls could not achieve. Her mother encouraged her to be the best she could be. Sadly, her mother died the day before Ruth graduated from high school, but her mother's hopes for Ruth remained an inspiration to her. These books describe the discrimination she faced in law school and in finding a law job. But Ruth never stopped pursuing what was just and fair for people and won many landmark cases as an attorney.

As a judge, she always sought justice for all. Throughout her life, Judge Ginsburg faced discrimination as a woman and as a Jew. How does a person overcome adversity to seek justice for others? In what ways was Judge Ginsburg a righteous person? How old do you need to be to be recognized as a righteous person? How many righteous acts must a person do to be considered righteous? Does a person have to be perfect to be considered righteous? In what ways do we recognize that everyone should be treated fairly and equitably, regardless of gender, religion, or other reasons? What does it mean to treat a person fairly and equitably? What does it mean to fight for people according to their universal rights? Sometimes it seems as if fairness, justice, and equity are very difficult to obtain. How can a person still have optimism when it is so difficult and we still have so far to go to ensure fairness, justice, and equity for all?

Many elementary students have heard of the Statue of Liberty, but do they know that the famous words, "Give me your tired, your poor, Your huddled masses yearning to breathe free" were written by a Jewish woman, Emma Lazarus, who was committed to social justice? Two picture-book biographies tell the story of Emma Lazarus: *Emma's Poem: The Voice of the Statue of Liberty* by Linda Glaser; and *Liberty's Voice: The Story of Emma Lazarus* by Erica Silverman.

Emma was born to a wealthy Jewish family in New York City. After meeting immigrants at Wards Island, Emma dedicated herself to helping them through raising funds, teaching English, and other efforts. As a writer, Emma used her pen in poems and newspaper articles to create awareness about the poor living conditions and needs of immigrants. Emma learned that France was building a statue for New York Harbor and that to finance the project, authors and poets were asked to write something for a book collection that would be sold.

Emma's poem "The New Colossus" expressed her views about oppressed people. Unfortunately, Emma passed away when she was thirty-eight, before the statue was completed, and her words were engraved on a plaque in the statue's pedestal.

What motivates a wealthy person—or anyone else—to relate to the needs of those less fortunate? How did Emma use her talent to inspire others to care about the immigrants to the United States? What do Emma's words—"Give me your tired, your poor, Your huddled masses yearning to breathe free"— mean for the experience of immigrants today? What are our obligations to people who want to immigrate? What are our obligations to people in our community who are immigrants? What are our obligations to people who are immigrants in communities beyond our own?

FINAL THOUGHTS

The wise rabbi in *The Peddler and the Baker* by Yael Molchadsky and illustrated by Liora Grossman teaches a valuable lesson on justice. A poor, hard-working peddler lives above a bakery. Although he cannot afford to buy the bread, he enjoys inhaling the smells from the bakery. The baker complains to the rabbi that the peddler is enjoying the smells of his bread without paying. The rabbi instructs the peddler to work extra hard during the week and return on Friday with his earnings. When the peddler returns, he gives his earnings to the rabbi. The rabbi takes the bag of coins and shakes it. The rabbi asks the baker if he enjoyed hearing the sound of the clinking coins. When the baker responds that he did, the rabbi explains that hearing the clinking coins is the baker's payment for allowing the peddler to smell the bread.

This story prompts many questions: Was it just for the baker to expect payment from someone smelling his bread? How has the rabbi taught the baker about fairness and justice? What things in the world should be free for everyone, regardless of how poor or rich they are? How can we teach others about what it means to be just?

THE PEDDLER AND THE BAKER

[*The Peddler and the Baker* by Yael Molchadsky and illustrated by Liora Grossman is a folktale about a poor peddler who lives over a bakery. The peddler loves the smells of fresh bread. The baker wants the peddler to pay for the smells.]

I used *The Peddler and the Baker* in my third-grade classroom as part of our unit on opinion writing. My students come from varying backgrounds, so before reading the book we discussed three vocabulary words: *peddler* (someone who travels to sell their merchandise/wares), *baker* (someone who cooks food to sell), and *rabbi* (a religious leader in a Jewish community) to ensure the understanding of the book.

While reading this book my students were extremely invested in the apparent injustice and possible outcomes. Students were frequently heard gasping or whispering, "That's not fair," or "Why would he do that?" This book led to a deeper discussion of human rights and what should innately be free for all people. The discussion quickly led from the literal comparisons from the book (smells, sounds) to higher-level concepts (attending school, fire department, police protection), and even to things that aren't always free that my students feel should be (e.g., college education, health care, visiting zoos).

In this chapter, books are discussed that explore justice, righteousness, and repairing the world in the Jewish tradition. Real and fictional people set about repairing the world in many different ways. In what ways can students themselves be agents of change? In addition to discussing the many enduring questions that these books foster, students can find concrete ways to seek justice and repair the world within their own school, community, or beyond. Children, indeed, can help to repair the world, and educators have a responsibility to prepare the next generation to do so.

Later, we were able to revisit the book when discussing the concept of empathy as the students discussed how they felt such strong feelings about what was happening to the peddler even though they had never been in that situation before. As a closing activity, I asked my students, "Should other teachers have this book in their classroom?" Their responses were an overwhelming "Yes." Their reasons included: "I liked the lesson that it taught," "Their students will start asking questions," and "I really liked the book."

JoAnne Boulware, third-grade teacher, public school, South Carolina

WORKS CITED

Children's Literature

Ades, Audrey. *Judah Touro Didn't Want to Be Famous*. Illustrated by Vivien Mildenberger. Minneapolis: Kar-Ben, 2020.

———. *The Rabbi and the Reverend: Joachim Prinz, Martin Luther King Jr., and Their Fight against Silence*. Illustrated by Chiara Fedele. Minneapolis: Kar-Ben, 2021.

Blankman, Anne. *The Blackbird Girls*. New York: Viking, 2020.

Churnin, Nancy. *Dear Mr. Dickens*. Illustrated by Bethany Stancliffe. Chicago: Albert Whitman, 2021.

Clinton, Chelsea. *She Persisted: 13 American Women Who Changed the World*. Illustrated by Alexandra Boiger. New York: Philomel, 2017.

Cohen, Tziporah. *No Vacancy*. Toronto: Groundwood Press, 2020.

Faruqi, Saadia, and Laura Shovan. *A Place at the Table*. New York: Clarion, 2020.

Finkelstein, Norman H. *Schools of Hope: How Julius Rosenwald Helped Change African American Education*. Honesdale, PA: Calkins Creek, 2014.

Glaser, Linda. *Emma's Poem: The Voice of the Statue of Liberty*. Illustrated by Claire A. Nivola. Boston: Houghton Mifflin Harcourt, 2010.

Korman, Gordon. *Linked*. New York: Scholastic, 2021.

Krull, Kathleen. *No Truth without Ruth: The Life of Ruth Bader Ginsburg*. Illustrated by Nancy Zhang. New York: HarperCollins, 2018.

Levinson, Cynthia. *The People's Painter: How Ben Shahn Fought for Justice with Art.* Illustrated by Evan Turk. New York: Abrams Books for Young Readers, 2021.

Levy, Debbie. *I Dissent: Ruth Bader Ginsburg Makes Her Mark.* Illustrated by Elizabeth Baddeley. New York: Simon & Schuster, 2016.

Macy, Sue. *The Book Rescuer: How a Mensch from Massachusetts Saved Yiddish Literature for Generations to Come.* Illustrated by Stacy Innerst. New York: Simon & Schuster, 2019.

Malaspina, Ann. *A Scarf for Keiko.* Illustrated by Merrilee Liddiard. Minneapolis: Kar-Ben, 2019.

Markel, Michelle. *Brave Girl: Clara and the Shirtwaist Makers' Strike of 1909.* Illustrated by Melissa Sweet. New York: HarperCollins, 2013.

Marshall, Linda Elovitz. *The Polio Pioneer: Dr. Jonas Salk and the Polio Vaccine.* Illustrated by Lisa Anchin. New York: Knopf Books for Young Readers, 2020.

Michelson, Richard. *As Good as Anybody: Martin Luther King, Jr., and Abraham Joshua Heschel's Amazing March toward Freedom.* Illustrated by Raul Colón. New York: Knopf, 2008.

———. *Fascinating: The Life of Leonard Nimoy.* Illustrated by Edel Rodriguez. New York: Knopf, 2016.

Molchadsky, Yael. *The Peddler and the Baker.* Illustrated by Liora Grossman. Translated by Annette Appel. S. Yorkshire, UK: Green Bean Books, 2020.

Pinkney, Andrea Davis. *A Poem for Peter: The Story of Ezra Jack Keats and the Creation of The Snowy Day.* Illustrated by Lou Fancher and Steve Johnson. New York: Viking, 2016.

Rappaport, Doreen. *Ruth Objects: The Life of Ruth Bader Ginsburg.* Illustrated by Eric Velasquez. New York: Disney-Hyperion, 2020.

Rose, Lisa. *The Singer and the Scientist.* Illustrated by Isabel Muñoz. Minneapolis: Kar-Ben, 2021.

Schwartz, Howard. *Gathering Sparks.* Illustrated by Kristina Swarner. New York: Roaring Brook Press, 2010.

Silverman, Erica. *Liberty's Voice: The Story of Emma Lazarus.* Illustrated by Stacey Schuett. New York: Dutton Children's Books, 2011.

Weatherford, Carole Boston. *Dear Mr. Rosenwald.* Illustrated by R. Gregory Christie. New York: Scholastic, 2006.

Winter, Jonathan. *Ruth Bader Ginsburg: The Case of R. G. B. vs. Inequality.* Illustrated by Stacy Innerst. New York: Harry N. Abrams, 2017.

References

Edelman, M. W. "Remembering the Rosenwald Schools." Child Watch Column. Children's Defense Fund, 2021. Retrieved April 24, 2022, from https://www.childrensdefense.org/child-watch-columns/health/2021/remembering-the-rosenwald-schools/.

McDew, C., with B. Gilfix. *Tell the Story: A Memoir of the Civil Rights Movement.* Newtown, MA: Beryl Gilfix, 2020.

New York Public Library. *Classic Children's Story* The Snowy Day *Tops the New York Public Library's All-Time Checkouts List*, 2020. Retrieved April 25, 2022, from https://www.nypl.org/press/press-release/january-13-2020/classic-childrens-story-snowy-day-tops-new-york-public-librarys.

Trotsky, L. *Literature and Revolution.* Translated by R. Strunsky. New York: International Publishers, 1925.

Chapter 8

How Might We Imagine Life for Ourselves Together in the World? Using Jewish Children's Literature in Multicultural Education

> Books are sometimes windows, offering views of worlds that may be real or imagined, familiar or strange. These windows are also sliding glass doors, and readers have only to walk through in imagination to become part of whatever world has been created or recreated by the author. (Bishop, 1990, ix)

Teachers often use children's literature to help students imagine themselves in a world marked by caring, acceptance, friendship, and fulfillment—a world in which their dreams and the dreams of others can be realized. Although Jewish children's literature may be used by itself to engage students in enduring questions, Jewish children's literature can also be used in combination with other multicultural children's literature. Indeed, the diversity of students in our schools, in our nation, and in the world calls for teachers to help students imagine (and work for) a world in which people take pride in themselves and in their own cultural backgrounds, histories, and literatures as well as respect and appreciate those of others. We hope this book will inspire educators of preschool–sixth grade to integrate Jewish children's literature within a body of diverse and multicultural children's literature.

The concept of addressing enduring questions with Jewish children's literature has been presented throughout the previous chapters, but teachers may still wonder:

- Where in their curriculum will they introduce Jewish children's literature and pose enduring questions?
- Are there specific questions to pose pertaining to a given story?
- How might enduring questions be used to encourage children to think deeply about their own heritage as well as connecting with other children's heritages?

Often, teachers implement curricula arranged in themes or topics (e.g., animals, family life, folktales, friendship, holidays, nature/environment), discipline areas (e.g., social studies, science, language arts), or set aside space within the curricula to specifically connect with children's interests and events in their own lives and the world. (Appendix A lists Jewish children's literature by themes traditionally used in preschool through elementary classrooms.) Implementing high-quality children's literature with enduring questions has many possibilities to become a part of your curriculum and instructional practices.

This chapter discusses ways to integrate Jewish children's literature with other high-quality multicultural literature to support all children in imagining lives for themselves with others in the world. Four themes are presented as examples to consider within your curriculum: exploring inclusivity, building community, keeping memories, and preserving nature and the environment. Many teachers are already using these themes in their curriculum.

These themes align with the Jewish concept of tikkun olam as protecting the health and welfare of humanity, the environment, the Earth, and pursuing justice. Each of the themes describes how a Jewish children's book might be paired with other multicultural books. Of course, these are only examples. You'll want to include other books such as your favorites or those books that have special relevance to your students or a particular period of the school year.

Each book is summarized to frame enduring questions. After the books and questions are introduced, ways to extend children's knowledge in the form of activities are provided. These activities help children better understand the messages from the books by being culturally relevant, hands-on, activity-oriented, inquiry-based, and/or project-based. In addition, action-based projects are included to help children address problems within their immediate lives and communities.

EXPLORING INCLUSIVITY

In Jewish tradition, an obligation exists to ensure equal access for all people and to help facilitate the full participation of individuals with disabilities. Furthermore, ethical teachings and rules of conduct from rabbinic Jewish tradition state that we must prevent anyone from being separated from the community against their will (Pirke Avot 2:5).

Young children often take the world for granted. Although children (and others) around them are excluded from activities and places because of a disability, or because, for example, they speak a different language, wear different clothes, eat different foods, or are racially different, young children often are not aware that this is wrong. They may be unaware that exclusion causes pain. Even if they are the ones excluded, they may believe their pain to be "normal."

In *Cakes and Miracles; A Purim Tale* by Barbara Diamond Goldin and illustrated by Erika Weihs, Hershel is a young child who is blind. (This book was described in chapter 4.) All he wants to do is help his mother with the household chores and do all the things other children do. He sees helping with chores as a way to express his love for his mother and for his family and a way to feel good about himself. Who will help her when she gets too old to bake, clean, cook, sew, and do household chores? He wants the opportunity to be that person.

In the story, the holiday of Purim is approaching. Purim is a holiday that children love. Not only do they dress up in costumes, but they also eat *hamantaschen*. Purim is an important holiday because it celebrates the courage and strength of Esther and women more generally as they saved the Jews from a genocide. Hershel would like to help his mother make hamantaschen and other baked goods, but his mother perceives his lack of vision as hindering his abilities to help with Purim festivities. Hershel struggles to consider how

CAKES AND MIRACLES

[Hershel wishes he would be allowed to help his mother bake hamantaschen pastries, but his mother thinks he's incapable because he is blind.]

I read the book to my first-grade class connecting it to our monthly skill builder, empathy. The class is primarily composed of children who are white. There are no Jewish students in the class.

We started by reviewing empathy and discussing how everyone is unique, special, and appreciating differences. Then, I explained the value of learning about people's cultures including their celebrations. I showed a video introducing the Jewish celebration, Purim, and we held a discussion about the importance of the holiday. We watched a few short clips showing the activities of Jewish people participating in this holiday. The children were engaged in the story of Esther having courage and standing up to the king. They were also excited about the yummy treats in the shape of hats.

Next, we read the story and thought about what it might feel like to be blind and not be allowed to do certain activities. The kids made connections to having a disability, which doesn't mean you can't do things, just like Hershel. The children also talked about how they might have empathy when they see someone different from them, and not stare or say mean things. We also talked about how we are all unique and might have struggles, but if others have empathy and help each other, we can achieve great he can help, especially given his mother's reluctance to view him as capable.

An angel appears to Hershel in a dream and helps him imagine how to cut out cookies from the dough. He does so and bakes the cookies. Hershel's mother now sees Hershel as having abilities and strengths that she had not imagined that he had. Is it a miracle that an angel came to help Hershel figure out how to cut cookie dough and bake cookies? Or is it a miracle that Hershel's mother came to see Hershel with a different attitude toward him?

We have other important questions to ask about Hershel's mother. Although she loved him, she might have perceived his blindness as an obstacle preventing him from demonstrating his abilities to be part of Jewish life and helping her. Was it fair for her not to let Hershel help with household chores and baking at the beginning? Why did she assume that he could not cut cookie dough and bake cookies? Is she showing her love by protecting him? Was it fair and just that Hershel had to prove that he could bake cookies and carry out household chores?

Often when a person is excluded for some type of difference, many people not only assume a negative attitude toward the person's abilities but also reject the whole person. This negative attitude is countered in the story *My Brother Charlie*. The story portrays an African American family that includes mother (author, Holly Robinson Peete), father, Charlie's twin sister (and coauthor), and Charlie, who has autism. They are a loving family but struggle to understand Charlie. The family wants to communicate with Charlie. Not only do they find it very difficult, but they are hurt by his lack of verbal sharing of feelings, particularly that he has never shown or told his mother that he loves her. Of course, he does love her, but he cannot show her that he loves her in ways that she will understand. The family doesn't give up. Through their love, courage, and patience, they slowly learn about Charlie's strengths, interests, dislikes, and how he demonstrates feelings. At the end of the story, his sister bangs her foot, and Charlie runs to her, patting her back and verbally stating his love for her.

After reading *My Brother Charlie*, additional enduring questions can be considered about Hershel from *Cakes & Miracles*. Charlie was unable to tell his mother that he loved her in ways his mother could easily understand; is

> things. It was wonderful to share a new cultural celebration with the children and help them build their eagerness to welcome all sorts of people into their worlds.
>
> They are very excited for the actual date of Purim, and I am going to look into finding the hamantaschen pastries for the kids.
>
> Katy McKenney, 1st grade, public school, Montana

Hershel's mother showing that she loves him by excluding him from doing household chores and baking? After all, she is trying to protect him. But is that a show of love? Did Hershel's mother realize how Hershel felt? Did Charlie's family realize how he felt? Do all human beings have this problem—that we find it difficult to know how others feel, especially if people are different? How are Charlie's strengths and Hershel's strengths recognized? How might Hershel's family and Charlie's family learn about their children's strengths? How might we all respect each other and feel worthy in this world? How do you express caring for others other than verbally to your family members, classmates, and others? How might you play with Charlie and Hershel? How are you like Charlie and Hershel?

Some ways to extend children's knowledge of the books and encourage children to explore these questions is to have them draw, write, or perform an activity they do well. Examples include

- an activity where they have helped a family or community member, or
- an interest they enjoy doing (singing, dancing, art, gardening).

In preparation, they might want to talk first with a family member or a teacher. The two books explained in this section are used mostly with young children as a read-aloud by the teacher.

The following two books in this theme of inclusivity are for older elementary-age children. These books are much longer and address more complex topics. They can be read to the whole class in chapters followed by discussion of enduring questions. They can also be used in book groups where students select a book to read and discuss enduring questions, exploring similarities and differences between the books, the characters, and the stories.

Bluish by Virginia Hamilton is a story about a fifth-grade girl. Her given name is Natalie, but her classmates nickname her "Bluish" for her skin color resulting from chemotherapy. She has a form of blood cancer and attends school periodically by traveling in a wheelchair with a small dog. Her classmates, except for Dreenie and Tuli, stay away from her. They exclude her from their conversations and treat her with contempt due to her fragile appearance and the fact that she wears a knitted hat to cover her head.

Why can't these children look beyond Natalie's appearance to see a caring individual? Dreenie is new to the school and becomes curious about Bluish. Dreenie keeps a diary of what she is learning about Bluish and begins to find ways to interact with her, such as moving her wheelchair and including her in a small-group class project. Bluish reciprocates by inviting Dreenie to her home to play and knitting special caps for Dreenie and Tuli.

The race and ethnicity of the children and their parents is unclear. The book cover shows a picture of three girls assumed to be Bluish, Tuli, and Dreenie. In the story, we know that Bluish's mother is Jewish because the family celebrates Hanukkah. Dreenie's family celebrates Kwanzaa and Christmas.

As students read, they can be encouraged to ask questions about why the author is ambiguous about the race of the characters in the story. Why is it that people feel awkward and reluctant to make friends with people who are ill or who are different from them? What does it take to see yourself in someone who is ill or who is different from you? Some may not know much about an illness such as cancer and be afraid. What does it take to overcome that fear and ignorance?

Lucky Broken Girl by Ruth Behar is about another fifth-grade girl and is a fictionalized recounting of part of Ruth Behar's youth. This award-winning historical novel is about Ruthie, who is bedridden for more than a year in a body cast from a broken leg she received in a terrible car accident. Ruthie and her family are Jewish and have emigrated from Cuba to New York, leaving behind Fidel Castro's communist government. During the time Ruthie is bedridden, she experiences physical exclusion from much of the world. Her life is rearranged by what and who come to her bedside. She learns important lessons about exclusion. For example, her good friend Ramu sneaks to visit her against his parents' wishes. Ramu's problem is that he must disobey his parents in order to be a good friend and visit Ruthie.

Ruthie learns of other forms of exclusion: her relatives tell her stories of her family being hated and expelled from Poland because they were Jewish. She discusses with her tutor, Joy, reasons Martin Luther King Jr. is protesting segregation and people who hate African Americans. For a while Ruthie hates the boys in the car who caused her accident. But during that year her feelings change, and she stops hating them.

When someone is excluded, like Ruthie, what is needed to break down the isolation? Is it enough just to let people visit, or is more needed? Ruthie has been in a car accident and is isolated for a long time. She is in a lot of mental and physical pain. She hates the boys who caused the accident. When people hate, what are the consequences of that hate (even if they feel justified in that hate)? What does it take to get over that hate?

BUILDING COMMUNITY

Kehillah (Hebrew for community) has historically been an important local, organizing, and communal structure for Jewish life. Like everyone else, Jews belong to many communities, including Jewish communities. Belonging to a community affirms one's social identities, values, and beliefs by providing for its members' physical and spiritual needs. In a society such as the United States where everyone lives in and among diverse communities, people continuously and frequently interact with others who may differ in their religion, culture, or other ways of being in the world. Unfortunately, too often people, including Jews, experience injustices due to differences. How might children become responsible and implement acts of social justice that support members in their community or other communities?

These types of discussions regarding responsibilities to one's community and other communities often provide connections to other children, their families, and teachers by learning about their similar and unique ways of life. Furthermore, once children understand what is happening in their local communities, it is easier for them to understand with some depth issues of justice and injustice globally. The following books with enduring questions and ways to respond to the books provide examples of how to help children further think about themselves as members of a community and their responsibilities to others.

In *Red and Green and Blue and White* by Lee Wind and illustrated by Paul O. Zelinsky, Isaac and his parents are the only family in their community who celebrate Hanukkah. They celebrate by decorating their window with a menorah and colors of blue and white while the other houses celebrate Christmas with decorative trees and colors of red and green.

Someone throws a stone through Isaac's window, extinguishing the menorah light. The culprit is unknown. After Isaac's family gives much consideration as to whether to relight the candles, they decide to do so. Once their candles are lit again, Teresa, Isaac's good friend, draws a menorah and places her drawing in the window of her house. Following on this sign of support, the rest of the community draws menorahs and hangs them in their houses or proudly shows them in the community. This picture book is based on a true incident that occurred in Billings, Montana, in 1993.

In *Red and Green and Blue and White*, the entire community showed their support. That doesn't happen in all cases. What makes people show their support publicly? Isaac's family had to be brave to relight the menorah candles. Why did they have to have courage to do so? Why did someone hate Isaac's family and their menorah so much that they threw a stone through the window at the menorah? What can we do to counter such hate?

In *Red and Green and Blue and White* the entire community came together to fight hate. However, sometimes people are not so brave. Often, barriers come between people and between communities. People do not know each other and do not learn to appreciate their differences. In the previous discussion of exploring inclusivity using children's literature, some children were excluded because of some type of difference. In a town, people may physically exclude themselves by separating in groups and by putting up signs or obstacles such as fences that keep certain groups from interacting with each other. How does one break down such barriers?

Breaking down a barrier is demonstrated in the story of *Daniel and Ismail* by Jan Pablo Iglesias and illustrated by Alex Peris. The story features two boys, Daniel and Ismail, who live in the same city, have the exact same birth date, and enjoy playing soccer. They are from two different nationalities that historically have been in conflict with each other. Daniel is Jewish and speaks Hebrew; Ismail is Palestinian and speaks Arabic.

The book is written in three languages, Hebrew, Arabic, and English. The use of Hebrew and Arabic values both boys' primary languages. The first page of the story opens from right to left, customary for Hebrew and Arabic books.

In this story, the reader learns that clothes might represent sacred traditions of their cultures but can also be negatively interpreted as an attempt to keep people apart. For his birthday, Daniel is given a *tallit*, a fringed garment with twined and knotted fringes (*tzitzit*) attached to its four corners. It is worn by Jews as a religious garment, and during prayers and worship. Ismail, for his birthday, is given a *keffiyeh*, shaped from a square scarf, commonly worn by Arabs and others who live in dry, hot regions providing protection from the sun, dust, and sand. The keffiyeh, worn by Palestinian men, has also become a symbol of Palestinian nationalism (Kim, 2007). The boys are also each given a soccer ball for their birthdays.

In the story, Daniel and Ismail, who haven't met previously, are having a good time playing soccer together in the park. Not keeping track of the time, they find themselves late for dinner and rush home in the dark, Daniel with the keffiyeh and Ismail with the tallit. Both boys' parents yell at their children for bringing the OTHER's item into the home.

The next day, both boys return to the park, and give back their respective pieces of clothing. They share with each other how difficult it is to be the other (a Jew and a Palestinian) and what their community thinks about the "other" community. The story ends with Daniel and Ismail continuing to play soccer together as they did the previous day.

What type of loyalty must you have to your parents for following their rules? How do you think Daniel and Ismail found the courage to go against their parents' wishes and play with each other? When is it OK to disobey one's parents? Daniel and Ismail are both proud of their own community, yet they enjoy playing soccer together. How can someone be proud and loyal to their own community, yet also be proud and enjoy having friends from other communities? Daniel and Ismail's continuing to play soccer together might be called an act of courage to interact with people considered different from themselves.

An act of courage is evident in *The Other Side* by Jacqueline Woodson, with illustrations by E. B. Lewis. On one side of a very long fence lives an African American girl, Clover, whose mother tells her not to go on the other side of the fence. On the other side of the fence lives a white girl, Annie, who is also told not to go on the other side of the fence. It is summer, and Clover sees Annie spending a lot of time by herself, hanging out on her side. Annie seems to be staring at Clover and her friends.

Early in the story, Annie asks to jump rope with Clover and her friends, but one of Clover's friends says no. Clover and Annie slowly get to know each other by sitting together on the fence, an action they think is allowed because neither has gone over the fence.

There seems to be a lot of pressure on Annie and Clover, both from peers and adults, not to become friends. What kind of courage does it take to resist that pressure to form new relationships and friendships? How is the situation in *The Other Side* the same or different from that in *Red and Green and Blue and White?* In *Daniel and Ismail?*

Here are some ways to extend children's understandings of the messages in these books:

- Walk around the community to explore rules, icons, signs, and written communications that exclude or include people. In addition to signs, are there subtle ways that people are excluded or included within and from the community? Are there unwritten rules that prevent people from being more inclusive and from interacting with others who might have a different culture, religion, language, or history?
- Design signs that are friendly and accessible to all people in your community and school.
- Learn through books and videos about the civil rights movement and other movements for inclusion, equity, and social justice.
- Invite into the classroom people in the community who have been leaders in advocating for inclusion, equity, and social justice.
- In *Red and Green and Blue and White*, an act of violence disturbed the right of Isaac and his family to celebrate Hanukkah. Think of a holiday that you like to celebrate. Imagine that for some reason, this year you wouldn't be allowed to celebrate this holiday in public. Express your feelings by writing a poem, drawing a picture, or composing a song.
- Select an injustice that occurred in your school, neighborhood, or city. Learn about it by having community members inform the students. Write letters, draw, or use other ways to show support for the people who are victims of this injustice.

In addition to addressing exclusion and hate based on differences, it is important for children to learn to help create an inclusive, caring, and just community. The award-winning book *The Last Stop on Market Street* by Matt de la Peña and illustrated by Christian Robinson provides important lessons about building community. Every Sunday after church, CJ and his Nana take the bus to its last stop on Market Street to volunteer at a soup kitchen. One Sunday, CJ begins to wonder why they don't have a car and have to wait in the rain to take a bus, and why they always make this same trip. Nana helps CJ appreciate his physical surroundings of their community, the special people who make up their community, and the importance of belonging to this community.

In *Red and Green and Blue and White* people from different communities come together after an act of hate. In *Daniel and Ismail* and *The Other Side*, children from different communities come together after refusing to accept being segregated. All of these actions require courage. In *Last Stop on Market Street*, CJ and Nana are proactive in building community and caring for others. This also takes courage. What kind of courage is needed to build community, to build caring across communities, and to enact caring and just relationships?

KEEPING MEMORIES

What is a memory? Why is it important to hold on to memories? How do memories impact us?

The Hebrew word for remember—*zakhor*—is noted multiple times in the Hebrew Bible. Traditions, rituals, and narratives are ways for keeping shared memories. For example, during the holiday of Passover, Jews retell the story of the exodus from slavery in Egypt. The story is told as if the people in the present are themselves being freed from slavery. Through these recollections and by telling their stories, we are reminded that we stand on the shoulders of our ancestors so their experiences, teachings, and sacrifices will never be forgotten. Rabbi Marc Baker of the Combined Jewish Philanthropies states, "We root ourselves in the past so we know where we come from and so we feel part of a People and a story that gives meaning to our lives. We learn lessons from the past to help us interpret and make meaning of the present, which in turn informs the choices we make today as we write the story of tomorrow" (2020).

Tía Fortuna's New Home: A Jewish Cuban Journey by Ruth Behar, illustrated by Devon Holzwarth, features Tía Fortuna sharing her Sephardic heritage with her granddaughter, Estrella. The story begins when her ancestors lived in Spain until they were forced to leave in 1492 because they were Jewish. Some settled in Cuba, such as Tía's family. Generations later, her family moved to Miami. In the story, Tía Fortuna is making still another move from a home in Miami to a different home in Miami. Estrella doesn't understand why Tía Fortuna is not bringing a lot of items to her new place. Tía responds that she is bringing her memories with her.

Why are memories so important to Tía Fortuna? She keeps her memories in her mind. How do memories shape our relationships with others? With family? With ourselves? What memories are worth remembering? What items are worth keeping? Some memories belong just to us. Other memories are shared. What makes a memory worth sharing?

Another story of memories is *The Bracelet* by Yoshiko Uchida, illustrated by Joanna Yardley. It is World War II, shortly after the outbreak of war with Japan. Emi, a second grader, and her family are very sad and angry. The U.S. government is forcing them and other people of Japanese descent, including U.S. citizens, to leave their homes. They are to be imprisoned in isolated camps. Shortly before the family leaves their home, Emi's best friend, Laurie, comes to say goodbye and gives her a bracelet to remember their friendship. Emi puts the bracelet on her wrist and vows to always wear it. But when she gets to the camp, Emi finds that her bracelet is lost. Emi fears that with its loss, she won't remember her best friend. However, the next day as she unpacks her clothes, she has memories of Laurie and realizes that she doesn't need the bracelet, after all, to remember her friend.

The U.S. government is treating Emi and her family as if they are enemies and criminals. They are being robbed of their dignity, their home, their livelihood, their neighborhood. All that Emi can take with her—besides a few items—is her memory of a friend. How is such a memory important? How does such a memory counter the nightmare of being unjustly imprisoned?

Why do we want to keep and cherish items that are given to us by special people in our lives? Do we need the items if we'll always have the memories? What memories are important to remember—only good memories, or should we remember bad memories as well?

Toni Morrison in *Remember: The Journey to School Integration* provides important reasons for remembering difficult memories. She takes the reader on a journey through pages of photographs before segregated schools were declared unconstitutional in *Brown v. Board of Education* in 1954. She writes about the importance of memories—even painful memories—and how they lead to understanding and to an open mind and heart.

Many of the photographs in this book are, indeed, painful but also provide a message of compassion for humanity and hope for a better future. The pictures in the book are not memories of events that children have themselves experienced. However, the pictures hold memories that, as a nation, belong to all of us. Reading *Remember: The Journey to School Integration* requires more than just understanding the times depicted in the pictures. It requires accepting the collective memories of those times as one's own. What obligations do people have to take hold of the collective memories of the communities to which they belong? What does accepting those collective memories do for us and for our communities? To our relationships with others? To how we conceive the future together with others who may or may not be like us?

Some of the memories in *Remember: The Journey to School Integration* are of segregation. Inherently, segregation is evil. How do we confront segregation? Why do people not like or interact with other people because of their skin color, their place of origin, their language, religion, or sexuality? How can memories of exclusion and pain be used to create a future of community, caring, and justice?

Extending the knowledge of students includes helping them to learn about their own histories and memories as well those of others. Here are a few activities that may be helpful:

- Interview a grandparent, an elderly member of your family, or a senior citizen in the community about when they were young. What games/activities did they engage in? What historical events do they remember from their childhood? What photographs do they have of themselves during this time?
- Interview a senior citizen from a community that is different than your own (perhaps teaming with someone else in the classroom).
- Explore your family's places of origin (and that of other families). On a world map, locate children's places of origin.
- Identify an artifact that holds memories of your family's or community's history and culture (e.g., recipes, items, jewelry, written texts).
- Select key events that have special memories for your family or for your community.

PRESERVING NATURE AND THE ENVIRONMENT

A philosophical principle that many Jews hold comes from the book of Genesis in the Hebrew Bible. The principle is that human beings have a responsibility to the world by cultivating it, protecting it, and using it wisely. This principle has become more critical as climate change has become more severe in damaging the environment.

The Jewish people were originally primarily an agrarian society, and many Jewish festivals are agricultural celebrations. For example, the Jewish holiday Tu B'Shevat is celebrated in many Jewish communities all over the world as an ecological awareness day, and trees are planted in celebration. Three books address this important theme of preserving nature and the environment.

In *Pearl Moscowitz's Last Stand* by Arthur A. Levine, Pearl recalls the many changes and lives shared on Gingko Street. The street was named after the many ginko trees that Pearl's mother advocated to have planted on the block. Immigrants of many different nationalities celebrate their traditions and other holidays with each other under these trees. Over generations trees had been struck down by lightning, decay, and urban renewal. But when a man from the city comes to take down the last tree, Pearl does all she can to prevent the tree from being cut down. She coaxes him with food, conversation, and persuasion. Her "last stand" involves chaining herself around the tree.

Why are trees important not only to this neighborhood but to the rest of the world? How do trees address climate change? How do you protect trees? What is the community's responsibility for keeping people in their community, especially those who have lived there and contributed to the community for generations? Why did Pearl need to put herself in danger to attract attention from the city officials not to cut down the tree? Pearl might have been taken to jail; what sacrifices should one consider taking to preserve the environment?

Pearl Moscowitz's Last Stand focused on preserving the environment by a little girl's protesting the cutting down of one tree in her neighborhood. How are lives protected when we preserve a forest of trees that seems so very far away from us? *Zonia's Rain Forest* by Jana Martinez-Neal provides an opportunity to address just such a situation, preserving a forest far away from children in the United States. The book is about a young girl who is part of the Asháninka community and lives in the Peruvian Amazon rain forest. The book portrays her bond with her family, the animals, fish, reptiles, and other creatures of the rain forest.

One day she is walking back to her mother from the forest when she finds part of the forest destroyed. Zonia brings back broken sticks from the destroyed area to her mother, exclaiming that the forest needs help. Her mother responds by stating that the forest is speaking to her. Then, Zonia states that she will answer.

The last words of the story call for all of us to answer. How will we answer? Will the rest of the world allow a young girl and her family to be the only ones to answer because they live in the forest? What is our responsibility to a place where we don't live? Are we able to protect every place on Earth, or do we choose places to protect? Why is it so important to protect forests?

Similar questions might also be asked about the Dakota Access Pipeline that has been the target of a movement to protect clean water and maintain wildlife and plants. In 2016, the Standing Rock Sioux tribe stood up against the oil industry protesting the building of this pipeline that would destroy sacred burial grounds and the waterways. This movement has extended to many tribal nations around the world. Although the industry insisted that the pipeline would be safe, many oil leaks have occurred each year in pipelines around the world.

The book *We Are Water Protectors* written by Carole Linds of the Ojibwe tribe and illustrated by Michaele Goade of the Tlingit and Haida Indian tribes tells this empowering story that won a Caldecott Medal as well as receiving other awards. A young Sioux girl recalls the story her grandmother told, warning that a black snake would come to contaminate the water source. The black snake in the story is a metaphor in response to the construction of the Dakota Access Pipeline.

The story highlights the importance of water to the Indigenous peoples described as the first medicine and nourishment of life. The young girl takes a social action stand against the black snake and encourages readers, similar to the Jewish tradition, to be stewards of the Earth.

All three books end with asking readers what they will do to protect the Earth. Some activities to extend student knowledge about protecting the environment are:

- Learn the impact of climate change through local newspapers, videos, and community members.
- List actions children and their families can perform to reduce their carbon footprint (many things we do in our daily lives create carbon dioxide, or greenhouse gases).
- Explore the potential of solar energy, hydropower, and wind power in helping to decrease fossil fuels.
- Sign the pledge at the end of *We Are Water Protectors*, or write and design your own pledge to protect the Earth.

In conclusion, if our children read any of these books, ponder any of these enduring questions, and engage in any of these action items—will that be enough? Elie Wiesel writes, "In a world of absurdity, we must invent reason; we must create beauty out of nothingness (Wiesel, 1967, 299). Jewish children's literature encompasses a wealth of emotions, history, and culture about the Jewish people. Their stories reflect a range of good and difficult times of a people, happy and sad times, perplexing times, as well as hope for a better future. Jewish children's literature is for everyone, not just children with Jewish backgrounds. Enduring questions provide opportunities to move beyond anti-Semitism and other forms of hate to a place that has more respect and love for our fellow people.

The introduction to this book shared the reactions that three children, Ezra, Sharon, and Bernie, had to the Jewish children's literature books they were reading—*Naftali the Storyteller and His Horse Sus, Berchick,* and *The Carp in the Bathtub*, respectively. The three children are now adults, and their children are not finding Jewish children's literature in their public school classrooms (except for Holocaust literature). This needs to change.

It is our hope that Jewish and non-Jewish teachers, teachers in schools in all kinds of geographies, whether they have many Jewish students in their classrooms or none, will incorporate Jewish children's literature as part of their multicultural literature curriculum and instruction. Both through Jewish children's literature and other multicultural children's literature, we hope more children will have opportunities in their classrooms to explore together what we have called enduring questions.

Liz Paige, who earlier shared how she used one of the books (see chapter 6), writes,

> I often use Jewish children's literature in my kindergarten through fifth-grade ethics and cultures classes. Not only do the books give the majority of my students a "window" into a different culture, but the stories teach values and life lessons that are important for all, regardless of religion, culture, or ethnicity: to be humble and to not take up more than one's space, to have awe and respect for the natural world, to recognize the good in everything, to be active in one's community, to keep traditions as part of one's heritage, to understand that within each tradition is an intention that goes deeper than the tradition itself, to do good and kind deeds, and the power of our words and actions to repair the world.

WORKS CITED

Children's Literature

Behar, Ruth. *Lucky Broken Girl*. New York: Nancy Paulsen Books, 2017.
———. *Tía Fortuna's New Home: A Jewish Cuban Journey*. Illustrated by Devon Holzwarth. New York: Knopf, 2022.
de la Peña, Matt. *Last Stop on Market Street*. New York: Putnam, 2015.
Goldin, Barbara Diamond. *Cakes and Miracles: A Purim Tale*. Illustrated by Erika Weihs. New York: Viking Penguin, 1991.
Hamilton, Virginia. *Bluish*. New York: Scholastic Press, 2005.

Iglesias, Juan Pablo. *Daniel and Ismail.* Illustrated by Alex Peris. Translated into English by Ilan Stavans. Translated into Hebrew by Eliezer Nowodworski and Frieda Press-Danieli. Translated into Arabic by Randa Sayegh. Brooklyn, NY: Restless Books, 2019.

Levine, Arthur. *Pearl Moscowitz's Last Stand.* Illustrated by Robert Roth. New York: HarperCollins, 1993.

Lindstrom, Carole. *We Are Water Protectors.* Illustrated by Michaela Goade. New York: Roaring Brook Press, 2020.

Martinez-Neal, Jana. *Zonia's Rain Forest.* Somerville, MA: Candlewick, 2021.

Morrison, Toni. *Remember: The Journey to School Integration.* Boston: Houghton Mifflin, 2004.

Peete, Holly Robinson, and Ryan Elizabeth Peete. *My Brother Charlie.* Illustrated by Shane W. Evans. New York: Scholastic, 2010.

Uchida, Yoshiko. *The Bracelet.* Illustrated by Joanna Yardley. New York: Putnam & Grosset Group, 1993.

Wind, Lee. *Red and Green and Blue and White.* Illustrated by Paul O. Zelinsky. Montclair, NJ: Levine Querido, 2021.

Woodson, Jacqueline. *The Other Side.* Illustrated by E. B. Lewis. New York: Putnam, 2001.

References

Baker, M. "Zachor: You Shall Remember." CJP, April 17, 2020. Retrieved April 27, 2022, from https://www.cjp.org/streams/a-message-from-marc/zachor-you-shall-remember.

Bishop, R. S. "Windows, Mirrors, and Sliding Glass Doors." *Perspectives* 6, no. 3 (1990): ix–xi.

Kim, K. "Where Some See Fashion, Others See Politics." *New York Times*, February 11, 2007. Retrieved April 25, 2022, from https://www.nytimes.com/2007/02/11/fashion/shows/11KAFFIYEH.html.

Wiesel, E. "Jewish Values in the Post Holocaust Future." *Judaism* 16 (1967): 299; cited in D. Diamond, "Elie Wiesel: Reconciling the Irreconcilable." *World Literature Today* 57 (1983): 228–34.

Glossary

The definitions below are informal ones, written to be helpful to teachers. More formal and technical definitions and accompanying references can be found at the following websites: *Glossary: Jewish Virtual Library*, www.jewishvirtuallibrary.org/glossary; the YIVO Encyclopedia of Jews of Eastern Europe, https://yivoencyclopedia.org; and the Union of Reform Judaism glossary, https://reformjudaism.org/glossary. Please note: many Jewish words have various spellings, especially those translated from Hebrew, Yiddish, or Ladino.

Ashkenazi Jews—Jews whose heritage derives at least in part from Eastern Europe.

Bar Mitzvah/Bat Mitzvah/B-Mitzvah—Bar mitzvah/bat mitzvah/b-mitzvah is a rite of passage that occurs for boys at the age of thirteen. A bat mitzvah occurs for girls at twelve or thirteen years old, depending on the Jewish denomination. A b-mitzvah is the name used increasingly for this rite of passage for nonbinary youth. At a bar mitzvah/bat mitzvah/b-mitzvah, the youth is called to read the Torah at a Shabbat service, and a celebration often follows.

Blood Lie—Anti-Semitic falsehood that Jews kill Christian children and use their blood to bake matzo and bread and for religious rituals. The blood lie was used to justify pogroms and other violent and murderous attacks against Jews.

The Bund—Also known as the General Jewish Labor Bund, it was established in 1897 in Eastern Europe to address oppressive labor, civil, and political conditions of Jewish workers. The Bund argued for equal rights for women and for establishing Yiddish as the national language of Jews. The Bund was also a self-defense organization fighting against pogroms.

Although the Bund dissolved as an organization in the 1920s, some Jews continue to define themselves as Bundists.

Cabala (see Kabbalah)

Challah—Special bread associated with Ashkenazi Jewish traditions, often used on Jewish holidays such as Shabbat and Rosh Hashanah. Challah is often braided and, according to Jewish tradition, when being made a small portion of the dough is set aside (originally to be given to the Temple, but more recently as symbolic of sharing and giving to those in need).

Chelm—In Jewish folklore, when God made fools, the angels carried the fools in a sack to distribute evenly around the world. However, one of the sacks ripped and dropped a large number of fools into the city of Chelm. Many humorous stories tell about the people of Chelm and their foolishness (which they consider wisdom). A real city named Chelm should not be confused with the city in Jewish folklore.

Chuppah—Canopy used during a Jewish wedding under which people are married.

Conversos—When Jews were forced to convert or be executed, as occurred in Spain in the fifteenth century, some Jews pretended to convert but continued being Jews in private (often called Marranos). Some Jews did convert but maintained or adapted some Jewish traditions. Both groups are called conversos.

Esrog (also etrog or ethrog)—Yellow citron. It is one of four species of plants important to the holiday of Sukkot. This fruit is taken in hand and held or waved during specific portions of the holiday prayers.

Golem—According to Jewish legend, a golem is a nonhuman figure made of clay and brought to life by a righteous rabbi with special magical powers. A golem was created to protect the Jewish community from attacks, although in some Jewish children's stories, a golem is created to help with chores such as making latkes (potato pancakes) for Hanukkah.

Hamantaschen—Three-cornered cookie/pastry, often filled with a sweet filling, usually eaten at Purim. The triangle shape of the hamantaschen represents the hat of Haman, the person who tried unsuccessfully to murder the Jews.

Hanukkah—Jewish holiday celebrating the rededication of the Temple after the victory of the Jews over the Greek King Antiochus. Antiochus had outlawed Judaism. The miracle of Hanukkah is that after the victory, the Jews found only enough oil to light the Temple lamp for one day; however, the light burned for eight days. In religious terms, Hanukkah is a minor holiday. However, in North America, Hanukkah has become a significant holiday.

Holocaust—The systematic murder of nearly six million Jews and the destruction of Jewish communities throughout Europe, carried out by the

Nazi-controlled German government and its collaborators from 1938 through 1945.

Kabbalah—Form of Jewish mysticism.

Kibitzers—Yiddish term for a spectator, usually one who offers advice or commentary.

Kosher—Food that has been prepared in accordance with Jewish rules and rituals.

Kristallnacht—Beginning on the night of November 9 and continuing through November 10, 1938, a pogrom was started by the Nazi government of Germany. Jews throughout Germany were violently attacked; their homes, synagogues, and places of work vandalized and destroyed; many Jews were murdered; and thirty thousand Jewish men were taken to concentration camps.

Ladino—Jewish language that originated among Jews in Spain. When Spain expelled Jews in 1492, Jews took Ladino to many countries in the Mediterranean region. It is also called Judeo-Spanish and Judesmo.

Latkes—Potato pancakes, often made during the holiday of Hanukkah.

Luftmench—Airhead; a person who is foolish.

Marranos (see Conversos)

Matzo (also spelled matzoh)—Unleavened bread. During the holiday of Passover, no leavened foods may be eaten, and thus matzo is often eaten instead of bread.

Mensch—Yiddish word for person. Often used as a compliment, meaning a true human being, a person of integrity and honor.

Mitzvah/Mitzvot (plural)—Literally meaning commandment, colloquially used to mean a good deed. According to some Jews, the Torah lists 613 mitzvot. Some Jews would argue that there are more.

Mizrahi Jews—Jews whose heritage derives from North Africa, the Middle East, and Eastern Europe.

Passover (also called Pesach)—Celebrates the freeing of the Jews from their enslavement in Egypt. The first night of Passover begins on the fifteenth day of the month of Nisan, typically in March or April of the Gregorian calendar. Some Jews celebrate Passover for seven days, whereas others celebrate for eight days.

Pogrom—Government-enabled violent attack on Jews and Jewish communities. The term is most often used to refer to attacks against Jewish communities in Eastern European countries.

Rakhmones (also spelled rachmones)—To have mercy, pity, and sympathy for another.

Rosh Hashanah—Jewish new year (means head of the year), celebrated during the first ten days of Tishri, an autumn month. Customs include tasting apples and honey to represent a sweet new year, sounding of the shofar, and often includes eating a round challah. The holiday begins a ten-day period ending with Yom Kippur, the Day of Atonement.

Rothschild—Although an actual wealthy Rothschild family (with interests in banking, mining, real estate, and other areas) exists, the term *Rothschild* has been used by Jews to refer to an extremely wealthy person. Anti-Semites have created lies about the Rothschilds controlling governments and politics through their wealth, part of the anti-Semitic lie about an international Jewish conspiracy controlling the world.

Schlemazel—Person who always seems to have bad luck.

Schlemiel—Clumsy person who is always dropping things or bumping into things. An old Jewish joke helps distinguish between a schlemiel and a schlimazel: a schlemiel always spills soup, and always spills it on a schlemazel.

Seder—Means order, but most Jews use the word *seder* to refer to a traditional meal held during Passover in which the story is told of the Jews' liberation from Egypt.

Sephardi or Sefardi; plural Sephardim or Sefardim—Descendants of the Jews who lived in Spain and Portugal from at least the later centuries of the Roman Empire until their persecution and mass expulsion from those countries in the last decades of the fifteenth century. The Sephardim who were able to flee mostly kept their native Judeo-Spanish language (Ladino), literature, and customs.

Shabbat (also Shabbos or Shabbot)—Jewish day of rest. Shabbat occurs each week from sunset on Friday to sunset on Saturday. During Shabbat, Jews remember the story from the Torah where God created the world in six days and rested on the seventh day.

Shewbread—Special bread given as a sacrifice at the Temple or at a synagogue. The term is no longer in use.

Shtetl—Yiddish word for town.

Shtot—Yiddish word for city.

Sukkot—Harvest holiday that follows four days after Yom Kippur. People often build a sukkah, a homemade shed or lean-to, covered with leafy branches to commemorate the Jews building only temporary huts during their forty years of wandering in the desert.

Synagogue—From the Greek word *synagein*, meaning to bring together, a synagogue is a dedicated place of Jewish worship.

Talmud—Collection of writings that include Jewish law, traditions, and commentary. It is the central text for Jewish religious study and provides guidance for many Jews on a broad range of daily and religious topics.

Tashlich—Ritual during Rosh Hashanah in which bread crumbs are thrown into a flowing body of water, symbolizing the casting away of sins.

Temple—The first temple was built in Jerusalem in the tenth century BCE. It was destroyed by Nebuchadnezzar in 586 BCE. The second temple was built on the site of the first temple in 515 BCE and significantly upgraded in 20 BCE. It was destroyed in 70 CE by the Romans, who exiled the Jews from what is now called Israel/Palestine. Reform Jews often call their synagogues "temple."

Tikkun Olam—Means repairing the world. It is often used to refer to the pursuit of social justice and freedom.

Tikvah—In Hebrew, tikvah means hope.

Torah—First five books of the Hebrew Bible; also called the Five Books of Moses.

Tzaddik—Righteous and spiritual person who is often a leader in the Jewish community, often a rabbi.

Tzedakah—Hebrew word for charity. The root of the word—*tzede*—means justice or righteousness.

Yiddish—Jewish language originating in Eastern European communities in the ninth century.

Zachor/Zakar/Zichron—Among many terms used for memory and remembrances.

Zayde—Yiddish for grandfather.

Appendix A
Select List of Jewish Children's Literature Organized by Topics/Themes
(Suggested Grade Levels Indicated)

ADVENTURE

Gidwitz, Adam. *The Inquisitor's Tale: Or, The Three Holy Children and Their Magical Dog.* New York: Dutton, 2016. (grades 4–6)

Ish-Kishor, Sulamith. *A Boy of Old Prague.* Illustrated by Ben Shahn. Mineola, NY: Dover, 1963. (grades 4–6)

Shulevitz, Uri. *The Travels of Benjamin of Tudela: Through Three Continents in the Twelfth Century.* New York: Farrar, Straus & Giroux, 2005. (grades 4–6)

Simon, Solomon. *The Clever Little Tailor.* Illustrated by Yehuda Blum. Translated by David Forman. New York: Kinder-Loshn, 2021. (kindergarten–grade 6)

ANIMALS

Cohen, Santiago. *The Yiddish Fish.* New York: Sky Pony Press, 2014. (preschool–grade 3)

Jules, Jacqueline. *The Generous Fish.* Illustrated by Frances Tyrrell. Bloomington, IN: Wisdom Tales, 2020. (preschool–grade 3)

Pinkwater, Daniel Manus. *Beautiful Yetta: The Yiddish Chicken.* Illustrated by Jill Pinkwater. New York: Feiwel and Friends, 2010. (preschool–grade 3)

Singer, Isaac Bashevis. *Naftali the Storyteller and His Horse, Sus, and Other Stories.* Illustrated by Margot Zemach. New York: Farrar, Straus & Giroux, 1976. (grades 2–6)

———. *Zlateh the Goat and Other Stories.* Illustrated by Maurice Sendak. Translated by Elizabeth Shub. New York: HarperCollins, 2001. (preschool–grade 3)

Stampler, Ann Redisch. *The Cats on Ben Yehuda Street.* Illustrated by Francesca Carabelli. Minneapolis: Kar-Ben, 2013. (preschool–grade 3)

ANTI-SEMITISM

Dublin, Anne. Anne. *A Cage Without Bars*. Toronto: Second Story Press, 2018. (grades 4–6)
Lasky, Kathryn. *Broken Song*. New York: Puffin Books, 2005. (grades 5–6)
———. *The Night Journey*. New York: Puffin Books, 1981. (grades 5–6)
Levine, Gail Carson. *A Ceiling Made of Eggshells*. New York: HarperCollins, 2020. (grades 4–6)
Rogasky, Barbara. *The Golem*. Illustrated by Trina Schart Hyman. New York: Holiday House, 1996. (grades 4–6)
Wisniewski, David. *Golem*. New York: Clarion, 1996. (grades 4–6)

BAR MITZVAH/BAT MITZVAH/B-MITZVAH

Freedman, Paula J. *My Basmati Bat Mitzvah*. New York: Abrams, 2015. (grades 4–6)
Kacer, Kathy. *The Diary of Laura's Twin*. Victoria, British Columbia: Orca, 2008. (grades 4–6)
Weissman, Elissa Brent. *The Length of a String*. New York: Dial, 2018. (grades 4–6)
Wolkenstein, M. Evan. *Turtle Boy*. New York: Delacorte, 2020. (grades 4–6)

BILINGUAL/MULTILINGUAL JEWISH CHILDREN'S LITERATURE (ENGLISH PLUS)

Aroeste, Sarah. *Ora de Despertar/Time to Wake Up*. Illustrated by Miriam Ross. Aroeste Music, 2017. (English/Ladino) (preschool–grade 1)
Iglesias, Juan Pablo. *Daniel and Ismail*. Illustrated by Alex Peris. Translated into English by Ilan Stavans. Translated into Hebrew by Eliezer Nowodworski and Frieda Press-Danieli. Translated into Arabic by Randa Sayegh. Brooklyn, NY: Restless Books, 2019. (preschool–grade 2)
Molodowsky, Kadya. *Through an Endless Stretch of Land*. Translated by Yaira Singer. Lund, Sweden: Olniansky Tekst Farlag, 2020. (English/Yiddish) (grades 1–6)
Nomberg, Hersh Dovid. *Between Parents*. Translated by Ollie Elkus and Daniel Kennedy. Farlag Press, 2021. (English/Yiddish) (grades 5–6)
Simon, Solomon. *The Clever Little Tailor*. Illustrated by Yehuda Blum. Translated by David Forman. New York: Kinder-Loshn, 2021. (English/Yiddish) (kindergarten–grade 6)

BIOGRAPHIES

Adler, David. *A Hero and the Holocaust: The Story of Janusz Korczak and His Children.* Illustrated by Bill Farnsworth. New York: Holiday House, 2002. (grades 4–6)

Anholt, Laurence. *Papa Chagall, Tell Us a Story.* Hauppauge, NY: Barron's Educational Services, 2014. (preschool–grade 3)

Drucker, Malka. *Portraits of Jewish-American Heroes.* Illustrated by Elizabeth Rosen. New York: Puffin, 2008. (grades 4–6)

Epstein, Nadine. *RBG's Brave & Brilliant Women: 33 Jewish Women to Inspire Everyone.* Illustrated by Bee Johnson. New York: Delacorte, 2021. (grades 5–6)

Landmann, Bimba. *I Am Marc Chagall.* Grand Rapids, MI: Eerdmans Books for Young Readers, 2006. (grades 3–6)

Lemke, Elisabeth, and Thomas David. *Marc Chagall: What Colour Is Paradise?* Translated by Rosie Jackson. Munich: Prestel Verlag, 2000. (grades 4–6)

Levinson, Cynthia. *The People's Painter: How Ben Shahn Fought for Justice with Art.* Illustrated by Evan Turk. New York: Abrams, 2021. (preschool–grade 4)

Levy, Debbie. *I Dissent: Ruth Bader Ginsburg Makes Her Mark.* Illustrated by Elizabeth Baddeley. New York: Simon & Schuster, 2016. (preschool–grade 4)

Lindauer, Bonnie. *Hannah G. Solomon Dared to Make a Difference.* Illustrated by Sofia Moore. Minneapolis: Kar-Ben, 2021. (kindergarten–grade 5)

Macy, Sue. *The Book Rescuer.* Illustrated by Stacy Innerst. New York: Simon & Schuster Books for Young Readers, 2019. (kindergarten–grade 4)

Marshall, Linda Elovitz. *The Polio Pioneer: Dr. Jonas Salk and the Polio Vaccine.* Illustrated by Lisa Anchin. New York: Knopf Books for Young Readers, 2020. (kindergarten–grade 4)

Michelson, Richard. *Fascinating: The Life of Leonard Nimoy.* Illustrated by Edel Rodriguez. New York: Knopf, 2016. (preschool–grade 3)

Newman, Tracy. *Itzhak: A Boy Who Loved the Violin—The Story of Young Itzhak Perlman.* Illustrated by Abigail Halpin. New York: Abrams, 2020. (preschool–grade 4)

Rose, Lisa. *The Singer and the Scientist.* Illustrated by Isabel Muñoz. Minneapolis: Kar-Ben, 2021. (kindergarten–grade 5)

Silverman, Erica. *Sholom's Treasure: How Sholom Aleichem Became a Writer.* Illustrated by Mordicai Gerstein. New York: Farrar, Straus & Giroux, 2005. (kindergarten–grade 5)

Stanley, Jerry. *Frontier Merchants: Lionel and Barron Jacobs and the Jewish Pioneers Who Settled West.* New York: Knopf Books for Young Readers, 1998. (grades 3–6)

EDUCATION/PHILOSOPHY

Adler, David. *A Hero and the Holocaust: The Story of Janusz Korczak*. Illustrated by Bill Farnsworth. New York: Holiday House, 2002. (grades 4–6)

Bogacki, Tomek. *The Champion of Children: The Story of Janusz Korczak*. New York: Farrar, Straus & Giroux, 2009. (grades 3–6)

Cohen, Barbara. *Even Higher*. Illustrated by Anatoly Ivanov. New York: Lothrop, Lee & Shepard, 1987. (kindergarten–grade 6)

Cohen, Santiago. *The Yiddish Fish*. New York: Sky Pony Press, 2014. (preschool–grade 3)

Cohen-Janca, Irene. *Mister Doctor: Janusz Korczak and the Orphans of the Warsaw Ghetto*. Illustrated by Maurizio A. C. Quarello. Translated by Paula Ayer. Toronto: Annick Press, 2015. (grades 3–6)

Davis, Aubrey. *Bagels from Benny*. Illustrated by Dušan Petričić. Toronto, ON: Kids Can Press, 2003. (preschool–grade 3)

Glaser, Linda. *On One Foot*. Illustrated by Nuria Balaguer. Minneapolis: Kar-Ben, 2016. (kindergarten–grade 6)

Jules, Jacqueline. *Drop by Drop: A Story of Rabbi Akiva*. Illustrated by Yevgenia Nayberg. Minneapolis: Kar-Ben, 2017. (preschool–grade 3)

———. *The Generous Fish*. Illustrated by Frances Tyrrell. Bloomington, IN: Wisdom Tales, 2020. (preschool–grade 3)

Kimmel, Eric A. *Even Higher*. Illustrated by Jill Weber. New York: Holiday House, 2009. (preschool–grade 6)

Macy, Sue. *The Book Rescuer*. Illustrated by Stacy Innerst. New York: Simon & Schuster Books for Young Readers, 2019. (kindergarten–grade 3)

Matas, Carol. *Sparks Fly Upward*. Boston: Clarion, 2002. (grades 5–6)

Spielman, Gloria. *Janusz Korczak's Children*. Illustrated by Matthew Archambault. Minneapolis: Kar-Ben, 2007. (grades 2–6)

Stampler, Ann Redisch. *The Rooster Prince of Breslov*. Illustrated by Eugene Yelchin. Boston: Clarion, 2010. (preschool–grade 4)

———. *The Wooden Sword*. Illustrated by Carol Liddiment. New York: Albert Whitman, 2012. (preschool–grade 3)

Stavans, Ilan. *Golemito*. Illustrated by Teresa Villegas. Montgomery, AL: NewSouth Books, 2013. (grades 2–6)

Uhlberg, Myron. *Lemuel the Fool*. Illustrated by Sonja Lamut. Atlanta: Peachtree, 2001. (kindergarten–grade 3)

Ungar, Richard. *Rachel Captures the Moon*. Toronto: Tundra, 2001. (grades 2–5)

Waldman, Debby. *A Sack Full of Feathers*. Illustrated by Cindy Revell. Victoria, BC, Canada: Orca. (preschool–kindergarten)

Select List of Jewish Children's Literature Organized by Topics/Themes

FAMILY LIFE

Aleichem, Sholem. *Hanukah Money.* Illustrated by Uri Shulevitz. Translated by Elizabeth Shub. New York: Greenwillow, 1978. (grades 2–4)

Aylesworth, Jim. *My Grandfather's Coat.* Illustrated by Barbara McClintock. New York: Scholastic, 2014. (preschool–grade 3)

Blanc, Esther Silverstein. *Berchick.* Illustrated by Tennessee Dixon. Volcano, CA: Volcano Press, 1989. (grades 2–4)

Byrne, Jennifer. *Adopting Ahava.* Illustrated by Oana Vaida. Sicklerville, NJ: My Family! Products/Dodi Press, 2013. (grades 4–6)

Cohen, Barbara. *The Carp in the Bathtub.* Illustrated by Joan Halpern. New York: Lothrop, Lee & Shepard, 1972. (kindergarten–grade 5)

Cohen, Santiago. *The Yiddish Fish.* New York: Sky Pony Press, 2014. (preschool–grade 1)

Edwards, Michelle. *Papa's Latkes.* Illustrated by Stacey Schuett. Cambridge, MA: Candlewick, 2004. (kindergarten–grade 2)

Ehrenberg, Pamela. *Queen of the Hanukkah Dosas.* Illustrated by Anjan Sarkar. New York: Farrar, Straus & Giroux, 2017. (preschool–grade 3)

Elon, Ori. *A Basket Full of Figs.* Illustrated by Menahem Halberstadt. Translated by Gilah Kahn-Hoffmann. Barnsley, England: Green Bean Books, 2017. (kindergarten–grade 3)

Fagan, Cary. *Oy Feh So?* Illustrated by Gary Clement. Toronto: Groundwood Books, 2013. (preschool–grade 3)

Herman, Michael. *Under the Sabbath Lamp.* Illustrated by Alida Masssari. Minneapolis: Kar-Ben, 2017. (preschool–grade 2)

Herron, Carolivia. *Always an Olivia: A Remarkable Family History.* Illustrated by Jeremy Tugeau. Minneapolis: Kar-Ben, 2012. (grades 2–6)

Hesse, Karen. *Letters from Rifka.* New York: Henry Holt, 1992. (grades 4–6)

Hyde, Heidi Smith. *Feivel's Flying Horses.* Illustrated by Johanna van der Sterre. Minneapolis: Kar-Ben, 2010. (kindergarten–grade 4)

Londner, Renee. *Stones for Grandpa.* Illustrated by Martha Avilés. Minneapolis: Kar-Ben, 2013. (kindergarten–grade 4)

Malaspina, Ann. *A Scarf for Keiko.* Illustrated by Merrilee Liddiard. Minneapolis: Kar-Ben, 2019. (kindergarten–grade 6)

Matas, Carol. *Sparks Fly Upward.* New York: Clarion, 2002. (grades 5–6)

Michelson, Richard. *Too Young for Yiddish.* Illustrated by Neil Waldman. Watertown, MA: Charlesbridge, 2002. (grades 1–4)

Perlov, Betty Rosenberg. *Rifka Takes a Bow.* Illustrated by Cosei Kawa. Minneapolis: Kar-Ben, 2013. (kindergarten–grade 4)

Pinkwater, Daniel Manus. *Beautiful Yetta: The Yiddish Chicken.* Illustrated by Jill Pinkwater. New York: Feiwel and Friends, 2010. (preschool–grade 3)

Rael, Elsa. *When Zaydeh Danced on Eldridge Street.* Illustrated by Marjorie Priceman. New York: Simon & Schuster Books for Young Readers, 1997. (grades 1–4)

Singer, Isaac Bashevis. *The Parakeet Named Dreidel.* Illustrated by Suzanne Raphael Berkson. New York: Farrar, Straus & Giroux, 2015. (grades 1–4)

———. *Zlateh the Goat and Other Stories*. Illustrated by Maurice Sendak. Translated by Elizabeth Shub. New York: HarperCollins, 2001. (grades 2–6)

Sinykin, Sheri Cooper. *Zayde Comes to Live*. Illustrated by Kristina Swarner. Atlanta: Peachtree, 2012. (preschool–grade 3)

Smith, Chris. *One City, Two Brothers.* Illustrated by Aurélia Fronty. Cambridge, MA: Barefoot Books, 2007. (grades 1–6)

Taylor, Sydney. *All-of-a-Kind Family*. Illustrated by Helen John. Westchester, IL: Follett, 1951. (grades 4–6)

FOLKTALES (OLD AND NEW) TOLD AND RETOLD

Elon, Ori. *A Basket Full of Figs.* Illustrated by Menahem Halberstadt. Translated by Gilah Kahn-Hoffmann. Barnsley, England: Green Bean Books, 2017. (kindergarten–grade 3)

Gershator, Phillis. *Honi and His Magic Circle.* Illustrated by Shay Rieger. Philadelphia: Jewish Publication Society, 1979. (grades 1–3)

Gilman, Phoebe. *Something from Nothing.* New York: Scholastic, 2008. (kindergarten–grade 6)

Hirsch, Marilyn. *Joseph Who Loved the Sabbath.* Illustrated by Devis Grebu. New York: Viking, 1986. (grades 2–5)

Howland, Naomi. *Latkes, Latkes, Good to Eat.* New York: Clarion, 2004. (preschool–grade 4)

Kimmel, Eric A. *The Adventures of Hershel of Ostropol.* Illustrated by Trina Schart Hyman. New York: Holiday House, 1995. (preschool–grade 3)

———. *Onions and Garlic: An Old Tale.* Illustrated by Katya Arnold. New York: Holiday House, 1996. (preschool–grade 4)

Nadler, Jill Ross. *Such a Library.* Illustrated by Esther van den Berg. Seattle: Intergalactic Afikoman, 2020. (preschool–grade 3)

Renberg, Dalia Hardof. *King Solomon and the Bee.* Illustrated by Ruth Heller. New York: HarperCollins, 1994. (kindergarten–grade 2)

Sheir, Rebecca. *Onions & Garlic*. Illustrated by Sabina Hahn. Agwam, MA: PJ Library, 2019. (preschool–grade 4)

Silverman, Erica. *Raisel's Riddle.* Illustrated by Susan Gaber. New York: Farrar, Straus & Giroux, 1999. (kindergarten–grade 3)

Singer, Isaac Bashevis. *Mazel and Shlimazel or The Milk of a Lioness*. Illustrated by Margot Zemach. Translated by Elizabeth Shub. New York: Farrar, Straus & Giroux, 1967. (kindergarten–grade 4)

———. *A Tale of Three Wishes.* Illustrated by Irene Lieblich. New York: Farrar, Straus & Giroux, 1976. (grades 2–4)

———. *Why Noah Chose the Dove.* Illustrated by Eric Carle. Translated by Elizabeth Shub. New York: Scholastic, 1973. (grades 2–6)

Smith, Chris. *One City, Two Brothers.* Illustrated by Aurélia Fronty. Cambridge, MA: Barefoot Books, 2007. (grades 1–6)

Stampler, Ann Redisch. *The Rooster Prince of Breslov*. Illustrated by Eugene Yelchin. Boston: Clarion, 2010. (preschool–grade 4)

———. *Shlemazel and the Remarkable Spoon of Pohost*. Illustrated by Jacqueline M. Cohen. Boston: Clarion, 2006. (grades 3–6)

———. *The Wooden Sword*. Illustrated by Carol Liddiment. Chicago: Albert Whitman & Company, 2012. (preschool–grade 3)

Taback, Simms. *Joseph Had a Little Overcoat*. New York: Viking, 1999. (preschool–grade 2)

———. *Kibitzers and Fools: Tales My Zayda Told Me*. New York: Viking, 2005. (preschool–grade 1)

Waldman, Debby. *A Sack Full of Feathers*. Illustrated by Cindy Revell. Victoria, BC, Canada: Orca, 2006. (preschool–kindergarten)

Yolen, Jane, and Heidi E. Y. Stemple. *Jewish Fairy Tale Feasts: A Literary Cookbook*. Illustrated by Sima Elizabeth Shefrin. Northampton, MA: Crocodile, 2013. (grades 3–5)

Zemach, Margot. *It Could Always Be Worse*. New York: Farrar, Straus & Giroux, 1976. (preschool–grade 3)

FRIENDSHIP

Altman, Linda Jacobs. *The Legend of Freedom Hill*. Illustrated by Cornelius Van Wright and Ying-Hwa Hu. New York: Lee & Low Books, 2000. (kindergarten–grade 4)

Berg, Melissa. *The Challah That Took Over the House*. Illustrated by Shiela Marie Alejandro. Eclectic Ivri Press, 2019. (grades 1–6)

Cohen, Tziporah. *No Vacancy*. Toronto: Groundwood Books, 2020. (grades 4–6)

Faruqi, Saadia and Laura Shovan. *A Place at the Table*. New York: Clarion, 2020 (grades 4–6)

Gilani-Williams, Fawzia. *Yaffa and Fatima Shalom, Salaam*. Illustrated by Chiara Fedele. Minneapolis: Kar-Ben, 2017. (preschool–grade 4)

Glaser, Linda. *Hannah's Way*. Illustrated by Adam Gustavson. Minneapolis: Kar-Ben, 2012. (kindergarten–grade 4)

Rosenberg, Madelyn, and Wendy Wan-Long Shang. *This Is Just a Test*. New York: Scholastic, 2017. (grades 4–6)

Shang, Wendy Wan-Long, and Madelyn Rosenberg. *Not Your All-American Girl*. New York: Scholastic, 2020. (grades 3–6)

Singer, Isaac Bashevis. *Naftali the Storyteller and His Horse, Sus, and Other Stories*. Illustrated by Margot Zemach. New York: Farrar, Straus & Giroux, 1976. (grades 5–6)

Stavans, Ilan. *Golemito*. Illustrated by Teresa Villegas. Montgomery, AL: NewSouth Books, 2013. (grades 2–6)

Zalben, Jane Breskin. *A Moon for Moe and Mo*. Illustrated by Mehrdokht Amini. Watertown, MA: Charlesbridge, 2018. (preschool–grade 2)

GRAPHIC NOVELS

Dauvillier, Loïc. *Hidden.* Illustrated by Marc Lizano. Translated by Alexis Siegel. New York: First Second, 2012. (grades 4–6)
Deutsch, Barry. *Hereville: How Mirka Caught a Fish.* New York: Abrams, 2015. (grades 3–6)
———. *Hereville: How Mirka Got Her Sword.* New York: Abrams, 2010. (grades 3–6)
———. *Hereville: How Mirka Met a Meteorite.* New York: Abrams, 2012. (grades 3–6)
Molodowsky, Kadya. *The Life of a Coat.* Illustrated by Batia Kolton. Translated by Ilana Kurshan. Seattle: Fantagraphics Books, 2019. (grades 1–3)
Palacio, R. J. *White Bird: A Wonder Story.* New York: Knopf Books for Young Readers, 2019. (grades 3–6)
Robbins, Trina. *Lily Renée, Escape Artist: From Holocaust Survivor to Comic Book Pioneer.* Illustrated by Anne Timmons and Mo Oh. Minneapolis: Lerner, 2011. (grades 5–6)
Watts, Irene N. *Seeking Refuge: A Graphic Novel.* Illustrated by Kathryn E. Shoemaker. Vancouver, Canada: Tradewind Books, 2016. (grades 4–6)

HOLIDAYS

Hanukkah

Aleichem, Sholem. *Hanukah Money.* Illustrated by Uri Shulevitz. Translated by Elizabeth Shub. New York: Greenwillow, 1978. (preschool–grade 1)
da Costa, Deborah. *Hanukkah Moon.* Illustrated by Gosia Mosz. New York: Scholastic, 2007. (grades 1–3)
Edwards, Michelle. *Papa's Latkes.* Illustrated by Stacey Schuett. Cambridge, MA: Candlewick, 2004. (kindergarten–grade 2)
Ehrenberg, Pamela. *Queen of the Hanukkah Dosas.* Illustrated by Anjan Sarkar. New York: Farrar, Straus & Giroux, 2017. (grades 1–3)
Goldin, Barbara Diamond. *Just Enough Is Plenty: A Hanukkah Tale.* Illustrated by Seymour Chwast. New York: Viking Kestrel, 1988. (kindergarten–grade 2)
Howland, Naomi. *Latkes, Latkes, Good to Eat.* New York: Clarion, 2004. (kindergarten–grade 3)
Jenkins, Emily. *All-of-a-Kind Family Hanukkah.* Illustrated by Paul O. Zelinksy. New York: Schwartz & Wade, 2018. (kindergarten–grade 3)
Kimmel, Eric A. *The Chanukkah Guest.* Illustrated by Giora Carmi. New York: Holiday House, 1988. (preschool–grade 3)
———. *Hershel and the Hanukkah Goblins.* Illustrated by Trina Schart Hyman. New York: Scholastic, 1985. (preschool–grade 3)
———. *The Magic Dreidels.* Illustrated by Katya Krenina. New York: Holiday House, 2014. (preschool–grade 3)

———. *Zigazak: A Magical Hanukkah Night.* Illustrated by Jon Goodell. New York: Doubleday Books for Young Readers, 2001. (preschool–grade 2)

Koffsky, Ann D. *Kayla and Kugel.* Springfield, NJ: Apples & Honey Press, 2015. (preschool–grade 2)

Passover/Pesach

Goldin, Barbara Diamond. *The Magician's Visit.* Illustrated by Robert Andrew Parker. New York: Viking, 1993. (preschool–grade 3)

Kusel, Susan. *The Passover Guest.* Illustrated by Sean Rubin. New York: Holiday House, 2021. (preschool–grade 3)

Peretz, I. L. "The Magician." In Esther Hautzig (translator), *The Seven Good Years and Other Stories of I. L. Peretz,* 37–46. Illustrated by Deborah Kogan Ray. Philadelphia: Jewish Publication Society, 1984. (grades 2–6)

Strauss, Linda Leopold. *The Elijah Door.* Illustrated by Alexi Natchev. New York: Holiday House, 2012. (preschool–grade 4)

Wayland, April Halprin. *More Than Enough: A Passover Story.* Illustrated by Katie Kath. New York: Dial Books for Young Readers, 2016. (preschool–kindergarten)

Yolen, Jane. *Miriam at the River.* Illustrated by Khoa Le. Minneapolis: Kar-Ben, 2020. (kindergarten–grade 3)

Purim

Berkowitz, Leah Rachel. *Queen Vashti's Comfy Pants.* Illustrated by Ruth Bennett. Millburn, NJ: Apples & Honey Press, 2021. (preschool–grade 3)

Goldin, Barbara Diamond. *Cakes and Miracles: A Purim Tale.* Illustrated by Jaime Zollars. Tarrytown, NY: Marshall Cavendish, 2010. (kindergarten–grade 3)

Kushner, Elisabeth. *The Purim Superhero.* Illustrated by Mike Byrne. Minneapolis: Kar-Ben, 2013. (preschool–grade 3)

Rosh Hashanah

Cohen, Barbara. *Even Higher.* Illustrated by Anatoly Ivanov. New York: Lothrop, Lee & Shepard, 1987. (kindergarten–grade 6)

Kimmel, Eric A. *Gershon's Monster.* Illustrated by Jon J. Muth. New York: Scholastic, 2000. (preschool–grade 3)

Shabbat

Barash, Chris. *Fridays Are Special.* Illustrated by Melissa Iwai. Agawam, MA: PJ Library, 2014. (preschool–grade 1)

———. *Wait! It's Friday.* Illustrated by Christine Grove. Millburn, NJ: Apples & Honey Press, 2019. (preschool)

Bietz, Barbara. *The Sundown Kid: A Southwestern Shabbat.* Illustrated by John Kanzler. Atlanta: August House, 2016. (kindergarten–grade 2)
Glaser, Linda. *Hannah's Way.* Illustrated by Adam Gustavson. Minneapolis: Kar-Ben, 2012. (kindergarten–grade 4)
Herman, Michael. *Under the Sabbath Lamp.* Illustrated by Alida Massari. Minneapolis: Kar-Ben, 2017. (preschool–grade 2)
Hirsch, Marilyn. *Joseph Who Loved the Sabbath.* Illustrated by Devis Grebu. New York: Viking, 1986. (grades 2–5)
Schur, Maxine Rose. *Day of Delight: A Jewish Sabbath in Ethiopia.* Illustrated by Brian Pinkney. New York: Dial Books for Young Readers, 1994. (kindergarten–grade 3)

Sukkot

Jaffe, Nina. "Sukkot—The Magician's Spell." In *The Uninvited Guest and Other Jewish Holiday Tales.* Illustrated by Elivia. New York: Scholastic, 1993. (kindergarten–grade 6)
Polacco, Patricia. *Tikvah Means Hope.* New York: Doubleday Books for Young Readers, 1994. (grades 1–3)

Tu BiShvat

Geffen, Shira. *The Heart-Shaped Leaf: A Magical Tale for Tu B'Shvat.* Illustrated by David Polonsky. Barnsley, England: Green Bean Books, 2010. (grades 4–6)
Levine, Arthur. *Pearl Moscowitz's Last Stand.* Illustrated by Robert Roth. New York: HarperCollins, 1993. (grades 1–6)
Rostoker-Gruber, Karen. *Happy Birthday Trees.* Illustrated by Holly Sterling. Minneapolis: Kar-Ben, 2020. (preschool–grade 1)

Yom Kippur

Adler, David A. *Yom Kippur Shortstop.* Illustrated by Andre Ceolin. Springfield, NJ: Apples & Honey Press, 2017. (grades 3–6)

HOLOCAUST

Adler, David. *A Hero and the Holocaust: The Story of Janusz Korczak and His Children.* Illustrated by Bill Farnsworth. New York: Holiday House, 2002. (grades 2–6)
Batalion, Judy. *The Light of Days Young Readers' Edition: The Untold Story of Women Resistance Fighters in Hitler's Ghettos.* New York: HarperCollins, 2020. (grades 5–6)
Borden, Louise. *The Journey That Saved Curious George: The True Wartime Escape of Margret and H. A. Rey.* Illustrated by Allan Drummond. New York: Houghton Mifflin Harcourt, 2005. (grades 3–6)

Dauvillier, Loïc. *Hidden*. Illustrated by Marc Lizano. Translated by Alexis Siegel. New York: First Second, 2012. (grades 4–6)

Fleischman, Sid. *The Entertainer and the Dybbuk*. New York: Greenwillow, 2007. (grades 5–6)

Frank, Anne. *The Diary of a Young Girl*. Translated by B. M. Mooyaart-Doubleday. New York: Modern Library, 1952. (grades 4–6)

Golabek, Mona, and Lee Cohen. *Hold On to Your Music*. Illustrated by Sonia Possentini. Adapted by Emil Sher. New York: Little, Brown, 2021. (kindergarten–grade 4)

Johnston, Tony. *The Harmonica*. Illustrated by Ron Mazellan. Watertown, MA: Charlesbridge, 2004. (grades 3–6)

Kacer, Kathy. *Shanghai Escape*. Toronto, ON: Second Story Press, 2013. (grades 4–6)

Kopelman, Judy Tal. *Grandpa's Third Drawer: Unlocking Holocaust Memories*. Philadelphia: Jewish Publication Society, 2014. (grades 4–6)

Kushner, Tony. *Brundibar*. Illustrated by Maurice Sendak. Westport, CT: Hyperion Books for Children, 2003. (grades 4–6)

Lowry, Lois. *Number the Stars*. Boston: Houghton Mifflin, 1989. (grades 4–6)

Meyer, Susan. *Black Radishes*. New York: Delacorte Press, 2010. (grades 4–6)

Orlev, Uri. *The Island on Bird Street*. Translated by Hillel Halkin. Boston: Houghton Mifflin, 1984. (grades 4–6)

Rappaport, Doreen. *Beyond Courage: The Untold Story of Jewish Resistance during the Holocaust*. Somerville, MA: Candlewick, 2012. (grades 5–6)

Richter, Hans Peter. *Friedrich*. New York: Puffin Books, 1987. (grades 5–6)

Shulevitz, Uri. *How I Learned Geography*. New York: Farrar, Straus & Giroux, 2008. (grades 2–5)

Upjohn, Rebecca. *The Secret of the Village Fool*. Illustrated by Renné Benoit. Toronto: Second Story Press, 2012. (grades 2–5)

Vaughn, Marcia. *Irena's Jars of Secrets*. Illustrated by Ron Mazellan. New York: Lee & Low, 2011. (grades 4–6)

Watts, Irene N. *Seeking Refuge: A Graphic Novel*. Illustrated by Kathryn E. Shoemaker. Vancouver, Canada: Tradewind Books, 2016. (grades 4–6)

Yolen, Jane. *The Devil's Arithmetic*. New York: Puffin Books, 1988. (grades 4–6)

Zullo, Allan. *We Fought Back: Teen Resisters of the Holocaust*. New York: Scholastic, 2012. (grades 5–6)

HUMOR AND FOOLISHNESS

Abas, Shlomo. *The Sages of Chelm and the Moon*. Illustrated by Omer Hoffman. Translated by Gilah Kahn-Hoffman. Yorkshire, England: Green Bean Books, 2019. (kindergarten–grade 2)

Kimmel, Eric A. *The Adventures of Hershel of Ostropol*. Illustrated by Trina Schart Hyman. New York: Holiday House, 1995. (preschool–grade 3)

———. *Right Side Up: Adventures in Chelm*. Illustrated by Steve Brown. Millburn, NJ: Apples & Honey Press, 2019. (grades 3–6)

McGinty, Alice B. *Rabbi Benjamin's Buttons*. Illustrated by Jennifer Black Reinhardt. Watertown, MA: Charlesbridge, 2014. (preschool–grade 3)

Taback, Simms. *Kibitzers and Fools: Tales My Zayda Told Me*. New York: Viking, 2005. (preschool–grade 1)

Uhlberg, Myron. *Lemuel the Fool*. Illustrated by Sonja Lamut. Atlanta: Peachtree, 2001. (kindergarten–grade 3)

Ungar, Richard. *Rachel Captures the Moon*. Toronto: Tundra Books, 2001. (grades 2–5)

IMMIGRATION

Cohen, Barbara, *Molly's Pilgrim*. Illustrated by Jennifer Bricking. New York: HarperCollins, 2018. (grades 1–4)

Heller, Linda. *Castle on Hester Street*. Illustrated by Boris Kulikov. New York: Simon & Schuster Books for Young Children, 1982. (preschool–grade 3)

Herman, Michael. *Under the Sabbath Lamp*. Illustrated by Alida Massari. Minneapolis: Kar-Ben, 2017. (preschool–grade 2)

Hest, Amy. *When Jessie Came Across the Sea*. Illustrated by P. J. Lynch. Cambridge, MA: Candlewick, 1997. (grades 1–4)

Hyde, Heidi Smith. *Feivel's Flying Horses*. Illustrated by Johanna van der Sterre. Minneapolis: Kar-Ben, 2010. (kindergarten–grade 4)

———. *Mendel's Accordion*. Illustrated by Johanna van der Sterre. Minneapolis: Kar-Ben, 2007. (grades 1–4)

Meyer, Susan. *Skating with the Statue of Liberty*. New York: Delacorte Press, 2016. (grades 4–6)

Moss, Morissa. *Hannah's Journal: The Story of an Immigrant Girl*. Boston: Houghton Mifflin Harcourt, 2000. (grades 4–6)

Newman, Lesléa. *Gittel's Journey: An Ellis Island Story*. Illustrated by Amy June Bates. New York: Abrams, 2019. (kindergarten–grade 3)

Pérez, Amado Irma. *My Diary from Here to There*. Illustrated by Maya Christina Gonzalez. New York: Children's Book Press, 2002. (grades 1–4)

Schubert, Leda. *Nathan's Song*. Illustrated by Maya Ish-Shalom. New York: Dial Books for Young Readers, 2021. (preschool–grade 3)

Schur, Maxine Rose. *When I Left My Village*. Illustrated by Brian Pinkney. New York: Dial Books for Young Readers, 1996. (grades 3–6)

Woodruff, Elvira. *The Memory Coat*. Illustrated by Michael Dooling. New York: Scholastic, 1999. (preschool–grade 3)

INCLUSION

Goldin, Barbara Diamond. *Cakes and Miracles: A Purim Tale*. Illustrated by Jaime Zollars. Tarrytown, NY: Marshall Cavendish, 2010. (preschool–grade 6)

Kushner, Elisabeth. *The Purim Superhero.* Illustrated by Mike Byrne. Minneapolis: Kar-Ben, 2013. (preschool–grade 3)

Pinkwater, Daniel Manus. *Beautiful Yetta: The Yiddish Chicken.* Illustrated by Jill Pinkwater. New York: Feiwel and Friends, 2010. (preschool–grade 3)

JEWS OF COLOR

Barash, Chris. *Fridays Are Special.* Illustrated by Melissa Iwai. Agawam, MA: PJ Library, 2014. (preschool–grade 1)

———. *Wait It's Friday!* Illustrated by Christine Grove. Millburn, NJ: Apples & Honey Press, 2019. (preschool)

Behar, Ruth. *Lucky Broken Girl.* New York: Nancy Paulsen, 2017. (grades 4–6)

da Costa, Deborah. *Hanukkah Moon.* Illustrated by Gosia Mosz. New York: Scholastic, 2007. (grades 1–6)

Ehrenberg, Pamela. *Queen of the Hanukkah Dosas.* Illustrated by Anjan Sarkar. New York: Farrar, Straus & Giroux, 2017. (preschool–grade 3)

Herron, Carolivia. *Always an Olivia: A Remarkable Family History.* Illustrated by Jeremy Tugeau. Minneapolis: Kar-Ben, 2007. (grades 2–6)

Rosenberg, Madelyn, and Wendy Wan-Long Shang. *This Is Just a Test.* New York: Scholastic, 2017. (grades 4–6)

Schur, Maxine Rose. *Day of Delight: A Jewish Sabbath in Ethiopia.* Illustrated by Brian Pinkney. New York: Dial Books for Young Readers, 1994. (preschool–grade 6)

———. *When I Left My Village.* Illustrated by Brian Pinkney. New York: Dial Books for Young Readers, 1996. (grades 3–5)

Schwartz, Ellen. *Stealing Home.* Toronto: Tundra Books, 2006. (grades 3–6)

Shang, Wendy Wan-Long, and Madelyn Rosenberg. *Not Your All-American Girl.* New York: Scholastic, 2020. (grades 3–6)

Stavans, Ilan. *Golemito.* Illustrated by Teresa Villegas. Montgomery, AL: NewSouth Books, 2013. (grades 2–4)

Weissman, Elissa Brent. *The Length of a String.* New York: Dial, 2018. (grades 4–6)

Wing, Natasha. *Jalapeño Bagels.* Illustrated by Robert Casilla. New York: Atheneum, 1996. (kindergarten–grade 3)

JUSTICE/SOCIAL JUSTICE

Berkowitz, Leah Rachel. *Queen Vashti's Comfy Pants.* Illustrated by Ruth Bennett. Millburn, NJ: Apples & Honey Press, 2021. (preschool–grade 3)

Cohen, Barbara. *Even Higher.* Illustrated by Anatoly Ivanov. New York: Lothrop, Lee & Shepard, 1987. (grades 2–4)

Goldin, Barbara Diamond. *The Magician's Visit.* Illustrated by Robert Andrew Parker. New York: Viking, 1993. (grades 1–4)

Kusel, Susan. *The Passover Guest.* Illustrated by Sean Rubin. New York: Holiday House, 2021. (preschool–grade 3)

Levine, Arthur. *Pearl Moscowitz's Last Stand.* Illustrated by Robert Roth. New York: HarperCollins, 1993. (grades 1–6)

Lindauer, Bonnie. *Hannah G. Solomon Dared to Make a Difference.* Illustrated by Sofia Moore. Minneapolis: Kar-Ben, 2021. (kindergarten–grade 5)

Markel, Michelle. *Brave Girl: Clara and the Shirtwaist Makers' Strike of 1909.* Illustrated by Melissa Sweet. New York: HarperCollins, 2013. (grades K–3)

Michelson, Richard. *As Good as Anybody: Martin Luther King, Jr., and Abraham Joshua Heschel's Amazing March toward Freedom.* Illustrated by Raul Colón. New York: Knopf Books for Young Readers, 2008. (grades 1–4)

Rose, Lisa. *The Singer and the Scientist.* Illustrated by Isabel Muñoz. Minneapolis: Kar-Ben, 2021. (kindergarten–grade 6)

Zalben, Jane Breskin. *A Moon for Moe and Mo.* Illustrated by Mehrdokht Amini. Watertown, MA: Charlesbridge, 2018. (preschool–grade 2)

LGBTQ+

Byrne, Jennifer. *Adopting Ahava.* Illustrated by Oana Vaida. Sicklerville, NJ: My Family! Product/Dodi Press. (grades 4–6)

Kushner, Elisabeth. *The Purim Superhero.* Illustrated by Mike Byrne. Minneapolis: Kar-Ben, 2013. (preschool–grade 3)

NATURE/ENVIRONMENT

Gellman, Ellie B. *Netta and Her Plant.* Illustrated by Natascia Ugliano. Minneapolis: Kar-Ben, 2014. (preschool–grade 2)

Levine, Arthur. *Pearl Moscowitz's Last Stand.* Illustrated by Robert Roth. New York: HarperCollins, 1993. (grades 1–6)

Rosenberg, Madelyn. *Happy Birthday, Tree! A Tu B'Shevat Story.* Illustrated by Jana Christy. Chicago: Albert Whitman, 2012. (preschool–grade 2)

Rostoker-Gruber, Karen. *Happy Birthday Trees.* Illustrated by Holly Sterling. Minneapolis: Kar-Ben, 2020. (preschool–grade 1)

PEACE

da Costa, Deborah. *Snow in Jerusalem.* Illustrated by Cornelius Van Wright and Ying-Hwa Hu. Chicago: Albert Whitman, 2001. (preschool–grade 3)

Gilani-Williams, Fawzia. *Yaffa and Fatima: Shalom, Salaam.* Illustrated by Chiara Fedele. Minneapolis: Kar-Ben, 2017. (preschool–grade 4)

Stampler, Ann Redisch. *The Wooden Sword.* Illustrated by Carol Liddiment. Chicago: Albert Whitman, 2012. (preschool–grade 3)

SPORTS

Adler, David A. *Yom Kippur Shortstop.* Springfield, NJ: Apples & Honey Press, 2017. (grades 3–6)

McDonough, Yona Zeldis. *Hammerin' Hank: The Life of Hank Greenberg.* Illustrated by Malcah Zeldis. New York: Walker, 2006. (grades 1–6)

Sommer, Shelley. *Hammerin' Hank Greenberg: Baseball Pioneer.* Honesdale, PA: Calkins Creek, 2011. (grades 4–6)

Winter, Jonah. *You Never Heard of Sandy Koufax?!* Illustrations by Andre Carrilho. New York: Schwartz & Wade, 2009. (preschool–grade 3)

STORYTELLING AND AUTHORING

Silverman, Erica. *Sholom's Treasure: How Sholom Aleichem Became a Writer.* Illustrated by Mordicai Gerstein. New York: Farrar, Straus & Giroux, 2005. (kindergarten–grade 6)

Singer, Isaac Bashevis. *Naftali the Storyteller and His Horse, Sus, and Other Stories.* Illustrated by Margot Zemach. New York: Farrar, Straus & Giroux, 1976. (grades 4–6)

Appendix B

Select Resources for Using Jewish Children's Literature in the Preschool through Elementary Classroom

DIGITAL RESOURCES

Numerous videos and audio recordings exist of many of the stories discussed in this book being read aloud. They include:

Always an Olivia, YouTube video of the reading of the story from Temple Emanu-El of San Diego, https://www.youtube.com/watch?v=1EBGMZhuBQk

Aviva Brown reading aloud her book *Ezra's Big Shabbat Question*, https://www.facebook.com/HinenuBaltimore/videos/author-aviva-l-brown-reads-ezras-big-shabbat-question/246782116429586/

Between Parents, read aloud by Ollie Elkus, translator of the book (only the first three chapters are read aloud), https://www.youtube.com/watch?v=iDtrTyx35bw

Cakes and Miracles, YouTube video of the reading of the story by Rabbi Joshua Fixler, https://www.youtube.com/watch?v=Nk1fIQASsr8

New Year at the Pier, read aloud, https://www.youtube.com/watch?v=NI0MjgEHzo4

Tale of Two Brothers, https://www.youtube.com/watch?v=m2t5fxK7Q8A and https://storiestogrowby.org/story/two-brothers/

Brief interview with Naomi Shmuel, author of *Too Far from Home*, https://www.youtube.com/watch?v=XSrtIoQd55A

Video reading of *When Jessie Came Across the Sea*, https://www.youtube.com/watch?v=XItyBTC2umo

Tales of Chelm enacted by the Jewish Arts Collaborative, https://www.youtube.com/watch?v=AM3mmRsLt9E&t=5s

Appendix B

SELECT DIGITAL RESOURCES RELATED TO THE HOLOCAUST

Interview with Judy Batalion, author of *The Light of Days: The Untold Story of Women Resistance Fighters in Hitler's Ghettos*, https://www.youtube.com/watch?v=COch-1dFbwY

Facing History and Ourselves has excellent resources on anti-Semitism, the Holocaust, genocide, and the teaching of history, https://www.facinghistory.org

Jewish Partisan Educational Foundation, https://www.jewishpartisans.org/

Video documentary on the Life of Janusz Korczak from Yad Vashem, https://www.youtube.com/watch?v=zGwnMgEx6b8

Kristallnacht video produced by Facing History and Ourselves, https://www.facinghistory.org/resource-library/video/kristallnacht-november-1938-pogroms

Montreal Holocaust Museum, https://museeholocauste.ca/en/resources-training/5-tips-teach-history-holocaust-elementary-school/

U.S. Holocaust Memorial Museum, https://www.ushmm.org/teach/fundamentals/guidelines-for-teaching-the-holocaust

OTHER DIGITAL RESOURCES FOR DISCUSSING THE STORIES WITH STUDENTS

Anti-Defamation League. Books Matter, https://www.adl.org/education-and-resources/resources-for-educators-parents-families/childrens-literature

It Could Always Be Worse, discussion of the story by the Prindle Institute for Ethics at https://www.prindleinstitute.org/books/it-could-always-be-worse/

Prindle Institute for Ethics guidelines for a philosophical discussion, https://www.prindleinstitute.org/teaching-children-philosophy/

ANTHOLOGIES AND COLLECTIONS OF JEWISH CHILDREN'S STORIES

Gaster, Moses. *Ma'aseh Book: Book of Jewish Tales and Legends*. Philadelphia: Jewish Publication Society, 1981.

Geras, Adèle. *My Grandmother's Stories: A Collection of Jewish Folktales*. Illustrated by Anita Lobel. New York: Knopf Books for Young Readers, 2003.

Kimmel, Eric A. *The Jar of Fools: Eight Hanukkah Stories from Chelm*. Illustrated by Mordicai Gerstein. New York: Holiday House, 2000.

Rossel, Seymour. *The Wise Folk of Chelm*. Houston: Rossel Books, 2013.

Schwartz, Howard, and Barbara Rush. *A Coat for the Moon and Other Jewish Tales*. Illustrated by Michael Iofin. Philadelphia: Jewish Publication Society, 1999.

Simon, Solomon. *The Wise Men of Helm and Their Merry Tales.* Illustrated by Lillian Fischel. Translated by Ben Bengal and David Simon. Springfield, MA: Behrman House, 1973.

Singer, Isaac Bashevis. *Stories for Children.* New York: Farrar, Straus & Giroux, 1984.

Taback, Simms. *Kibitzers and Fools: Tales My Zayda Told Me.* New York: Viking, 2005.

Udel, Miriam, ed. and trans. *Honey on the Page: A Treasury of Yiddish Children's Literature.* New York: New York University Press, 2020.

Yolen, Jane, and Heidi E. Y. Stemple. *Jewish Fairy Tale Feasts: A Literary Cookbook.* Illustrated by Sima Elizabeth Shefrin. Northampton, MA: Crocodile Books, 2013.

BIBLIOGRAPHIES OF JEWISH CHILDREN'S LITERATURE

100 Jewish Children's Books for the Family Book Shelf from the Association of Jewish Libraries and the Jewish Grandparents Network, https://jewishlibraries.org/wp-content/uploads/2021/04/100-Best-Books.pdf

Be'chol Lashon Children's Books, https://globaljews.org/resources/childrens-books/

Harrison, C. E., 11 Great Books about and for Jewish Children of Color, https://reformjudaism.org/blog/11-great-books-about-and-jewish-children-color

Institute for Translation of Hebrew Literature, https://www.ithl.org.il

Jewish Multiracial Network Books for Children, https://www.jewishmultiracialnetwork.org/books-for-children/

National Jewish Book Award, https://www.jewishbookcouncil.org/awards/national-jewish-book-awards

The Noah Costen Library of Yiddish Children's Literature: Annotated Bibliography. Amherst, MA: National Yiddish Book Center, 2003. Each item listed is available from the digital library of the National Yiddish Book Center, https://www.yiddishbookcenter.org/collections/yiddish-book-centers-noah-cotsen-library-yiddish-childrens-literature

Pinchuck, C., ed. *The Sydney Taylor Book Award: A Guide to the Winners, Honor Books and Notables, 1968–2018.* Association of Jewish Libraries, 2018.

PJ Library, https://pjlibrary.org/home

Rabinowitz, H., ed. *Evaluating Jewish Representation in Children's Literature: A Guide for Libraries*, https://jewishlibraries.org/wp-content/uploads/2020/08/Evaluating-Jewish-Kidlit-Guide.pdf

Silver, L. R. *Best Jewish Books for Children and Teens.* Philadelphia: Jewish Publication Society, 2010.

———. *Jewish Classics for Kids.* Philadelphia: Association of Jewish Libraries, 2006.

Sydney Taylor Book Award, https://jewishlibraries.org/sydney_taylor_book_award/

Tablet Magazine Children's Books, https://www.tabletmag.com/search?search=Children%27s%20Books

Appendix C

Select List of Professional and Scholarly Books and Articles on Jewish Children's Literature

Aarons, V., and P. Lassner. *The Palgrave Handbook of Holocaust Literature and Culture.* London: Palgrave Macmillan, 2020.

Banks, C., and L. Silverman. "The Quest for Excellence in Jewish Children's Literature." *Judaica Librarianship* 12 (2006): 69–78.

Bishop, R. S. "Reframing the Debate about Cultural Authenticity." In K. Short and D. Fox, eds., *Stories Matter: The Complexity of Cultural Authenticity in Children's Literature*, 25–37. Urbana, IL: National Council of Teachers of English, 2003.

Cummins, J.. *From Sarah to Sydney: The Woman behind All-of-a-Kind Family.* New Haven, CT: Yale University Press, 2021.

———. "What Are Jewish Boys and Girls Made Of?: Gender in Contemporary Jewish Teen and Tween Fiction." *Children's Literature Association Quarterly* 36, no. 3 (2011): 296–317.

Estraikh, G., K. Hodge, and M. Krutikow. *Children and Yiddish Literature: From Early Modernity to Post-Modernity.* London and New York: Routledge, 2016.

Frankel, E. "Legend in Jewish Children's Literature." *Judaica Librarianship* 8, nos. 1–2 (1994): 97–99.

Freeman, E. B. "Jewish Folk Tales: From Elijah the Prophet to the Wise Men of Chelm." In T. A. Young, ed., *Happily Ever After: Sharing Folk Literature with Elementary and Middle School Students,* 181–191. Newark, DE: International Reading Association, 2003.

Haynes, B. D. *The Soul of Judaism.* New York: New York University Press, 2018.

Horn, D. Who Doesn't Love Roald Dahl? *Jewish Review of Books*, 2021. Retrieved April 8, 2022, from https://jewishreviewofbooks.com/articles/9145/who-doesnt-love-roald-dahl/.

Kimmel, E. A. "Joy on Beale Street." *The Lion and the Unicorn* 27 (2003): 410–15.

Larsen, K. M. "Navigating Worlds of 'Trouble and Woe and Worse' in Children's Literature." *Children's Literature in Education* 43 (2012): 27–47.

May, J. "Envisioning the Jewish Community in Children's Literature: Maurice Sendak and Isaac Singer." *Journal of the Midwest Modern Language Association* 33/34, no. 1 (2000): 137–51.

Monsters and Miracles: A Journey through Jewish Picture Books. I. Stavans and N. Sokol, guest curators. Skirball Cultural Center and The Eric Carle Museum of Picture Book Art, 2010.

Rabinowitz, H. "Finally, Jewish Kids' Books Are Starting to Reflect the Diversity of Judaism." *Forward*, July 22, 2020. Retrieved April 27, 2022, from https://forward.com/culture/451036/finally-jewish-kids-books-are-starting-to-reflect-the-diversity-of-judaism/.

Rabinowitz, H., and K. Bloomfield. "'Love Your Neighbor': An AJL Project to Combat Anti-Semitism." *Judaica Librarianship* 27 (2020): 105–18.

Ressler, P., and B. Chase. *Meaningful Encounters: Preparing Educators to Teach Holocaust Literature.* Lanham, MD: Rowman & Littlefield, 2019.

Sonheim, A. "Picture Books about the Golem: Acts of Creation Without and Within." *The Lion and the Unicorn* 27 (2003): 377–93.

Zaltzman, L. "A Jewish Anti-Racist Reading List for Children of All Ages." *Baltimore Jewish News*, June 18, 2020. Retrieved April 29, 2022, from https://www.jewishtimes.com/a-jewish-anti-racist-reading-list-for-children-of-all-ages/.

Index

Adopting Ahava, 43–44, 55, 177, 186
Adventures of Hershel of Ostropol, 89–92, 101, 178, 184
African American, 18, 135, 138, 139, 140–41, 154, 159;
    African American Education, 140–41
    African American literature, 18, 34–35, 138
    Black History Month, 17
    See also Brown v. Board of Education
    See also civil rights movement
    See also Jews of Color
Agnon, S. Y., 29
Aleichem, Sholom, 28, 63–64, 76, 175, 187
All-of-a-Kind Family, 16, 23, 30–31, 38, 41–42, 55, 178, 180, 193
Always An Olivia: A Remarkable Family History, 18, 22, 34–35, 37, 177, 185, 189
Anderson, Marian, 138
animals, 1–4, 6, 10, 31, 33, 35, 37–38, 43–44, 50–51, 52–55, 86, 94–97, 101, 103, 163, 165, 173, 177–78
Anne Frank: Diary of a Young Girl, 3, 10, 30, 37, 183
anti-Semitism, 3–4, 7, 28, 103–30, 139, 165, 174, 190, 194;

    See also blood lie
    See also ghetto
    See also Holocaust
    See also pogrom
Arabic culture, 6, 158
Arabic language, 5, 158, 166
art, x, 9, 17, 35, 138–40, 148, 155, 175, 189;
    art and justice, 35, 138–40, 148, 175
    cover illustrations, 9, 10, 35–36, 39, 66, 86, 92, 156, 194
As Good as Anybody: Martin Luther King, Jr., and Abraham Joshua Heschel's Amazing March toward Freedom, 18, 22, 136, 148, 186
Ashkenazi, 14, 83, 138, 167, 168
Association of Jewish Libraries, xi, 16, 18, 19, 23, 30, 34–35, 191
awards, 8, 11, 15, 18, 21, 27, 31–33, 122, 132, 156, 160, 164;
    Caldecott Award, 17, 20, 31, 107, 139, 164
    Hans Christian Andersen Award, 15, 32, 122
    Israel Prize, 33
    Kate Greenaway Medal, 17
    Mildred L. Batchelder Award, 31, 32

National Jewish Book Award, 14, 15, 16–17, 19, 20, 30, 34, 35, 46, 47, 191
Newbery Award, 15, 31, 52
Sydney Taylor Book Award, 14, 15–17, 19, 20, 30, 34, 35, 46, 47, 191
Vine Award for Canadian Literature, 122
See also Nobel Prize for Literature
autobiography. See biography

Bagels from Benny, 47–48, 55, 99, 176
A Basket Full of Figs, 54–55, 177, 178
Bar/Bat Mitzvah/B-Mitzvah, 61, 72–74, 76, 133, 167, 174
Beautiful Yetta: The Yiddish Chicken, 50–51, 55, 173, 177, 185
Berchick, 2–3, 10, 14, 165, 177
Between Parents, 45–46, 55, 174, 189
Beyond Courage: The Untold Story of the Jewish Resistance during the Holocaust, 126–27, 129, 183
Bialik, Hayyim Nahman, 26, 37, 178
Bible, 5, 20–21, 26, 29, 33, 131, 160, 162, 171
bilingual, 29, 45, 86, 174
biography, 14–15, 17–18, 31, 35, 118, 136, 138–46
bisexual. See LGBTQ+
Bishop, Rudine Sims, 16, 23, 151, 166, 193
Black History Month. See African American
The Blackbird Girls, 132–33, 147
blood lie, 110–14, 132, 167;
See also anti-Semitism
Bluish, 155–56, 165
Bone Button Borscht, 92–93, 101
The Book Rescuer: How a Mensch from Massachusetts Saved Yiddish Literature for Generations to Come, 137, 148, 175, 176;
See also National Yiddish Book Center

A Boy of Old Prague, 113–14, 129, 173
The Bracelet, 161, 166
Brave Girl: Clara and the Shirtwaist Makers' Strike of 1909, 143–44, 148
Broken Song, 112–13, 129, 174
Brown v. Board of Education, 161;
See also African American
Brundibar, 103–5, 129, 183
Bund, 12, 112–13, 167

Cakes and Miracles: A Purim Tale, 69, 76, 98, 153–55, 165, 181, 189
Caldecott Award. See awards
calendar, 58–63, 70, 169
The Carp in the Bathtub, 2–3, 10, 95, 101, 165, 177
A Ceiling Made of Eggshells, 27, 37, 106–7, 129, 174
challah, 41, 81, 98, 99, 168, 170, 179
The Chanukkah Guest, 67, 76, 92–93, 180
Charlottesville, 115
Chelm, 81–85, 99–100, 168, 183, 189, 190, 193
Chelm for the Holidays, 83, 99, 101
civil rights movement, 18, 135–36, 148, 159;
See also Brown v. Board of Education
The Clever Little Tailor, 86–89, 100, 101, 173, 174
climate change. See Environment
community, 7, 27, 44, 50, 51, 59, 63, 65, 74, 84, 121, 132, 141, 152, 156–60
converso, 98, 168;
See also Marrano
See also Spanish inquisition
culture, 5, 12, 19, 20, 58, 63, 151–60, 165, 193
cultural heritage, 12, 26, 57–78
Jewish Culture, 7–8, 12, 20, 51, 57–78, 128, 137–38, 143
Curious George, 15, 119–20, 129, 183

Daniel & Ismail, 158–60, 166, 174
Day of Delight: A Jewish Sabbath in Ethiopia, 74–75, 76, 182, 185
Dear Mr. Dickens, 137, 147
Dear Mr. Rosenwald, 141–42, 148
death, 3, 4, 27, 44, 49–50, 58, 81, 98, 103, 105–8, 111–13, 115–20, 123–26, 135, 167, 168, 169
Devil's Arithmetic, 3, 10, 123, 124, 130, 183
The Diary of Laura's Twin, 73, 76, 174
Dickens, Charles, 137
discrimination, 139, 144, 145;
  See also anti-Semitism
  See also civil rights movement
  See also Japanese internment
divorce, 45
diversity, 4, 9, 12, 13, 16, 17, 20, 23, 32, 34, 41, 68, 116, 151, 194

Edelman, Marian Wright, 140, 148
Einstein, Albert, 138
Elijah, 51–52, 71, 124
Elijah's Door, 71, 77, 93, 181, 193
Emma's Poem: The Voice of the Statue of Liberty, 145, 147
environment, 97, 152, 162–64, 186
Even Higher, 16, 22, 23, 61–62, 76, 176, 181, 186
evil, 3, 4, 7, 68, 69, 103–28, 162
exceptionalities, 69, 92–93, 153–54
exodus from Egypt, 3, 52, 70, 125, 160;
  See also Pesach

Facing History and Ourselves, 115, 118, 130, 190
family, 2–3, 6, 9, 11, 18, 20, 30, 34–35, 41–54, 57–60, 62–69, 71–74, 80, 85–86, 91, 95, 97–100, 106–7, 113, 118–21, 124, 132–34, 136, 154–57, 161–64, 177–78, 191
fantasy, 14, 18–19, 33
farm life, 2, 7, 44, 63, 75, 112
Feivel's Flying Horses, 44–45, 55, 177, 184

fool(s), 25, 79–86, 92–93, 100, 121, 128, 168, 169, 183–84
freedom, 3, 7, 18, 65, 66, 70, 91, 136, 142
Freedom Summer: The Struggle for Civil Rights in Mississippi, 135
friendship, 6, 15–16, 18, 27, 29, 64–65, 67, 73, 118, 132, 138, 151–52, 159, 161, 179
folktales, 6, 14, 25–27, 33, 46, 54, 71, 80, 96, 146, 152, 178–79, 198

Gathering Sparks, 46, 55, 131, 148
Gay. See LGBTQ+
gender stereotypes, 8, 42
genocide, 44, 49, 119, 122, 153, 190
  See also Holocaust
ghetto, 81, 106, 113–14, 118, 122–27
Ginsburg, Ruth Bader, 14–15, 144–45;
  See also *I Dissent: Ruth Bader Ginsburg Makes Her Mark*
  See also *No Truth without Ruth: The Life of Ruth Bader Ginsburg*
  See also *Ruth Bader Ginsburg: The Case of R. B. G. vs. Inequality*
  See also *Ruth Objects: The Life of Ruth Bader Ginsburg*
Gittel's Journey: An Ellis Island Story, 11–13, 22, 184
golem, 19, 107–9, 111, 168, 194
Golem, 31, 37, 38, 107–9, 111, 168, 194
Golemito, 109–11, 129, 176, 179, 185
The Grand Mosque of Paris: A Story of How Muslims Rescued Jews during the Holocaust, 121, 129
grandfather, 20–21, 44, 46–50, 54, 106–7, 117–18, 124, 131, 162, 171
grandmother, 11, 17, 34–35, 44, 46–47, 118, 124, 132, 137, 160, 162
Grandpa's Third Drawer, 117, 129
graphic novels, 35, 73, 120, 122, 180
Gregorian Calendar. See calendar

Hannah Szenes: A Song of Light, 126, 129

Hannah's Way, 59–60, 76, 179, 182
Hanukkah, 19, 23, 34, 37, 65–67, 76, 91–93, 101, 156–57, 159, 168, 177, 180, 185, 190;
  See also latkes
Hans Christian Andersen Award. *See* awards
Hebrew, 5, 8, 13, 15, 21, 27, 32, 43, 46, 65, 69, 74, 117, 124, 131, 156, 158, 160
Hebrew Bible. *See* Bible.
A Hero and the Holocaust: The Story of Janusz Korczak, 125, 129, 175, 176, 182
Hershel and the Hanukkah Globlins, 91–93, 101
Hershel of Ostropol, 89–91, 101, 178, 184
Hidden, 120, 129, 180, 183
Hillel, 52, 80
Hitler, 35, 105, 115, 118, 127, 133, 135;
  See also Holocaust
  See also World War II
Holiday Tales of Sholom Aleichem, 63–64, 76
Holocaust, 3, 4, 5, 13, 14, 27, 30, 33, 34, 44, 73, 114–16
Holocaust education guidelines, 116
  See also Montreal Holocaust Museum
  See also The United States Holocaust Memorial Museum
Holocaust literature, 3, 7, 29, 30, 32, 64, 103–4, 106, 114–28, 129–30
homesteading, 2, 14
humor, 3, 7, 79–102

I Dissent: Ruth Bader Ginsburg Makes Her Mark, 14, 22, 144, 148, 175
immigration, 3, 11–14, 17, 28–30, 44–45, 50, 57–58, 110–13, 122, 143–46, 184
inclusivity, 152–56, 159
The Inquisitor's Tale: Or, the Three Magical Children and Their Holy Dog, 18–19, 22, 27, 37, 173

intergenerational love (l-dor vador), 46–50
Islam. *See also* Muslim.
The Island on Bird Street, 15, 22, 32, 37, 122, 129, 183
Israel Prize. *See awards*
It Could Always Be Worse, 31, 38, 86, 102, 179

Janusz Korczak's Children, 125, 129, 176
Japanese Internment, 20, 136, 161
Jewish Book Council, 33–34, 191
Jewish calendar. *See* calendar
Jewish Fairy Tale Feast: A Literary Cookbook, 98–99, 102, 179, 191
Jews of Color, 9, 10, 18, 21, 34–35, 67, 74–75, 108–9, 156, 160, 185, 191
Joseph Who Loved the Sabbath, 75, 76, 178, 182
The Journey That Saved Curious George: The True Wartime Escape of Margret and H. A. Rey, 15, 119–20, 129, 183
Judah Touro Didn't Want to Be Famous, 142, 147
justice, 4, 7, 15, 18, 20, 64, 68, 71, 72, 93, 111, 131–47, 152, 157, 159, 162, 186;
  See also tikkun olam
  See also tzedakah

kabbalah, 108, 169
Kate Greenaway Medal. *See* awards
Keats, Ezra Jack, 15, 31, 37, 139–40, 148
The Keeping Quilt, 57–59, 76
kehillah. *See* community
Kibitzers and Fools, 83, 102, 179, 184, 191
kindertransport, 122;
  See also Holocaust
King Matt the First, 28, 37, 125, 129;
  See also Korczak, Janusz
Kishinev pogrom. *See* pogrom

Korczak, Janusz, 28, 110, 125–26
kosher laws, 95, 107, 169
kristallnacht, 118, 169;
　See also anti-Semitism

Ladino, 5, 8, 13, 26, 167, 169, 174
Lansky, Aaron, 137–38;
　See also The Book Rescuer: How
　　a Mensch from Massachusetts
　　Saved Yiddish Literature for
　　Generations to Come
　See also National Yiddish Book
　　Center
The Last Stop on Market Street, 160, 165
latkes, 66–67, 76, 92, 98, 169, 177, 179–80
Latkes, Latkes, Good to Eat, 76, 178, 180
Lemuel the Fool, 85–86, 102,176, 184
Lesbian. See LGBTQ+
LGBTQ+, 5, 9, 16, 162, 186
Liberty's Voice: The Story of Emma Lazarus, 145, 148
The Light of Days: The Untold Story of Women Resistance Fighters in Hitler's Ghettos, 127–29, 182, 190
Linked, 133, 147
The Longest Night: A Passover Story, 70, 77
love, 1, 6, 7, 27, 41–55, 62, 65–67, 70–71, 91, 95, 101, 114, 117, 132, 143, 153–55
Lucky Broken Girl, 21–22, 156, 165, 185

The Magician, 51–52, 55, 70–71, 76, 181
The Magician's Visit, 71, 76, 181, 186
The Magician's Visit: A Passover Story, 71, 76
Marrano, 98–100, 168, 169;
　See also converso
McDew, Charles, 135, 148
memory, 7, 21, 30, 49, 58, 74, 128, 160–61, 171, 21, 23, 166

Mildred L. Batchelder Award. See awards
miracle, 62, 65–67, 71, 91–93, 98–101, 123, 154, 168
Mishnah, 26
Mister Doctor: Janusz Korczak and the Orphans of the Warsaw Ghetto, 125, 129, 176;
　See also Korczak, Janus
Mitzvah / Mitzvot, 27, 52, 80, 91, 142, 169
Monsters and Miracles: A Journey through Jewish Picture Books, 9, 10, 39, 194
Montreal Holocaust Museum, 115–16, 130, 190;
　See also Holocaust
multicultural literature, 5, 10, 23, 133, 151–54, 165
My Basmati Bat Mitzvah, 73–74, 76, 174
My Brother Charlie, 154–55, 166
My Grandmother's Stories: A Collection of Jewish Folk Tales, 86, 101, 190

Nachman of Breslov, 27–28, 80
Naftali the Storyteller and His Horse, Sus, 1, 10, 165, 173, 179, 187
National Jewish Book Award. See awards
National Yiddish Book Center, 137–38
nature, 6, 7, 53, 83, 97, 152, 162–64, 186–87
Newbery Award. See Awards
New Year at the Pier, 62, 77, 189
Night, 3, 10
No Truth without Ruth: The Life of Ruth Bader Ginsburg, 144, 147
No Vacancy, 133, 147, 179
Nobel Prize for Literature, 4, 29, 31, 52, 100
nonbinary. See LGBTQ+

Old Testament. See Bible
One City, Two Brothers, 6, 10, 166, 178, 179, 189

The Other Side, 159–60, 166

A Parakeet Named Dreidel, 65–67, 77, 177
parents, 3, 4, 9, 17, 42–50, 62, 63, 73, 95, 104–5, 114–17, 119–22, 128, 144, 155–58, 174
Passover. *See* Pesach
Pearl Moscowitz's Last Stand, 163, 166, 182, 186
The Peddler and the Baker, 146–47, 148
The People's Painter: How Ben Shahn Fought for Justice, 146–47, 148; *See also* Shahn, Ben
Pesach, 2–3, 51–52, 70–71, 111, 169, 181
philosophy for children, 3–7, 42, 125, 128, 176–77, 190
PJ Library, 26, 33
A Place at the Table, 134, 147, 179
A Poem for Peter: The Story of Ezra Jack Keats and the Creation of The Snowy Day, 139–40, 148; *See also* Keats, Ezra Jack
pogrom, 3, 44, 50, 111–18, 167, 169
The Polio Pioneer: Dr. Jonas Salk and the Polio Vaccine, 17, 22, 142–43, 148, 175
Purim, 61, 68–70, 153–54, 181, 185
Purim Superhero, 69, 76, 185, 186

Queen Esther, 68
The Queen of the Hanukkah Dosas, 67, 68, 76
Queen Vashti's Comfy Pants, 68–69, 76

The Rabbi and the Reverend, 135, 147
Rachel Captures the Moon, 84, 102, 176, 184
racial diversity. *See* diversity
Red and Green and Blue and White, 157, 159–60, 166
Remember: The Journey to School Integration, 161–62, 166
resistance, 15, 112, 119, 120, 123, 126–28

Rifka Takes a Bow, 42–43, 55, 177
Right Side Up: Adventures in Chelm, 82–83, 85, 101, 184
righteous (righteousness), 7, 20, 68, 72, 108–9, 131–46;
The Rooster Prince of Breslov, 28, 38, 79–81, 100, 101, 176, 179
Rosenwald, Julius, 140–42
Rosh Hashanah, 44, 61–63, 83, 169–70
Ruth Bader Ginsburg: The Case of R. B. G. vs. Inequality, 144, 148
Ruth Objects: The Life of Ruth Bader Ginsburg, 144, 148

Sabbath. *See* Shabbat
A Sack Full of Feathers, 95–96, 102, 176, 179
The Sages of Chelm and the Moon, 84, 101, 183
A Scarf for Keiko, 20, 22, 136, 148, 177
Schools of Hope: How Julius Rosenwald Helped Change African American Education, 140–41, 147;
See also African American education
The Secret of the Village Fool, 121–22, 129, 183
Seder. *See* Pesach
Seeking Refuge, 122, 129, 180, 183
segregation, 138, 162;
See also Brown v. Board of Education
See also ghetto
Sephardic, 14, 27, 28, 160, 170
The Seven Good Years and Other Stories, 55, 70, 76, 181
Shabbat, 1, 20, 41, 57, 59–61, 74–75, 99, 167, 170, 181, 189
Shahn, Ben, 113, 129, 138–40, 148, 173, 175
shalom bayit (peace in the family), 42, 44–46
Shanghai Escape, 118, 129, 183
Shanghai Sukkah, 64, 76

Singer, Isaac Bashevis, 1, 4, 10, 28, 31, 38, 52–54, 55, 65–67, 77, 173, 177, 178, 179, 187
The Singer and the Scientist, 138, 148, 175, 186
social justice. *See* justice
See also Tikkun Olam
Spanish, 5, 9, 12, 26, 27, 50
Spanish inquisition, 14, 27, 34, 106–7; *See also* converso
Sparks Fly Upward, 44, 55, 176, 177
Statue of Liberty, 145, 147, 184
Stone Soup, 92–93, 101
Stones for Grandpa, 49–50, 55, 177
Stories for Children, 4, 10
Such a Library!, 86, 101
Sukkot, 17, 61, 63–65, 168, 170, 182
Sweet Tamales for Purim, 69–70, 76
Sydney Taylor Book Award. *See* awards
synagogue, 28, 47–49, 62, 91–93, 99, 108, 115, 135, 142, 170, 171

Tablet Magazine, 19
Talmud, 19, 20, 26–27, 33, 42, 101, 112, 131, 132, 170
teacher stories of using Jewish children's literature, 6, 12–13, 34–35, 47–48, 50–51, 58–60, 63–64, 66, 73–74, 92–93, 104–5, 110–11, 132–33, 140–41, 143–44, 153–54
Tia Fortuna's New Home: A Jewish Cuban Journey, 160–61, 165
tikkun olam (repair the world), 4, 7, 10, 91, 131–47, 171
time, 7, 57–77, 125–25
Torah, 5, 42, 43, 45, 49, 53, 56, 59, 70, 72, 74, 99, 112, 125, 131, 167, 169, 170, 171
Transgender. *See* LGBTQ+
tree(s), 1, 7, 53–54, 163

Tu BiShvat, 163, 186
Turtle Boy, 72, 77, 174
tzaddik, 108, 131, 171; *See also* righteous (righteousness)
Tzedakah, 48, 72, 73, 171

Uncle Misha's Partisans, 127–28, 129
The United States Holocaust Memorial Museum, 9, 115, 116, 118, 130, 190

Warsaw ghetto uprising, 122–23, 125–27; *See also* Holocaust
Washington, Booker T., 140–41
We Are Water Protectors, 164, 166
When Zaydeh Danced on Eldridge Street, 48–49, 55, 177
Wiesel, Elie, 3, 10, 100–2, 164, 166
wisdom, 4, 7, 20, 41, 79–101, 106, 168
witness (witnessing), 7, 128
The Wooden Sword, 97–99, 101, 178, 187

Yaffa and Fatima: Shalom, Salaam, 7, 10, 179, 187
Yiddish, 5, 8, 13, 15, 16, 20, 21, 26, 27–29, 38, 42–43, 45, 48, 50–51, 55, 65–66, 74, 80, 83, 86–87, 94, 101, 112, 137–38, 143, 148, 171, 174, 191, 193
The Yiddish Fish, 94–95, 101, 173, 176, 177
Yom Kippur, 61, 62–64, 76, 182
Yom Kippur Shortstop, 62–64, 76, 182

Zayde. *See* grandfather
Zayde Comes to Live, 49, 55, 178
Zlateh the Goat and Other Stories, 31, 38, 52–53, 55
Zonia's Rain Forest, 163, 166

About the Authors

David Bloome is professor emeritus in the Department of Teaching and Learning of The Ohio State University College of Education and Human Ecology. For more than four decades, he has been researching and writing about the teaching of reading and writing and the use of reading and writing in people's lives. Prior to his university career, he was a classroom teacher at the middle-school and high-school levels. He is a former president of the National Council of Teachers of English and of the National Conference on Research in Language and Literacy. In 2008, Bloome was inducted into the Reading Hall of Fame. He is the coauthor or coeditor of twenty books on language and literacy in education, and author or coauthor of more than one hundred journal articles and book chapters.

Bloome's interest in Jewish children's literature originally came from reading books to his children when they were young and, more recently, to his grandchildren. A student of Yiddish language, culture, and literature, he has been enjoying reading Yiddish children's literature in Yiddish and in translation. Bloome was an originator of the National Council of Teachers of English Jewish Caucus, which sought to expand awareness of the diverse range of Jewish children's literature.

Evelyn B. Freeman is professor emerita at The Ohio State University, where she taught courses in children's literature and language arts, prepared elementary teachers, and worked with graduate students. She retired as dean and director of The Ohio State University at Mansfield. During her appointment, she also served as executive dean for Ohio State's regional campuses. After her retirement, Freeman worked as special assistant for international projects in the College of Education and Human Ecology. She has served as coeditor of the *Journal of Children's Literature*, for which she received the James P.

Barry Ohioana Award for Editorial Excellence, and *Bookbird: A Journal of International Children's Literature*. She has coauthored five books on topics related to children's literature, and numerous book chapters and journal articles. Freeman is past president of the Children's Literature Assembly of the National Council of Teachers of English and the United States Board on Books for Young People. She also served as vice president of the International Board on Books for Young People.

Freeman has a long-standing interest in Jewish children's literature. As an affiliated faculty member with The Ohio State University Melton Center for Jewish Studies, she taught a module on Jewish children's literature for the Center's summer workshops for teachers. She has presented at professional conferences on the topic, written reviews of Jewish children's books for various publications, and has a published book chapter on Jewish folktales for children. Freeman is a founding member of the Jewish Caucus of the National Council of Teachers of English.

Rosemary Horowitz was a member of Appalachian State's faculty for more than a quarter century. A highly committed Holocaust educator and English professor—greatly admired by her students and colleagues alike—she was an accomplished scholar, patron of the arts, and fierce opponent of anti-Semitism and any form of hostility against Israel. Dr. Horowitz dedicated her first major work, her 1995 study of Yisker Bikher, "to the six million"—a dedication that powerfully captured one of the central commitments of her life and career.

Dr. Horowitz was born to Holocaust survivors and spent the first decades of her life mainly in the northeastern United States. She earned a BA in English and education from Brooklyn College in the mid-1970s and subsequently worked as a writer, editor, trainer, and board member for several organizations. She returned to school and was bestowed a doctor of education degree from the University of Massachusetts–Amherst in 1995. In the course of her career, Dr. Horowitz became one of the foremost experts on *Yisker Bikher*, speaking and publishing widely on the topic.

Laurie Katz is a professor in the Department of Teaching and Learning of The Ohio State University College of Education and Human Ecology. She received her doctorate from University of Massachusetts–Amherst in 1992 with a specialization in early childhood education/early childhood special education. For the past thirty years, her research, teaching, and service have focused on teacher preparation of early childhood educators; inclusion issues; relationships between families, communities, and schools; and narrative styles and structures of young children. Before her university career, she worked as a social worker strengthening relationships between families, schools, and communities.

Katz's interest in Jewish children's literature comes predominantly from her passion for promoting the lives of all young children and their families. She has been a champion within her communities and internationally for breaking down the barriers for young children who have special needs as well as for children and their families from all cultural, linguistic, and socio-economic backgrounds. Her international connections include designing and implementing coursework, presentations, and publications with colleagues in Oranim College in Tiv'on, Israel, and Universidade Federal de Minas Gerais in Belo Horizonte, MG Brasil. Katz has served on many local and national boards focusing on improving lives of early childhood educators and young children and their families. Katz is a cofounder of the National Council of Teachers of English Jewish Caucus.